MW01593523

EXPERIENCE
HEAVEN
ON EARTH

A PRAYER TO UNLOCK THE KINGDOM

GARY HARGRAVE

Experience Heaven on Earth: *A Prayer to Unlock the Kingdom*
Copyright 2020 by Hargrave Ministries

Unless otherwise designated, all Scripture quotations are taken from the New American Standard Bible®, © 1960, 1962, 1963, 1968, 1971, 1972, 1973, 1975, 1977 by The Lockman Foundation. Used by permission.

Religious writing styles vary greatly among writers. This book follows the standards developed by Hargrave Ministries. Words such as: Father, Son, Word, Living Word, Gospel and Scripture are capitalized for emphasis, while the name "satan" is purposefully not capitalized. Additional style guides consulted for this book include The Chicago Manual of Style and The Associated Press.

For your convenience, Scriptures are included as footnotes on each page; if a Scripture appears more than once in a single chapter it is footnoted at its first reference.

Printed in the U.S.A.
ISBN 978-1-7356021-0-3

Hargrave Ministries
9018 Balboa Blvd, #579
Northridge, CA 91325-2610

HARGRAVE™
MINISTRIES

MATTHEW 6:9-13

[9] Our Father who art in heaven,
Hallowed be Thy name.
[10] Thy kingdom come.
Thy will be done,
On earth as it is in heaven.
[11] Give us this day our daily bread.
[12] And forgive us our debts,
as we also have forgiven our debtors.
[13] And do not lead us into temptation,
but deliver us from evil.
For Thine is the kingdom, and the power,
and the glory, forever. Amen.

CONTENTS

Introduction

I am excited that you are about to embark on an adventure in reading this book about the Lord's Prayer. I believe that these messages are thoroughly anointed by the Holy Spirit, and have the ability to change your prayer life and your relationship with the heavenly Father. These messages were originally delivered to a congregation in church services, and they retain that style. For this reason, some of the chapters end with a prayer, and occasionally there is a reference to the churches where these messages were delivered. As individual messages, these chapters will challenge you to reach into a greater understanding of Christ's teaching. Together, they form a powerful and deeply profound study of the Lord's Prayer.

The chapters of this book are expository in their presentation and many comprise a verse-by-verse explanation or understanding of the Lord's Prayer. Different types of Bible texts require different methods of interpretation, simply because of the nature of the writing. With poetry, you often have to explain the text; you cannot simply take the words at their face value. With parables, or with apocalyptic writings such as the Book of Revelation, you truly do have to interpret the meaning of the text. However, text that is just the author speaking in a straightforward manner does not require interpretation, but instead calls for explanation or teaching. In the science of interpreting the Bible, when you come across text that is a simple communication from author to listener, you simply take the words at face value. You do not need an interpretation; you simply rely on the fact that the author is saying what he means, and meaning what he says.

That is what we are doing with this book. We are simply accepting the words that Christ spoke, just as He spoke them, and making that the basis of our understanding of the Lord's Prayer. This prayer is not a parable or poetry or apocalyptic writing; Jesus was saying exactly what He meant. When He said, "Go into your inner room, and when you have shut your door, pray to your Father who is in secret" (Matthew 6:6), that is what He meant. He meant to go into the presence of God and, from that place, pray to the Father. It is a relationship. When Jesus said to pray, "Thy kingdom come" (Matthew 6:10), He really meant it. This confronts us with the fact that we really do not pray the Lord's Prayer in that way. When you take the concepts of this prayer just as Jesus spoke them, and begin instilling them in your prayer life, it can truly be revolutionary.

This leads us to how to approach this book. My mentor taught us to read the Bible until a verse or a passage comes alive, then hold that Word in your heart and incorporate it into your being by the Holy Spirit. This process is reflected in his personal thoughts concerning the Lord's Prayer:

> I think it would be a great blessing to us if we really learned how to pray the Lord's Prayer. The Lord's Prayer was given in response to a request, by the disciples, to learn to pray. And they said, "John taught his disciples; will You teach us to pray?" And Jesus gave them a prayer that could be quoted in a minute; and yet to really pray this prayer is often the exercise of a number of hours....I rely on this prayer, which is based more

upon a relationship to God than anything else, and I spend much time praying over it.…We have not made it a part of the liturgy of the service, because I think that people run through the scope of saying it and not really knowing what they're doing. To me, it is better termed the Disciples' Prayer…because it was what He gave to the disciples to pray.[1]

One of the motivating factors for writing this book is that, despite the vast familiarity throughout Christianity with this prayer, we have not had the necessary understanding of its depth and practical instruction for our lives. As Stevens said in the above quote, the Lord's Prayer has become a form of liturgy, something that is spoken by rote. The way we as believers tend to approach the Lord's Prayer, in effect, makes it similar to a mantra. It is something that we rattle off with no real depth of meaning. This book is necessary to break down the callousness and the lack of comprehension that is on us as we voice this prayer. Something has to take it out of rote memory, plant it in our hearts anew, and allow it to take root in our lives on another level.

Again, this quote provides a guideline for how to derive the greatest benefit from this book. This book is not a novel. It is not a quick read. You have to spend time with it. It is not a book that you should read through in one night. This book is a meditation on each verse of the Lord's Prayer. When I was working on the book, I would live for days in one chapter. Then when I prayed, I found these teachings coming alive and being incorporated into my prayer life.

The way to read this book is to make it your personal devotional and the focus of your meditation. Get up in the morning and read

---

[1] John Robert Stevens, *The Lord's Prayer, a Relationship to the Father – Part II*, Living Word Publications 201308271R (CD), 2013.

a chapter, then absorb that chapter, by the Holy Spirit, into your heart all day long. You may even want to go back and read the same chapter the next day. When you do that, I believe that the depth of what the Lord can reveal to you about prayer is unending.

1 | Our Door to the Father

The world is experiencing a period of great need, and Christians everywhere are entering into times of prayer to see the Lord bring answers. It is very important that our prayers be as effective as possible. Prayer is not just an exercise; when we pray, something is supposed to happen. Whether it be in our own hearts, in our community, or in the entire world, we must have a faith that when we pray, something will happen. We should not grow accustomed to our prayers not getting answered. On the contrary, we should sharpen our expectation to receive great things from the Lord.

To learn the secret of effective prayer, we need to look no further than a passage of Scripture that is very familiar to us: the Lord's Prayer. This is more than something to recite; it is Christ telling us how He wants us to pray. In the first place, it should be called the Disciples' Prayer. It is the prayer that Christ taught His disciples to pray. It was born out of the fact that the disciples saw Christ praying. When He finished, one of them asked Him, "Lord, teach us to pray" (Luke 11:1). In response to the request, He began

---

Luke 11:1 And it came about that while He was praying in a certain place, after He had finished, one of His disciples said to Him, "Lord, teach us to pray just as John also taught his disciples."

His marvelous teaching. We all know how the prayer begins in Matthew 6:9: "Our Father." It may seem like this is stating the obvious, that the Lord's Prayer is a prayer to the Father. However, we need a new understanding of this simple truth: when the Lord taught the disciples to pray, He taught them to address the Father.

As Christians we focus very much on having a relationship with Christ. We often lose sight of the fact that Christ came to bring us into a relationship with the Father. Christ is the very reason we are able to have a relationship with the Father. So it is extremely important that we do not stop at a relationship with Christ, but through Christ we begin to relate to the Father. This does not take away from Christ. This does not take anything away from what He is, what He has done, or why we must first come to Him. However, once we come to Him, we must relate to what the Father is doing in Him and through Him.

Read 2 Corinthians 5:17-19:

> Therefore if any man is in Christ, he is a new creature; the old things passed away; behold, new things have come. Now all these things are from God, who reconciled us to Himself through Christ, and gave us the ministry of reconciliation, namely, that God was in Christ reconciling the world to Himself.

We are all familiar with the Scripture, "For God so loved the world, that He gave His only begotten Son" (John 3:16). God sent Christ into the earth, but He had a purpose in sending Christ to the earth; He had an objective. If we lose the concept that the primary purpose of Christ is to reconcile us to the Father, then we are missing God's objective.

Matthew 6:9 "Pray, then, in this way: 'Our Father who art in heaven, hallowed be Thy name.'"

We know that Christ is our Savior and He is our Lord, but it doesn't end there. His purpose is to reconcile us to the Father. As a Christian you know that you are saved. Do you know why He saved you? What did He save you for? The purpose of Christ being your Savior is to reconcile you to the Father. You may say, "Well, He saved me to take away my sins." Yes, but why did He take away your sins? There was a reason. He removed your sin to reconcile you to the Father, so you could stand in the Father's presence (Colossians 1:21-22). Christ died to get rid of your sin, but He did it so that God could be your Father. It is the Father who was in Christ reconciling you to Himself.

Christ came preaching and teaching about the Kingdom of God; yet when He taught about prayer, He described it as an intimate relationship with the Father. "But you, when you pray, go into your inner room, and when you have shut your door, pray to your Father who is in secret, and your Father who sees in secret will repay you" (Matthew 6:6). Christ taught that you go into your closet with the Father and shut the door. Don't lose that idea in your relationship with Christ.

You cannot stop halfway in these relationships that God has established. The Holy Spirit is within us to teach us, to impart to us the things of Christ (1 John 2:27; John 16:14). He reminds us of all that Christ said and all that He did (John 14:26). We also

---

Colossians 1:21-22 And although you were formerly alienated and hostile in mind, engaged in evil deeds, [22] yet He has now reconciled you in His fleshly body through death, in order to present you before Him holy and blameless and beyond reproach.

1 John 2:27 And as for you, the anointing which you received from Him abides in you, and you have no need for anyone to teach you; but as His anointing teaches you about all things, and is true and is not a lie, and just as it has taught you, you abide in Him.

John 16:14 "He shall glorify Me; for He shall take of Mine, and shall disclose it to you."

John 14:26 "But the Helper, the Holy Spirit, whom the Father will send in My name, He will teach you all things, and bring to your remembrance all that I said to you."

see that Christ is within us to take us to the Father (John 14:6). Christ is the way to the Father. He said about Himself, "I am the door of the sheep" (John 10:7). We construct doors for one reason: to go through them. A door is not built so that you stand in the doorway. A door is built so that you can walk into a room. You cannot minimize the importance of a door. A room would be completely useless without it. Without a door to a building, we would all be standing outside scratching our heads, thinking, "How do I get in?" For us to enter into the presence of the Father, we need this door.

The way Christ taught us to pray is to enter into the inner room. What do you use to get into the inner room? You use the door, which is Christ. Christ lets you into the presence of the Father. Then something else happens, according to Matthew 6:6. He tells you to close the door. So Christ lets you in, but He also locks you into the presence of the Father. He holds you there. This is why He is always in intercession at the right hand of the Father, praying for us—to hold us in the Father's presence (Romans 8:34; Hebrews 7:25). Come through the door into the inner room. Then close the door and let Christ hold you in that secret place. Stay in that place, the presence of the Father, that God in Christ has made possible.

Let's go to Matthew 6:9: "Pray, then, in this way: 'Our Father who art in heaven.'" The very foundation of prayer is to begin your

---

John 14:6 Jesus said to him, "I am the way, and the truth, and the life; no one comes to the Father, but through Me."

John 10:7 Jesus therefore said to them again, "Truly, truly, I say to you, I am the door of the sheep."

Romans 8:34 Who is the one who condemns? Christ Jesus is He who died, yes, rather who was raised, who is at the right hand of God, who also intercedes for us.

Hebrews 7:25 Hence, also, He is able to save forever those who draw near to God through Him, since He always lives to make intercession for them.

prayer by addressing the Father, but don't forget where you are when you start praying. As we read in Matthew 6:6, we first enter into the secret place, the heavenlies, through Christ. From there we address the Father who is in heaven. When you pray, don't pray from down here. Don't pray from the earth as if you are throwing your prayers up to God. That is not the way Christ said to pray. He said, "I am the door to His presence. I am the way to the Father." If you are going to pray, first get into the realm of spirit in the heavens. Enter into where He is.

You may say, "How can I get into heaven? How do I get to where the Father is?" By faith, when you begin to pray, you enter through Christ. Enter by faith, in your spirit, into the heavenly places, seated with Christ as He is seated with the Father (Ephesians 2:6). Enter into the secret place. A secret place is something you don't know about, some place you cannot seem to go; but He opens the door. The Scripture says that where He is, we should be also (John 14:3). You may think, "I don't know how to do that. It is too hard to be spiritual." It is not too hard because it is done by faith, and all the faith you need is the size of a mustard seed (Matthew 17:20). Everyone has that much faith! If you received salvation, then you must have that much faith. That is all the faith you need to walk through the door. Use that faith to come into the heavenly place with the Father.

Look at Matthew 6:9 again: "Our Father who art in heaven [and now we are there with Him], hallowed be Thy name." When you

---

Ephesians 2:6 And raised us up with Him, and seated us with Him in the heavenly places, in Christ Jesus.

John 14:3 "And if I go and prepare a place for you, I will come again, and receive you to Myself; that where I am, there you may be also."

Matthew 17:20 And He said to them, "Because of the littleness of your faith; for truly I say to you, if you have faith as a mustard seed, you shall say to this mountain, 'Move from here to there,' and it shall move; and nothing shall be impossible to you."

pray, lock yourself in with the Father and begin your prayer in this way: "Hallowed be Your name." Bless the Father. Bless Him! Love and worship Him. Thank Him. He sent His Son to die for us that we might be able to enter into His presence. We thank You, Father. We are not here because of our worthiness, because of our spirituality, or because of our abilities. We are only here because You made the door to Your presence. You opened the door and allowed us to come in. Thank You, God, because You are going to do everything else just as perfectly as You worked our salvation.

Is that your attitude when you come into His presence? Or do you take out your list and say, "Now God, this is what I'm here for. I have worked on this list for a long time. I have some real needs here and these are the things I want"? Think about how that worked with your father on a natural level. That would be no way to get anything from him. If you ran through the door of the house, closed the door and started making demands of your father, you know what you would get, don't you? You would get corrected. That is no way to approach your heavenly Father either. We approach the heavenly Father in worship: "Hallowed be Your name." The truth is, when you come into His presence, you will forget your list and begin to worship.

We do not want to pray in a way that takes us nowhere. We do not want to pray, "O Jesus, we need this; we need that. Lord Jesus, take care of all these things." That is not how He taught us to pray. Matthew 6:8 explains this principle: "Therefore do not be like them [speaking of the Gentiles]; for your Father knows what you need, before you ask Him." Now that is something to think about if you are going to pray, isn't it? Before you pray, He already knows everything you need. So why pray? The reason is—God wants you. God was in Christ reconciling the world to Himself. He wants you. He wants you to come to Him. He wants you to approach Him. He wants you to be locked in with Him in that secret place. He wants you to go there with Him and lock the door. He already knows what you are going to ask, but He wants your presence with Him.

Something begins to happen in your relationship with the Father, and it begins in your worship: "Hallowed be Your name. I worship You, Father. I come to You, and I stand in Your presence. Father, I recognize that You have the answers. I recognize that Your presence is the answer to whatever I could ask and whatever I need. Your presence alone is the answer." All it takes is His presence. You enter into the Father's presence in order to bring His presence into every need. Your worship of Him brings the solution to every problem. And if you want to really worship, take the reins of your heart and give them to Him. Let Him father you. You may think you know what the needs are, but the Father knows what they really are. The true sense of a father is that he knows what you need, and he has what you need. He provides what you need. Our heavenly Father is called *El-Shaddai*,[2] the Almighty, the bountiful giver, because He has everything we need.

We have a greater need than to just know Christ as our Savior and Lord. The Body of Christ needs a Father. We need a relationship with the Father if we are to grow up and become mature sons of God. That is what Christ was; He was the Son of God who grew into a mature man (Luke 2:52). We also must grow up into the measure of the stature of the fullness that is in Christ (Ephesians 4:13). You cannot grow up or mature without a father. We know this is not always easy, because as a Father He disciplines us. He corrects

---

Luke 2:52 And Jesus kept increasing in wisdom and stature, and in favor with God and men.

Ephesians 4:13 Until we all attain to the unity of the faith, and of the knowledge of the Son of God, to a mature man, to the measure of the stature which belongs to the fulness of Christ.

[2.] Robert Baker Girdlestone, *Synonyms of the Old Testament: Their Bearing on Christian Doctrine.* (Oak Harbor, WA: Logos Research Systems, Inc., 1998), 32-33.

us, but always with one purpose: that His nature be imparted to us (Hebrews 12:5-11). "Be perfect, as your heavenly Father is perfect" (Matthew 5:48). This perfection can only come by having a relationship with the Father, and by impartation from Him.

As a child you often do not understand your need for a father. It is only as you get older that you begin to understand that need. The Body of Christ is growing up, and as we mature, we are beginning to understand our need for the Father. Therefore, we enter into the secret place and worship Him. Say to Him, "I know I have a Savior. I know I have a Lord. I know I have a King. But now I need You to be my Father. Teach me and train me as Your son. Let Your presence come." We enter in through the door to the secret place of His presence and say, "Be our Father. We commit our lives to You. We do not want to be Christians only; we want to be the sons of God (Romans 8:14). We want You to be our Father and we ask You to adopt us as Your sons." There is a cry that arises in our hearts: "Abba! Father!" (Romans 8:15). We enter into His Fatherhood over us. Our Father, who art in heaven, hallowed be Your name.

Hebrews 12:5-11   And you have forgotten the exhortation which is addressed to you as sons, "MY SON, DO NOT REGARD LIGHTLY THE DISCIPLINE OF THE LORD, NOR FAINT WHEN YOU ARE REPROVED BY HIM; [6] FOR THOSE WHOM THE LORD LOVES HE DISCIPLINES, AND HE SCOURGES EVERY SON WHOM HE RECEIVES." [7] It is for discipline that you endure; God deals with you as with sons; for what son is there whom his father does not discipline? [8] But if you are without discipline, of which all have become partakers, then you are illegitimate children and not sons. [9] Furthermore, we had earthly fathers to discipline us, and we respected them; shall we not much rather be subject to the Father of spirits, and live? [10] For they disciplined us for a short time as seemed best to them, but He disciplines us for our good, that we may share His holiness. [11] All discipline for the moment seems not to be joyful, but sorrowful; yet to those who have been trained by it, afterwards it yields the peaceful fruit of righteousness.

Romans 8:14   For all who are being led by the Spirit of God, these are sons of God.

Romans 8:15   For you have not received a spirit of slavery leading to fear again, but you have received a spirit of adoption as sons by which we cry out, "Abba! Father!"

2 | And I Will Be a Father to You— 2 Corinthians 6:18

When Christ taught His disciples to pray, He said, "Pray, then, in this way: 'Our Father who art in heaven'" (Matthew 6:9). Christ did not tell the disciples to pray to Himself; He taught them to pray to the Father. The anointing of Christ is to teach us of the Father and to lead us into a relationship with Him (Matthew 11:27). The process begins when you receive salvation through Christ, and then you receive the Holy Spirit (John 14:16-17). Then what does the Holy Spirit teach you? The Holy Spirit teaches you about Christ (John 15:26; 16:14). What does Christ teach you? He teaches you

---

Matthew 11:27 "All things have been handed over to Me by My Father; and no one knows the Son, except the Father; nor does anyone know the Father, except the Son, and anyone to whom the Son wills to reveal Him."

John 14:16-17 "And I will ask the Father, and He will give you another Helper, that He may be with you forever; ¹⁷ that is the Spirit of truth, whom the world cannot receive, because it does not behold Him or know Him, but you know Him because He abides with you, and will be in you."

John 15:26 "When the Helper comes, whom I will send to you from the Father, that is the Spirit of truth, who proceeds from the Father, He will bear witness of Me."

John 16:14 "He shall glorify Me; for He shall take of Mine, and shall disclose it to you."

about the Father (John 14:9-10; 17:7-8). Christ is always leading you to the Father. It is a progressive step-by-step relationship, and we have to reject any tendency in us that says, "We have a revelation of Christ and that is enough. That is what it's all about." No, if you really know Christ by the Holy Spirit, He will lead you to the Father.

Our concept of prayer is to pray for answers; however, this does not accomplish God's purpose. 2 Corinthians the 6th chapter contains a great picture of the objective that God has set for Himself in His dealings with man. It describes His goal for the earth from the beginning of creation up to this point. God's objective, His goal, His plan, and His purpose, that which He is driven to see unfold, is all expressed in this one verse: "'And I will be a father to you, and you shall be sons and daughters to Me,' says the Lord Almighty" (2 Corinthians 6:18). Everything that God is doing, everything that He is intending, has its conclusion in this fact: God is determined to be a Father to us, and He is determined that we become His sons and daughters.

Children who grow up without a father often have developmental and behavioral problems. The term "dysfunctional family" is used to describe families with certain behavioral and relationship problems, and in a sense, Christianity could be considered a dysfunctional family. We as Christians are dysfunctional because, up to this point, we have been robbed of the experience of having

---

John 14:9-10 Jesus said to him, "Have I been so long with you, and yet you have not come to know Me, Philip? He who has seen Me has seen the Father; how do you say, 'Show us the Father'? [10] Do you not believe that I am in the Father, and the Father is in Me? The words that I say to you I do not speak on My own initiative, but the Father abiding in Me does His works."

John 17:7-8 "Now they have come to know that everything Thou hast given Me is from Thee; [8] for the words which Thou gavest Me I have given to them; and they received them, and truly understood that I came forth from Thee, and they believed that Thou didst send Me."

God as a Father who is raising us up as His sons. You may think, "Well, I had a father and it wasn't much help," but God knows how to be a Father; and there is nothing better for a child than to have the security of a father who really knows how to be a father.

When you have a true father, you have an ability to move out into the world and do what you were created to do. You are able to find your destiny. You have confidence. Yet "confidence" is not a word I would necessarily use to describe many believers I know. Instead of confidence, they have a lot of self-condemnation, second-guessing, and questioning of themselves. All of those things are a result of not really having a father. When you have a father, the mistakes you make do not become an issue. All that matters is that you are growing. As we grow, we are able to step out by faith and do or speak the things we have seen with our Father (John 8:38). Then when you make a mistake, your Father is right there picking you up, dusting you off, and saying, "That was a great try." Think about your reactions when you make a mistake. Do you pick yourself up and say, "That was a great try," or do you say, "Oh, dear God, I did it again! What a mess I am!" If my confidence is never built up after I stumble, then that is the lack of a father. If there is never a release and a dynamic change in my life when I receive discipline, then that is the lack of a true father.

This concept requires a transition out of religion as we have known it, because His purpose is not only to be our God; He is determined to be our Father. Imagine being a kid whose dad is the king of a country. To everyone else, he is the king, but when he is with his children, he is still the king, but to them, he is their father. It is a different relationship, and God's relationship with us does not end with Him being our God. When you think about it, it is phenomenal that God Himself would act as God, move through

---

John 8:38 "I speak the things which I have seen with My Father; therefore you also do the things which you heard from your father."

the world as God, speak the Word as God, and use His godliness all for the purpose of being our Father. He is using His power and authority as God to become our Father. When you see this, it is no wonder that from the outset of the creation of man, satan has been set to stop that from happening.

Satan brought an accusation about God to Adam and Eve. He made God look like something other than what He really is. He made God out to be a liar and someone who was trying to cheat them. He asked, "Did God say to you, 'Don't eat of this fruit'? He just doesn't want you to become what He is" (Genesis 3:1-5). Thus, satan continually works to get you to mistrust God so that you don't see Him as a Father. You must understand that God's whole drive is to be your Father, and satan's drive is to block God's appearance to you as a Father. We have been robbed of the perception of Him as our Father. Jesus told His disciples, "These things I have spoken to you in figurative language; an hour is coming when I will speak no more to you in figurative language, but will tell you plainly of the Father" (John 16:25). Christ's promise to us is that He will teach us plainly about the Father, and it is time for us as Christians to see the truth about God and not be moved by any false perception of Him.

We labor so much with the appearance of things. Magic tricks work because our perception is so easily fooled into seeing one thing and thinking it is something else. Your eyes don't necessarily see the truth. Your ears don't necessarily hear the truth. A good

---

Genesis 3:1-5 Now the serpent was more crafty than any beast of the field which the Lord God had made. And he said to the woman, "Indeed, has God said, 'You shall not eat from any tree of the garden'?" 2 And the woman said to the serpent, "From the fruit of the trees of the garden we may eat; 3 but from the fruit of the tree which is in the middle of the garden, God has said, 'You shall not eat from it or touch it, lest you die.'" 4 And the serpent said to the woman, "You surely shall not die! 5 For God knows that in the day you eat from it your eyes will be opened, and you will be like God, knowing good and evil."

magician uses your senses against you so that you are deceived about what is happening right in front of your eyes, even up close. We do not yet understand how good a magician satan really is, and how much he has created an appearance of God that is false. We go through our lives, we get up close to situations, we watch things happen, and we are absolutely convinced about what we just saw, but it is an illusion. When it comes to relating to one another and relating to the Lord and thinking about life, the reality is that we draw conclusions based on these deceptive images—these magic tricks. Consequently, we have many distorted conclusions about God and what He is and what He isn't, but what is the truth?

God is driven to be our Father. He wants to be a Father to us, to care for us, to raise us up as His sons and daughters, and to really engage us in a relationship with Himself. The problem is that everything we observe tells us the opposite. We would say that God is off in His own world and doesn't care about us and doesn't communicate with us. When we experience the difficult circumstances of our lives, we think, "He can't be trying to help!" Have you ever felt that way? "God, I love you, but just leave me alone. You're not helping me. Just sit on Your throne and get out of my life." That is a reaction to an illusion about God. It is difficult for us to understand the drive of satan, the accuser of the brethren, to not only accuse us before God, but to accuse Him before us (Revelation 12:10). Christ is the first-born among many brethren, and so the accuser of the brethren also brings accusations against Him. More than accusations, satan uses our senses to actually bring an image before us to convince us that God is doing something to us that He really is not. It is satan's magic trick, and it will probably take more faith than we have ever exercised, in the midst of all that

---

Revelation 12:10 And I heard a loud voice in heaven, saying, "Now the salvation, and the power, and the kingdom of our God and the authority of His Christ have come, for the accuser of our brethren has been thrown down, who accuses them before our God day and night."

we are going through in our lives, to really forgive God for how we believe He has related to us. It is so difficult for us to believe that God is actually different than how we have perceived Him.

The prophecy concerning Christ was that He would not judge by what His eyes saw or what His ears heard (Isaiah 11:3). Christ came into the world and related to the world on that basis. He refused to see people according to what His eyes saw or what His ears heard or the picture that had been painted about mankind. He saw mankind with the heart of God. In turn, it is time for us to relate to God according to a different perception. We must start relating to God not according to what our eyes see or what our ears hear, but by a completely different standard. We must relate to God based on the true revelation of Him in His Word. When we ask, "Who is God?" the answer is in the Scriptures. He is the One who is determined to be our Father. He is the One who is determined to make us His sons and daughters. When we see all the problems that are happening in our generation and begin to form conclusions about God, there has to be something in us that says, "Wait! It's all an illusion. That is not from God. There is something else that God has for us."

We have many definitions and interpretations of what an appearing of the Lord will be. Maybe there will be a big cloud of glory or He will suddenly appear in our midst. I am far more interested, however, in an appearing that clears up our perceptions. You can be around people and never see them as they really are. That is the way accusations work; they create an image. According to the Hebrew Scriptures, there was great judgment upon idolatry, because idolatry is imagery. It is the act of making an image of God, or saying that an image is God, when it is not. If we are

---

Isaiah 11:3 And He will delight in the fear of the LORD, and He will not judge by what His eyes see, nor make a decision by what His ears hear.

honest, we have to admit that a great deal of the image we have of God is not God. In a very real sense, we are idolaters because we relate to an image in our minds that we are calling God, but that image is not God.

Now let's go back to the verse we read in 2 Corinthians 6, but start reading earlier in the chapter. This refers to God's judgment on idolatry:

> Do not be bound together with unbelievers; for what partnership have righteousness and lawlessness, or what fellowship has light with darkness? Or what harmony has Christ with Belial, or what has a believer in common with an unbeliever? Or what agreement has the temple of God with idols? For we are the temple of the living God; just as God said, "I WILL DWELL IN THEM AND WALK AMONG THEM; AND I WILL BE THEIR GOD, AND THEY SHALL BE MY PEOPLE. Therefore, COME OUT FROM THEIR MIDST AND BE SEPARATE," says the Lord. "AND DO NOT TOUCH WHAT IS UNCLEAN; and I will welcome you. And I will be a father to you, and you shall be sons and daughters to Me," says the Lord Almighty. (2 Corinthians 6:14-18)

Normally, when we look at all these dichotomies and comparisons between righteousness and unrighteousness, we think, "I have to stop being unrighteous and start being more righteous." So we strive to be righteous and strive to be clean, and we get into a very religious mode. Get out of that mode and look at it from a different perspective. If we would separate the filthiness of the lie from the truth about God, He would be a Father to us.

Religion makes relating to God all about striving: "I have to strive to be pure! I have to strive to not be unbelieving!" However, if you could simply extract satan's accusations from your thinking, God would already be your Father. Don't think, "I am worn out from working so hard, but finally, because I am so wonderful and have done all these great things, now God will be my Father." No, He already is your Father. He already exists as that. He is right here as our Father, but there is a screen between us and Him that projects all of these illusions. How do we get rid of that screen? We cast away the lies and simply remove the accusations about God, about ourselves, and about one another. It can happen immediately. As quickly as we can honestly break the lie, we will see Him as our Father. He already is our Father, but we do not yet perceive Him that way, so we do not relate to Him that way. We can't relate to Him as our Father until we stop believing the accusations against Him.

Some say, "Oh no, I have proof! I have absolute proof that these accusations are real!" There is no such thing as "proof" on a natural level. We read in Romans 8:20 that all of creation was subjected to futility, and the definition of the word "futility" in the original Greek is "devoid of truth."[3] What we call "truth" based on our natural senses is literally what God calls "devoid of truth." The natural senses will never lead us to a revelation of God as our Father. Our natural senses are always seeing the magic show being presented by satan, who is able to convince you, by your natural senses, of everything but the truth. Believe for the separation of the precious from the vile (Jeremiah 15:19, KJV). We separate the truth from the lie, the righteousness from the unrighteousness, and the clean from the unclean. We can do it by faith.

Romans 8:20 For the creation was subjected to futility, not of its own will, but because of Him who subjected it, in hope.

Jeremiah 15:19, KJV Therefore thus saith the LORD, If thou return, then will I bring thee again, and thou shalt stand before me: and if thou take forth the precious from the vile, thou shalt be as my mouth: let them return unto thee; but return not thou unto them.

[3.] Joseph Henry Thayer, *A Greek-English Lexicon of the New Testament: Being Grimm's Wilke's Clavis Novi Testamenti* (New York: Harper & Brothers, 1889), 393.

We read in 1 John 3:1-2,

> See how great a love the Father has bestowed upon us,
> that we should be called children of God; and such we
> are. For this reason the world does not know us, because
> it did not know Him. Beloved, now we are children of
> God, and it has not appeared as yet what we shall be.
> We know that when He appears, we shall be like Him,
> because we shall see Him just as He is.

The appearance of things now is not as it shall be. Our religiosity makes us strive for something. "Oh yes, it will appear because we will grow and change." No, now we are children of God. It does not appear what we are right now. Likewise, it does not appear to us what God is right now. We need to loose ourselves from the appearance of things. We do not have to strive to believe for something. It is simply a matter of breaking the illusion.

Believe for an appearing of the Lord where you simply see Him as He really is. Get rid of the idols and the idolatry that satan has thrust upon the world for so long. Stop looking up to heaven for some great appearing. Simply let Him appear, as He really is, to your mind and heart. When the veil is removed we see Him as He is. It actually takes very little to make someone disappear. If you were to hold a sheet up in front of someone, that person would magically disappear. Yet how thin a layer that is, and when you pull that sheet away, the person magically appears again. That is how simple this is. Lord, just pull the sheet away. Appear to us by removing satan's illusion or that which makes You disappear completely (Isaiah 25:7; 2 Corinthians 3:16-18).

Isaiah 25:7   And on this mountain He will swallow up the covering which is over all peoples, even the veil which is stretched over all nations.

2 Corinthians 3:16-18   But whenever a man turns to the Lord, the veil is taken away. [17] Now the Lord is the Spirit; and where the Spirit of the Lord is, there is liberty. [18] But we all, with unveiled face beholding as in a mirror the glory of the Lord, are being transformed into the same image from glory to glory, just as from the Lord, the Spirit.

"When He appears, we shall be like Him, because we shall see Him just as He is" (1 John 3:2); and He is our Father. Lord, appear to us today as our Father, and let us appear to You as Your children. Let us appear to one another as brothers and sisters, all with the same heart, born of the same Father. Let us be done with the lies and deceptions. Let us be done with the illusions and accusations. We reject them from our hearts absolutely. It is time for us to have a Father. It is time for God to be the Father to us that He wants to be. Study the Scriptures, such as 2 Corinthians 6:18, and the Gospels that show us how God the Father thinks, how He sees us, and how He treats us. Rehearse the Scriptures about the Father and how He loves us and provides for us. If we ask Him for bread, He will not give us a stone (Matthew 7:9). Every time you have a thought or image or situation in which God looks different to you than what you read in the Word, stop and say, "Father, I refuse to think this about You. I refuse to accept this illusion. I refuse to bow down to this image that is being created by my natural senses. Instead, I believe what Your Word says You are and what it says about how You care for me. You care even for the sparrows (Luke 12:6), and whatever I ask from You, I will receive (John 16:23). You will do all of these good things for me that You promised, and that is what I believe about You."

Violently and intensely reject the accusations and the lies about God, and believe what He has said about Himself in His Word. Do not accept the accusations about Him as the confirmation of what you are believing to receive. "Well, I asked for this bread and it

---

Matthew 7:9 "Or what man is there among you, when his son shall ask him for a loaf, will give him a stone?"

Luke 12:6 "Are not five sparrows sold for two cents? And yet not one of them is forgotten before God."

John 16:23 "And in that day you will ask Me no question. Truly, truly, I say to you, if you shall ask the Father for anything, He will give it to you in My name."

seems like I got this stone instead." You will always get the illusion first. Do not take that illusion and say, "Here's the answer to my prayer; this is what I believe about God. I asked for bread and I got a stone." No, throw out the illusion and say, "God, that's not You. That is not how You answer. You told me to ask and keep on asking until I receive what I requested" (Matthew 7:7-8). Don't stop with the stone. Stop accepting the accusation as the truth. Reject the accusation and do what He told us to do. Come back to Him and say, "Lord, that's not it. Now I'm going to have what I asked for."

Remember the story of how Daniel sought the Lord (Daniel 10:2-3). God started delivering the answer from the moment Daniel prayed, but satan, in order to keep the illusion about God not answering prayer and not being a loving Father, delayed the answer (Daniel 10:12-13). Every minute an answer is delayed, it paints a negative picture about God. We should be determined in our knowledge of the Word to constantly reject any false picture of God and say, "That is not it. That picture is not the God and Father that He has promised to be according to His Word." Throw out the illusion and say, "Lord, I asked You for these things, and it is Your desire and Your heart to give them to me." We need to end the delay. However, if we keep believing the magic tricks, then we are stuck with the illusions. Satan's magic show is specifically tailored

---

Matthew 7:7-8 "Ask, and it shall be given to you; seek, and you shall find; knock, and it shall be opened to you. [8] For everyone who asks receives, and he who seeks finds, and to him who knocks it shall be opened."

Daniel 10:2-3 In those days I, Daniel, had been mourning for three entire weeks. [3] I did not eat any tasty food, nor did meat or wine enter my mouth, nor did I use any ointment at all, until the entire three weeks were completed.

Daniel 10:12-13 Then he said to me, "Do not be afraid, Daniel, for from the first day that you set your heart on understanding this and on humbling yourself before your God, your words were heard, and I have come in response to your words. [13] But the prince of the kingdom of Persia was withstanding me for twenty-one days; then behold, Michael, one of the chief princes, came to help me, for I had been left there with the kings of Persia."

for each individual, to convince us to buy the illusions. We must reject them day by day and minute by minute. We stop believing the illusion, and we ask the Holy Spirit to move in us by wisdom and revelation to show us Christ, and we ask Christ to show us the Father. We ask Him to let us plainly see everything that happens, whether it is or is not the Father. When it is not, we reject it. When it is, we worship the Father in thanksgiving for who He is, what He is, and what He is giving us.

God has planted a seed of revelation that is increasing and multiplying. He is in the process of really delivering us from the things that have kept us from seeing Him as He really is. This is the revelation of being the sons of God who are restoring everything back to Him, and whose cry is, "Abba! Father!" (Romans 8:15). Our brains may not be accepting it, but our hearts are. Our spirits are bearing witness to the revelation that it is true. We do not realize how deeply the lies and accusations of satan, the accuser of the brethren, have robbed us of a true relationship with God as our Father. God's solitary goal, in all that He is doing with creation, is to be our Father, and the greatest crime in the history of the world is that we have been robbed of our Father. However, things are going to change; we are going to be free. We turn off the magic show that deceives, that alters the very appearance of God to us. The fact is that God is our Father and there is a revelation of the Father that is coming to us. Let there be revelation. Let Christ who richly dwells in our hearts break the bondage of deception and illusion and accusation, and anoint our eyes to see the truth of who the Father really is.

Romans 8:15 For you have not received a spirit of slavery leading to fear again, but you have received a spirit of adoption as sons by which we cry out, "Abba! Father!"

3 | Call Him Father!

In the previous chapter, we examined how satan has distorted man's perception of God. Satan is always trying to do that. He cannot create anything, so all he can do is attempt to pervert what God is doing. He can delay, he can deceive, but he cannot change the truth. He is the father of lies, so he tries to make a lie out of the truth (John 8:44). We have to be aware that the potential for deception rests on everything we know or think we know. A great deal of confusion has entered into traditional church teaching about God and Christ. One of the things we have been robbed of is a clarity concerning Jesus. Jesus has been presented to believers in many ways that paint a wrong picture of who He was and who He is in relation to God and to us. Jesus was sent by the Father, but more than that, Jesus was the Father ministering to mankind. You cannot read the Gospels without being aware that everything people were hearing or seeing about Jesus was the expression of the Father.

John 8:44 "You are of your father the devil, and you want to do the desires of your father. He was a murderer from the beginning, and does not stand in the truth, because there is no truth in him. Whenever he speaks a lie, he speaks from his own nature; for he is a liar, and the father of lies."

This really needs to be clear because you need to know who Jesus is and what He did. According to a familiar verse, "For God so loved the world, that He gave His only begotten Son" (John 3:16). We don't read in this verse that Jesus loved the world. We read that God loved the world. The Greek word for "world" here is *kosmos*,[4] which can be translated as "world," but it can also be translated as "universe," or even "people." I think it is more accurately translated as "people," because God so loved people that He sent Christ. So take it out of the generalized concept of God saving the world. If you have to generalize it, then at least use the term "mankind." God didn't really even send Christ into the earth to deliver the earth, because it is the sons of God who deliver creation (Romans 8:19-21). Christ did not come to deliver creation; He came to set mankind free. He loved mankind, human beings, even in our fallen state. Even while we were yet sinners, Christ died for us (Romans 5:8). God so loved man "that He gave His only begotten Son, that whoever believes in Him should not perish, but have eternal life" (John 3:16). God did this, and Jesus was His representative. As we read in 2 Corinthians 5:18, "Now all these things are from God, who reconciled us to Himself through Christ." God is determined to reconcile you to Himself through Christ.

These may seem like minor points, but we are not splitting hairs; we are fixing Grand Canyons in our thinking. Our concepts of God, even the very name "God," tend to make Him distant and

---

Romans 8:19-21 For the anxious longing of the creation waits eagerly for the revealing of the sons of God. [20] For the creation was subjected to futility, not of its own will, but because of Him who subjected it, in hope [21] that the creation itself also will be set free from its slavery to corruption into the freedom of the glory of the children of God.

Romans 5:8 But God demonstrates His own love toward us, in that while we were yet sinners, Christ died for us.

[4.] James Strong, *Enhanced Strong's Lexicon* (Bellingham, WA: Logos Bible Software, 2001).

unattainable in our thinking. Our perceptions of Him make Him essentially unreal, someone we cannot approach or have anything to do with. Try something for a while. Instead of calling Him "God," call Him "Father." Don't worry, the earth won't collapse. Of course He is God. He is the God of the universe, and He is God to unbelievers, but in the family, He is our Father. Think of how many times you refer to Him as God. What are your feelings toward Him when you do that? Now every time you refer to Him, say, "Father." I believe that you will feel resonating out of your being a significant difference in the way you relate to Him. You may be thinking, "I had some issues with my father, so I don't even know how to relate to God as my Father." Don't worry. I don't think anyone has truly had a father who could honestly compare with our heavenly Father. He is your Father and He loves you so much that He sent His Son to die for you. If you are tired of being separated from Him, understand that He is gut-wrenchingly tired of being separated from you. For this reason, He sent Jesus to reconcile you to Himself.

The 23rd chapter of Matthew records an exhortation by Jesus to a group of people, including His disciples. Near the end of the chapter we read,

> "O Jerusalem, Jerusalem, who kills the prophets and stones those who are sent to her! How often I wanted to gather your children together, the way a hen gathers her chicks under her wings, and you were unwilling. Behold, your house is being left to you desolate!" (Matthew 23:37-38)

This was the Father speaking through Jesus to Jerusalem. Obviously, He was not talking to a city; He was speaking to the people of Israel. He was expressing His feelings about sending Christ to them. He said, "I am only after one thing. All I want is to gather you under My wings." The analogy is that of a hen who is in some kind of danger, drawing all of her chicks to herself. If you have ever seen that, it is interesting to watch all of the chicks running back to mama as she puffs herself up and puts out her wings. The little chicks get under those wings because they know she will protect them, not only by covering them, but even by fighting for them if necessary. That is a picture of the Father. He was coming through Christ as their Father, and He wanted to draw His people back to Himself. He told them, "That is what I wanted, but you would not."

Christ said, "If you really understood Me, you would understand that I am trying to draw you to Myself," but they did not see Him as someone who was drawing them. Jesus was seen by most of them as something negative, as someone who was confrontational, who was criticizing them, who was tearing down their belief system. They did not feel drawn to Jesus; they felt repulsed by Jesus. Everything about Christ was the Father drawing them, and yet everything in their reaction to Christ was the opposite feeling. They felt pushed away, whether they were pushing themselves away or felt that He was pushing them away. He did, after all, call them a brood of vipers as well as use other negative terms to describe them (Matthew 23:33, 24-27). From their perspective, they had many good excuses to justify their feeling of repulsion.

If you truly examined your heart, you would probably find similar feelings that have built up over years of walking with the Lord. You feel put off, or you feel a lack of fulfillment, or you feel that

---

Matthew 23:33 "You serpents, you brood of vipers, how shall you escape the sentence of hell?"

Matthew 23:24-27 "You blind guides, who strain out a gnat and swallow a camel! [25] Woe to you, scribes and Pharisees, hypocrites! For you clean the outside of the cup and of the dish, but inside they are full of robbery and self-indulgence. [26] You blind Pharisee, first clean the inside of the cup and of the dish, so that the outside of it may become clean also. [27] Woe to you, scribes and Pharisees, hypocrites! For you are like whitewashed tombs which on the outside appear beautiful, but inside they are full of dead men's bones and all uncleanness."

God doesn't love you. A major focus of satan's attack against you is to block you from being aware of God's love. The people who were listening to Jesus back then did not feel that He loved them. They did not feel the love of God drawing them like a mother hen. The question is, will you believe those feelings, or will you believe that God is telling the truth when He says, "I am drawing you"? Let God be true and every man a liar (Romans 3:4). Right now God is repeating this to you: "I am drawing you unto Myself. I am gathering you." Believe it. From this moment on, everything that makes you feel repelled, isolated, independent, or separated from the Father is a lie. God is drawing you into a relationship with Himself, and you have to believe that.

The Father is drawing you. He is only concerned about one thing: "I want you under My wing. I want you in My presence. I want you with Me." If you are personally blocked from entering the Father's presence, or have any resistance to coming into a relationship with Him, the first thing that is stopping you is condemnation. You must not have condemnation. Condemnation makes you withdraw from God's presence (Genesis 3:8-11). "I would have drawn you, but you were unwilling," Jesus said (Matthew 23:37). Condemnation is the very definition of "you were unwilling." It must be a revelation deeper than your breath, more real than your heartbeat, that "there is therefore now no condemnation for those who are in Christ Jesus" (Romans 8:1). More than anything

---

Romans 3:4   May it never be! Rather, let God be found true, though every man be found a liar, as it is written, "THAT THOU MIGHTEST BE JUSTIFIED IN THY WORDS, AND MIGHTEST PREVAIL WHEN THOU ART JUDGED."

Genesis 3:8-11   And they heard the sound of the LORD God walking in the garden in the cool of the day, and the man and his wife hid themselves from the presence of the LORD God among the trees of the garden. [9] Then the LORD God called to the man, and said to him, "Where are you?" [10] And he said, "I heard the sound of Thee in the garden, and I was afraid because I was naked; so I hid myself." [11] And He said, "Who told you that you were naked? Have you eaten from the tree of which I commanded you not to eat?"

else, you need to get this one point: Christ, whom the Father sent, provides you with the end of condemnation. A relationship with the Father has to start there. This means that there is nothing that can stop you from being in His presence (Romans 8:38-39). There is no reason for you not to be drawn to Him as to a mother hen and to enter into His presence, to get under His wings and be with Him all the time. Condemnation stops you from doing that.

The Lord's emphasis is not a negative focus on the sins of the flesh. Our separation from the Father is more satanically contrived than it is something of our own choice. When the Father was entreating Jerusalem through Christ, He recognized that satan had plotted against Israel as the chosen people of God. Satan knew that he could effectively destroy the entire plan of God in one move if he could make them resist coming to the Father. We fall into the same trap when our concept about approaching God is, "Unless I clean up my act and get right with God, I can't be in His presence. I have to perfect myself; I have to be righteous. I have to crucify my flesh; I have to get rid of all my bad habits. If I do that, then I will be able to stand in the presence of the Father." That is a lie, but it is promoted by church and religion. Think about how Christ is taught. In church we preach about people's sin and preach about their flesh and preach about their problems. Many churches operate on the idea, "You can be part of our church, but if you do this or that, then you're out." What does "out" mean? It means having no access to God. This is so contrary to what God is actually doing. Everything He has done has been to draw people to Himself. Jesus said, "It is not those who are healthy who need a physician, but those who are sick; I did not come to call the righteous, but sinners" (Mark 2:17).

Romans 8:38-39   For I am convinced that neither death, nor life, nor angels, nor principalities, nor things present, nor things to come, nor powers, [39] nor height, nor depth, nor any other created thing, shall be able to separate us from the love of God, which is in Christ Jesus our Lord.

The Book of Zechariah describes Joshua the high priest standing in the presence of the Father with all of his filthy garments (Zechariah 3:3). This is a picture of how we come before the Father. The great old song "Just As I Am" has been sung in many meetings where people are invited to come up to the front and accept Jesus. Many people remember how wonderful that initial experience was when they honestly allowed themselves to go to Jesus just as they were. Remember that you do not only stand before Jesus just as you are. He is the way to the Father, so that you can stand before the Father just as you are. Jesus said, "I am the way" (John 14:6). He is the way to the Father. He is how we get there. He is the blood that covers us so that we can go into the Father's presence. Again, that does not only happen when you are perfect. You stand in the presence of God in your worst, filthiest state. What are you waiting for? Why are you resisting His call to be drawn to Him as to a mother hen? Why do you resist going in, right at this moment, to live in the presence of the Father? Whatever is wrong, Christ is the covering for us to be in the presence of God. Once we are in His presence, He will work out all other issues.

For the most part, we are off on our own trying to deal with our issues by ourselves. We continually try to work out our problems, our needs, our situations, even our promises from God—the ministry and anointing God gave us. Jesus said, "I am able to do nothing of Myself" (John 5:19, 30). Why then do we function independently

---

Zechariah 3:3 Now Joshua was clothed with filthy garments and standing before the angel.

John 14:6 Jesus said to him, "I am the way, and the truth, and the life; no one comes to the Father, but through Me."

John 5:19 Jesus therefore answered and was saying to them, "Truly, truly, I say to you, the Son can do nothing of Himself, unless it is something He sees the Father doing; for whatever the Father does, these things the Son also does in like manner."

John 5:30 "I can do nothing on My own initiative. As I hear, I judge; and My judgment is just, because I do not seek My own will, but the will of Him who sent Me."

from God? The Father is saying to us, "I want you under My wing. I want you with Me. I cannot handle being separated and isolated from you anymore. I cannot stand it that you function and act independently of Me." We are like the disciples who told Jesus, "Lord, we have been fishing all night long and we haven't caught anything." He told them to do something that they probably already had done. He said, "Put the net down on the other side of the boat." When they did that, they were not even able to haul in the huge number of fish they caught (Luke 5:4-7; John 21:3-6). The difference was that they did it with Him. They had fished all night long without Him, but when they were connected to Him, they could not even handle the blessing that came. Everything we have tried that has never worked will work if we do it in His presence, in a connection with Him.

We are doing exactly what satan wants when we act independently. After accepting Jesus as our Savior and receiving the baptism of the Holy Spirit, the first time we run into a problem in our life we are off on our own trying to bind and loose things. What is the first lesson about spiritual warfare? You submit yourself to God. You

---

Luke 5:4-7 And when He had finished speaking, He said to Simon, "Put out into the deep water and let down your nets for a catch." ⁵ And Simon answered and said, "Master, we worked hard all night and caught nothing, but at Your bidding I will let down the nets." ⁶ And when they had done this, they enclosed a great quantity of fish; and their nets began to break; ⁷ and they signaled to their partners in the other boat, for them to come and help them. And they came, and filled both of the boats, so that they began to sink.

John 21:3-6 Simon Peter said to them, "I am going fishing." They said to him, "We will also come with you." They went out, and got into the boat; and that night they caught nothing. ⁴ But when the day was now breaking, Jesus stood on the beach; yet the disciples did not know that it was Jesus. ⁵ Jesus therefore said to them, "Children, you do not have any fish, do you?" They answered Him, "No." ⁶ And He said to them, "Cast the net on the right-hand side of the boat, and you will find a catch." They cast therefore, and then they were not able to haul it in because of the great number of fish.

go into the presence of God, and from there you resist the devil (James 4:7). You don't have to make it a complicated effort. This is not about defeating satan, or binding him or loosing yourself. It's not even about agreeing together with two or three until whatever you ask for is happening (Matthew 18:19-20). If you want to do that, start with you and the Father. That's two. Now you can include Jesus and that's three. We have to get over this idea that we are accomplishing anything in ourselves apart from His presence.

We know that Jesus died for us, and that His blood cleanses us from our sins. But we do not stay there with Jesus; we go into the presence of God. Let's look at where the separation of God and man occurred in the first place. What happened according to Genesis? Don't focus on the forbidden fruit and the disobedience. Those who were in the presence of God were dismissed from His presence. They were separated from God. God Himself said, "Get out of the garden. You cannot be in My presence" (Genesis 3:22-24). From that time on, man and God were separate and distant from each other. That is the history of mankind up to Jesus, and God was determined to solve that problem. He created the separation, but He also resolved it by sending Jesus into the world.

Jesus came to take away our sins because our sins were separating us from the Father. Again, in our separation and independence we

---

James 4:7 Submit therefore to God. Resist the devil and he will flee from you.

Matthew 18:19-20 "Again I say to you, that if two of you agree on earth about anything that they may ask, it shall be done for them by My Father who is in heaven. [20] For where two or three have gathered together in My name, there I am in their midst."

Genesis 3:22-24 Then the LORD God said, "Behold, the man has become like one of Us, knowing good and evil; and now, lest he stretch out his hand, and take also from the tree of life, and eat, and live forever"— [23] therefore the LORD God sent him out from the garden of Eden, to cultivate the ground from which he was taken. [24] So He drove the man out; and at the east of the garden of Eden He stationed the cherubim, and the flaming sword which turned every direction, to guard the way to the tree of life.

think, "I just sinned. Now let me go to Jesus and take His blood, and then perfect myself." Stop focusing on sin. Sin is a leaf. It is a branch. It is a secondary issue. Come to Jesus and appropriate the victory He won, and then stand in the presence of the Father. The victory He won wasn't just a victory over satan. It was a victory over your isolation from God. It was a victory over what separates you from the Father. That is the victory that was won. You don't have to battle satan. I guarantee that if you are in the presence of the Father, you are exercising the victory of Jesus Christ, and satan at some point will become a mist that disappears. Right now, no matter what circumstance you are in, you can stand in the presence of the Father. And that does not mean standing in front of Him trying to hide. If you are going to confess something, go into His presence and say, "Father, I did this and I thought that, and this and that happened." He is your Father. Go talk to Him.

In situation after situation, our tendency is to deal with things ourselves. We think independently, and we move independently. The excuse is, "I learned that because God doesn't come through. I learned to be independent and do things myself because I have prayed for miracles to happen, and for promises to be fulfilled, and nothing has happened." You were not in His presence if they didn't happen. We have to stop believing the lie of satan that we did our part and it didn't work. Whatever makes you feel that way is a lie. You have to know, more than you know your own name, that the Father is constantly drawing you. He sent Jesus here for you so that you can now be in His presence—not in the future, not when you are perfected, not when you have your life in order, not when you are being a good father or mother or employee or whatever you think you are supposed to be. Whatever prophecies you have, whatever promises you have from the Word of God, they are all dependent upon Him being in your life, upon you being reconciled to the presence of the Father.

Jesus said to the people in His day, "The door is open for you to come under the shadow of the Almighty, but you would not" (Psalm 91:1; Luke 13:34). Today, no matter what condemnation you may be feeling, refuse it and say, "I am going into the presence of the Father." Your mind will tell you, "No, you can't go into His presence like that. He is God. He will be sitting there on His throne of judgment waiting for you to walk in and He is going to blow you away!" Somewhere along the line you got in your mind that you have to do something before you go into His presence. That is satan's thinking. That, pure and simple, is the biggest satanic lie that has ever existed. He knows that all he has to do is get you to flinch about going into the presence of the Father and he has won. Christ died on the cross 2,000 years ago, and how many times have people said, "Then, where is the fulfillment?" It is right there in His presence. Christ lived in the Father's presence, and we must follow that example. "The Father and I are one. I can do nothing of Myself but what I see My Father do (John 5:19). I can speak nothing but what I hear the Father speak." Now, that may not happen for you overnight, but let me tell you where it starts. It starts by simply huddling under His wings and staying there.

If you are having a hard time finding Jesus, it is because you are not trying to step into the presence of the Father. When you are determined to step into the presence of the Father, then you will find Jesus, because He is the way in. He said of Himself, "I am the door of the sheep" (John 10:7). If you want to find Him, He is the doorway. He is your ticket into the presence of the Father.

Psalm 91:1 He who dwells in the shelter of the Most High will abide in the shadow of the Almighty.

Luke 13:34 "O Jerusalem, Jerusalem, the city that kills the prophets and stones those sent to her! How often I wanted to gather your children together, just as a hen gathers her brood under her wings, and you would not have it!"

John 10:7 Jesus therefore said to them again, "Truly, truly, I say to you, I am the door of the sheep."

There is no reason for you not to be in God's presence. There is no reason for you to flinch or resist. God Himself, in Jesus, took care of everything so that you don't have to draw back at the door.

I once had a vision in which I walked up to a door that was like a large archway. On the other side of this archway I could see the Kingdom of God. As I entered through the archway, suddenly a waterfall of blood came down, and as I walked through it, I was covered by the blood of Christ. From that moment on I had absolute and complete access to every aspect of the heavenly realm in the Kingdom. I believe it really is that simple. We have stood and peered into the things of the Kingdom for a long time. Now is the time to enter in through Christ. We don't have to resist or even delay. All we have to do is walk through the door.

We are exhorted by Paul to take every thought captive in obedience to Christ, and the thoughts we take captive are all those thoughts that make us flinch from going into the Father (2 Corinthians 10:5). Take this verse, "There is therefore now no condemnation for those who are in Christ Jesus" (Romans 8:1), and start applying it continuously, because everything that comes against you is about keeping you out of the Father's presence. You have to start there, because if you can't break the sense of condemnation, you will not stand before Him. We have everything we need right now to end futility, but the first place futility ends is in us. The sons of God don't deliver creation from futility without themselves being free. When we read that all creation comes into the freedom of the sons of God, it means that the freedom in the sons is simply imparted to all creation. It is time to end futility, but we cannot pretend that we are sons of God taking authority over futility when we are not in His presence. Until we stop prophesying in independent isolation

---

2 Corinthians 10:5 We are destroying speculations and every lofty thing raised up against the knowledge of God, and we are taking every thought captive to the obedience of Christ.

from the Father, we will continue to have limited effect. When we are in the presence of the Father, however, the effect will be as when Jesus stopped the wind and the disciples said, "What kind of a man is this?" (Matthew 8:27). He was simply the only one who knew the Father (Matthew 11:27). That is still true. But the Body of Christ is going to change that, because everything that Christ did was so that we too could enter in and know the Father. Today we take the first step.

Matthew 8:27 And the men marveled, saying, "What kind of a man is this, that even the winds and the sea obey Him?"

Matthew 11:27 "All things have been handed over to Me by My Father; and no one knows the Son, except the Father; nor does anyone know the Father, except the Son, and anyone to whom the Son wills to reveal Him."

4 | Now We Abide in the Father

As we have studied in this book, Jesus is the door, the way to the Father. He came to end the separation between God and man. He came to end futility. What is futility? When we think of futility, we think of man's fall in the Garden of Eden, but what is it that really happened in the Garden of Eden? The real significance of what happened is that mankind was separated from God, and everything that we have experienced from that time on is by virtue of that reality. After the story of the fall of man, we read in the very next chapter of Genesis that "men began to call upon the name of the LORD" (Genesis 4:26). Upon leaving the Garden, one of the first things people did was build altars to try to find a way back to God.

Everything about religion, everything that we tend to do to relate to God, is from a place of being separated from God. Being separated from God is the very definition of futility, but according to Romans 8, creation was subjected to futility in hope that it will

---

Genesis 4:26 And to Seth, to him also a son was born; and he called his name Enosh. Then men began to call upon the name of the LORD.

be delivered at some point (Romans 8:20-21). This is why we are continually striving to get out of this futility (Romans 8:22-23). This is why we strive to break free from that which isolates us from the Father. It is time for the sons of God to come forth to free creation from futility so that the Father can once again dwell in this earth and be one with us and with His creation.

As long as we allow ourselves to be in a place of separation from God, we are not actually getting anywhere. We are not going where He wants to lead us. We know that we have salvation in Jesus Christ, but our relationship with Christ and with the Father does not stop there. According to Romans 8:10, even though Christ is in us, our body is dead because of sin. There is something more that God wants to bring us into (Romans 8:11-14). This does not mean that we do not want Christ dwelling in us. The opposite is true. Christ comes to take up His abode in us, but that is only the beginning (John 14:20). The Father is also coming to take up His

---

Romans 8:20-21 For the creation was subjected to futility, not of its own will, but because of Him who subjected it, in hope [21] that the creation itself also will be set free from its slavery to corruption into the freedom of the glory of the children of God.

Romans 8:22-23 For we know that the whole creation groans and suffers the pains of childbirth together until now. [23] And not only this, but also we ourselves, having the first fruits of the Spirit, even we ourselves groan within ourselves, waiting eagerly for our adoption as sons, the redemption of our body.

Romans 8:10 And if Christ is in you, though the body is dead because of sin, yet the spirit is alive because of righteousness.

Romans 8:11-14 But if the Spirit of Him who raised Jesus from the dead dwells in you, He who raised Christ Jesus from the dead will also give life to your mortal bodies through His Spirit who indwells you. [12] So then, brethren, we are under obligation, not to the flesh, to live according to the flesh— [13] for if you are living according to the flesh, you must die; but if by the Spirit you are putting to death the deeds of the body, you will live. [14] For all who are being led by the Spirit of God, these are sons of God.

John 14:20 "In that day you shall know that I am in My Father, and you in Me, and I in you."

abode in us (John 14:23). That is what is pleasing to the Father. That is what He is looking for. Yes, Christ came to save us; but He came to take us out of being humans in a religious relationship of futility with the Father, and to give us a way to abide with the Father. He said, "I am the way" (John 14:6). He is the way into abiding in the Father and the Father abiding in us so that we break out of this futility.

Becoming the sons of God who release creation from futility may be something we believe in and profess, but we will never be those who free creation until we are free in ourselves. We will never be free, or make any forward progress to becoming sons of God, until we break out of this long-distance relationship with God. The very term "God" gives us a convenient excuse to remain at arm's distance from Him. Using the term "God" evokes in the human brain something so great and so awesome and so distant and so unattainable that what else can we do but build altars? Our very form of worship recognizes our distance from Him, and we excuse it by thinking, "I can't be like God. I'm not supposed to be like God." That thinking evades what God really wants. Jesus said, "My Father and I will come and take up Our abode in you. We will abide in you, and you will abide in Us" (John 14:23).

The purpose of Jesus coming to earth was to end the isolation between God and man. Jesus related to God as His Father, and if you believe in Jesus Christ, then God is your Father. This does not mean that He is not God. He is God. He is all things to the world as God, but to you He is your Father. When I was a boy the kids in the neighborhood knew my father by what he did—he was a military pilot. I knew he was a pilot too, but to me he was my

---

John 14:23 Jesus answered and said to him, "If anyone loves Me, he will keep My word; and My Father will love him, and We will come to him, and make Our abode with him."

John 14:6 Jesus said to him, "I am the way, and the truth, and the life; no one comes to the Father, but through Me."

dad. God will always be God, but in your personal relationship with Him, He is your Father. We know that Jesus was crucified because He made Himself out to be as God, but what was the statement that made them accuse Him of that crime? He said, "I and the Father are one" (John 10:30). The fact that He said, "God is My Father" was considered blasphemy (John 5:18; 10:33-36; Matthew 26:63-65). Why was it blasphemy? By saying that, Jesus was turning upside down the entire foundation of man's religions, which are completely and thoroughly based on God being unattainable.

When Jesus talked about God being His Father, the scribes and Pharisees understood the meaning. In the culture of that day, fathers and sons were essentially the same. As an inheritance, the firstborn son received the father's occupation and everything that the father owned. Sons were named after their fathers. That is why the naming of John the Baptist was such an issue, because his parents named him John, instead of Zacharias after his

---

John 5:18 For this cause therefore the Jews were seeking all the more to kill Him, because He not only was breaking the Sabbath, but also was calling God His own Father, making Himself equal with God.

John 10:33-36 The Jews answered Him, "For a good work we do not stone You, but for blasphemy; and because You, being a man, make Yourself out to be God." [34] Jesus answered them, "Has it not been written in your Law, 'I SAID, YOU ARE GODS'? [35] If he called them gods, to whom the word of God came (and the Scripture cannot be broken), [36] do you say of Him, whom the Father sanctified and sent into the world, 'You are blaspheming,' because I said, 'I am the Son of God'?"

Matthew 26:63-65 But Jesus kept silent. And the high priest said to Him, "I adjure You by the living God, that You tell us whether You are the Christ, the Son of God." [64] Jesus said to him, "You have said it yourself; nevertheless I tell you, hereafter you shall see THE SON OF MAN SITTING AT THE RIGHT HAND OF POWER, and COMING ON THE CLOUDS OF HEAVEN." [65] Then the high priest tore his robes, saying, "He has blasphemed! What further need do we have of witnesses? Behold, you have now heard the blasphemy."

father (Luke 1:59-63). In our Western culture today we don't think in those terms. However, in the mindset of Christ's day, by simply uttering the word "Father" in reference to God He was turning religion on its head. Saying that God was His Father rejected the entire religious system of the day, which was based on the concept that mankind could never be one with God (Hebrews 10:1-4).

We have to see that Jesus not only brought salvation, He connected us with the Father. You may say, "The goal of Jesus was the cross." Yes, but what was He doing through the cross? He was coming as the great ambassador to reconcile us to the Father (2 Corinthians 5:18-20). Regardless, the primary focus of Christianity is on Jesus with very little focus on the Father. Many make the cross into a symbol, and come and worship Jesus from a place of futility and separation from the Father. We must not make Jesus so high and so lifted up and divine that we lose the fact that He was just like us. He was like us, and in that state, He and the Father became one.

Luke 1:59-63 And it came about that on the eighth day they came to circumcise the child, and they were going to call him Zacharias, after his father. [60] And his mother answered and said, "No indeed; but he shall be called John." [61] And they said to her, "There is no one among your relatives who is called by that name." [62] And they made signs to his father, as to what he wanted him called. [63] And he asked for a tablet, and wrote as follows, "His name is John." And they were all astonished.

Hebrews 10:1-4 For the Law, since it has only a shadow of the good things to come and not the very form of things, can never by the same sacrifices year by year, which they offer continually, make perfect those who draw near. [2] Otherwise, would they not have ceased to be offered, because the worshipers, having once been cleansed, would no longer have had consciousness of sins? [3] But in those sacrifices there is a reminder of sins year by year. [4] For it is impossible for the blood of bulls and goats to take away sins.

2 Corinthians 5:18-20 Now all these things are from God, who reconciled us to Himself through Christ, and gave us the ministry of reconciliation, [19] namely, that God was in Christ reconciling the world to Himself, not counting their trespasses against them, and He has committed to us the word of reconciliation. [20] Therefore, we are ambassadors for Christ, as though God were entreating through us; we beg you on behalf of Christ, be reconciled to God.

A great deal of Christian doctrine right now is incorrect in that it fails to acknowledge that Jesus was a man who **became** to us salvation (Hebrews 5:9). What we need is access to the Father. What we don't need is a religion that keeps God as someone who is absolutely unattainable, a religion in which we are believers and worshipers but never enter into a relationship with the Father. Jesus came to break down the walls and barriers between us and the Father. But satan wants us to do the same thing with Jesus that we have done with God, and that is to make Him so unattainable that there is no way we can relate to Him. Everything about satan and his kingdom is dependent on keeping you isolated from the Father, and keeping you relating to Jesus as a God figure who is afar off and is just as unattainable in your mind as God. Yet everything about Jesus coming to earth was to end that condition.

Jesus was just like you. He lived as a human being just as you have to live. However, in that state, He and the Father became one. He now has all the power and all the authority of the Godhead bodily (Colossians 2:9). He is the fullness of the Father, and according to the Scriptures we are supposed to be that too (Ephesians 3:19; 4:13). "As He is, so also are we in this world" (1 John 4:17). It is His purpose to bring many sons to glory (Hebrews 2:10). It may shock

---

Hebrews 5:9 And having been made perfect, He became to all those who obey Him the source of eternal salvation.

Colossians 2:9 For in Him all the fulness of Deity dwells in bodily form.

Ephesians 3:19 And to know the love of Christ which surpasses knowledge, that you may be filled up to all the fulness of God.

Ephesians 4:13 Until we all attain to the unity of the faith, and of the knowledge of the Son of God, to a mature man, to the measure of the stature which belongs to the fulness of Christ.

1 John 4:17 By this, love is perfected with us, that we may have confidence in the day of judgment; because as He is, so also are we in this world.

Hebrews 2:10 For it was fitting for Him, for whom are all things, and through whom are all things, in bringing many sons to glory, to perfect the author of their salvation through sufferings.

you to realize that in the very beginning, in the first century, the original Christians did not relate to Jesus as God. They related to Him as the Messiah, who is a man, and to the fact that He was resurrected (Acts 2:22-24). They made an issue out of the resurrection, because that was the proof that He and the Father were one (Acts 2:31-36; 3:13-15; 4:10; 5:30-31). Eventually, due to various influences and pressures, Christians became embroiled in very contentious debates about the nature of Christ.

In 325 AD, the emperor Constantine convened the Council of Nicaea in an attempt to unite Christians who were divided over, among other things, doctrines about Christ's nature as the Word.

Acts 2:22-24 "Men of Israel, listen to these words: Jesus the Nazarene, a man attested to you by God with miracles and wonders and signs which God performed through Him in your midst, just as you yourselves know— [23] this Man, delivered up by the predetermined plan and foreknowledge of God, you nailed to a cross by the hands of godless men and put Him to death. [24] And God raised Him up again, putting an end to the agony of death, since it was impossible for Him to be held in its power."

Acts 2:31-36 "He looked ahead and spoke of the resurrection of the Christ, that HE WAS NEITHER ABANDONED TO HADES, NOR DID His flesh SUFFER DECAY. [32] This Jesus God raised up again, to which we are all witnesses. [33] Therefore having been exalted to the right hand of God, and having received from the Father the promise of the Holy Spirit, He has poured forth this which you both see and hear. [34] For it was not David who ascended into heaven, but he himself says: 'THE LORD SAID TO MY LORD, "SIT AT MY RIGHT HAND, [35] UNTIL I MAKE THINE ENEMIES A FOOTSTOOL FOR THY FEET." ' [36] Therefore let all the house of Israel know for certain that God has made Him both Lord and Christ—this Jesus whom you crucified."

Acts 3:13-15 "The God of Abraham, Isaac, and Jacob, the God of our fathers, has glorified His servant Jesus, the one whom you delivered up, and disowned in the presence of Pilate, when he had decided to release Him. [14] But you disowned the Holy and Righteous One, and asked for a murderer to be granted to you, [15] but put to death the Prince of life, the one whom God raised from the dead, a fact to which we are witnesses."

Acts 4:10 Let it be known to all of you, and to all the people of Israel, that by the name of Jesus Christ the Nazarene, whom you crucified, whom God raised from the dead—by this name this man stands here before you in good health.

Acts 5:30-31 "The God of our fathers raised up Jesus, whom you had put to death by hanging Him on a cross. [31] He is the one whom God exalted to His right hand as a Prince and a Savior, to grant repentance to Israel, and forgiveness of sins."

Think about that. Imagine all of these bishops being called together by a pagan Roman ruler and forced to decide who and what Jesus was. Was Jesus God? Was Jesus man? They were so far removed from the event of Christ's resurrection that there really was no way for them to decide who and what Jesus was. Yet because of this drive to unify the Roman empire under Christianity, which was begun by Constantine and continued on through several Roman emperors presiding over Church councils, Christian doctrine was shaped by unending debates to emphasize that Jesus is God. I'm sure people will criticize and say, "Isn't this heresy? Are you saying that Jesus was not God?" Of course Jesus was God by virtue of the fact that the Father dwelt in Him. He was the fullness of the Godhead bodily (Colossians 2:9). How could He not be God? The issue is that we do not understand how He became that, because our tendency is to think that He dropped into earth that way.

Jesus came into the earth as a human, just like you and me, just like all of mankind (Philippians 2:5-8). God brought Him into the earth as a human being, and what He obtained by abiding in the Father in oneness, He obtained while in the exact same condition that we are in as humans. He is the way for us, because we can literally follow Him into the Father through the same process that He walked through. We read in the Word that He became perfect by the things that He suffered (Hebrews 2:10). He experienced the discipline of the Father. We also experience the discipline of the Father, but when we are disciplined by the Father, it is such a hard thing for us because we feel separated from Him. There is nothing worse than discipline without a relationship. What makes

---

Philippians 2:5-8 Have this attitude in yourselves which was also in Christ Jesus, [6] who, although He existed in the form of God, did not regard equality with God a thing to be grasped, [7] but emptied Himself, taking the form of a bond-servant, and being made in the likeness of men. [8] And being found in appearance as a man, He humbled Himself by becoming obedient to the point of death, even death on a cross.

discipline easy is that He is your Father (Hebrews 12:6-7). It is easy when God is a real person in your life and you know His love is real.

Are you confused by the circumstances of your life, because one thing after another seems to be going wrong? You can be assured that everything will go wrong under futility and religion that separates you from God. Religion, in its separation from God, makes discipline a matter of striving. Religion makes you believe, "We have to find some way to suffer pain in order to connect back to God." No, Jesus already connected you back to God. Your circumstances may seem to rule and reign, but God is not trying to torture you. He is only trying to get you to open your eyes and open your heart to Him. Jesus said, "If you abide in Me, everything is different. I am the vine and you are the branches. If you abide in Me, you will bear fruit" (John 15:4-5). The fruit, the resulting works, will be awesome. You will be blessed.

Again, He said, "If you abide in Me, and My words abide in you, ask whatever you wish, and it shall be done for you" (John 15:7). Christ is looking for us to abide in Him. Still, on a daily basis, we tend to live and move in isolation from Him. We still function and operate as people under futility. The way we function in our relationship with Christ resembles the way heavy equipment operators function. They use machinery to perform many powerful tasks. You can't say that they are one with the equipment; they are simply operating it. Similarly, we do not function as those

---

Hebrews 12:6-7 "For those whom the Lord loves He disciplines, and He scourges every son whom He receives." 7 It is for discipline that you endure; God deals with you as with sons; for what son is there whom his father does not discipline?

John 15:4-5 "Abide in Me, and I in you. As the branch cannot bear fruit of itself, unless it abides in the vine, so neither can you, unless you abide in Me. 5 I am the vine, you are the branches; he who abides in Me, and I in him, he bears much fruit; for apart from Me you can do nothing."

who are one with God, but as those who try to operate His power. We tend to look for the mechanics that make God move. We know what we want, so we pray to make Jesus move on our behalf. If we need a healing, then we try to evoke Jesus to move in healing for us. If we want more love, then we look to operate Jesus to bring us more love.

The mechanics we use to operate God may be scriptural mechanics, but they are still mechanics. It is wonderful when we receive the baptism of the Holy Spirit. It is awesome to speak with new tongues and see God give us the gifts of the Spirit. Then what happens? What do we do with the gifts and the anointing that God has given us? We become operators. We are always pulling levers. We are always operating things. We want God to move on our behalf, and we know the right things to do. We fast, we pray, we intercede, and we try to evoke the moving of God. We try to evoke the blessings of God or His presence, but we are always under futility. By operating God from a distance, separate from Him, we are still relating to God from a position of religious futility.

Jesus was pleasing to the Father because He was willing to abide in the Father. Jesus recognized Him as Father. He told people, "You do not know the Father. No one knows the Father but the Son" (Matthew 11:27). Philip asked Jesus to show them the Father:

> Jesus said to him, "Have I been so long with you, and yet you have not come to know Me, Philip? He who has seen Me has seen the Father; how do you say, 'Show us the Father'? Do you not believe that I am in the Father, and the Father is in Me? The words that I say to you I do not

---

Matthew 11:27 "All things have been handed over to Me by My Father; and no one knows the Son, except the Father; nor does anyone know the Father, except the Son, and anyone to whom the Son wills to reveal Him."

speak on My own initiative, but the Father abiding in Me does His works." (John 14:9-10)

Why did Jesus have no initiative, no ability of His own? It was because He abode in the Father, and every miracle that He performed came from that state of abiding with the Father. Jesus was not a heavy equipment operator. He did not come into the world as the one who was the most capable of getting God to do things for Him. We read in the Gospels that He stopped the wind, He healed the sick, He raised the dead, and we say, "I want to be like Jesus!" (Matthew 8:26-27; 4:23-24; Luke 7:14-15). Then when we prophesy and pray, we want to see these things happen, because we still think of Jesus as someone separate from the Father who was able to have God move at His request or on His behalf. That is how we relate to Him. That is our picture of how Jesus functioned.

We need to get rid of this false picture of who and what Jesus was, how He functioned, what He did, and how He did it. Jesus was abiding in the Father and the Father was abiding in Him. When you move into abiding in God, it is as different as leaving the wilderness and moving into the land of Canaan (Joshua 5:12). It

---

Matthew 8:26-27 And He said to them, "Why are you timid, you men of little faith?" Then He arose, and rebuked the winds and the sea; and it became perfectly calm. [27] And the men marveled, saying, "What kind of a man is this, that even the winds and the sea obey Him?"

Matthew 4:23-24 And Jesus was going about in all Galilee, teaching in their synagogues, and proclaiming the gospel of the kingdom, and healing every kind of disease and every kind of sickness among the people. [24] And the news about Him went out into all Syria; and they brought to Him all who were ill, taken with various diseases and pains, demoniacs, epileptics, paralytics; and He healed them.

Luke 7:14-15 And He came up and touched the coffin; and the bearers came to a halt. And He said, "Young man, I say to you, arise!" [15] And the dead man sat up, and began to speak. And Jesus gave him back to his mother.

Joshua 5:12 And the manna ceased on the day after they had eaten some of the produce of the land, so that the sons of Israel no longer had manna, but they ate some of the yield of the land of Canaan during that year.

is literally a different world. God wants to unplug you from one world, which is religion that man has developed under futility, and plug you into Jesus who is the way. If I am in God and God is in me, I do not need to pray for healing, because there is no sickness in God. God is "I Am." The holy name of God, which He revealed to Moses, is "I Am" (Exodus 3:14). God simply is. We are always trying to be, but God is. When we are trying to manipulate God to do something, we are like heavy equipment operators. When we abide in God, what we manifest simply is.

Jesus said, "The works and the words are God. Because I abide in God, the works happen" (John 14:10). Why? They happen because God is "I Am." Jesus stood before those Jews who had believed Him and said, "Before Abraham was born, I am" (John 8:58). You can make a doctrine out of that and say, "Let's figure out who Jesus was and how He existed with God before the foundations of the world." No, back up a minute and just recognize that Jesus is "I Am." God the Father is "I Am," isn't He? How did Jesus become "I Am"? He did it by abiding. If you abide in God, then you are what He is. This does not mean that you will be turned into a god. That is not the concept at all. Very simply, if God abides in you, it becomes difficult to separate between you and God. Then the works and miracles and healings just happen. As Jesus said, "All the words are at the initiative of the Father because the Father abides in Me and I abide in the Father" (John 14:10). Jesus did not pray to ask God to heal someone. When He raised Lazarus from the dead, Jesus prefaced His prayer by saying, "I don't even have to

---

Exodus 3:14 And God said to Moses, "I AM WHO I AM"; and He said, "Thus you shall say to the sons of Israel, 'I AM has sent me to you.' "

John 8:58 Jesus said to them, "Truly, truly, I say to you, before Abraham was born, I am."

say this prayer. I'm doing it for the benefit of those standing here" (John 11:41-42).

All the gifts and ministries that come to us from God are not separate from Him. They are Him. They are not things to be manipulated. Life is God. Health is God. Joy is God. Love is God. You don't need to pray, "Oh God, I need more love. Throw some down. I know You have it packaged up there around the throne. Just throw me another bundle." No, just abide in Him and you will abide in His love (1 John 4:16). All the things that you are seeking will happen when you are able to stand as Jesus did and say, "I am." You will not have attained them. They will not be promises fulfilled. They will simply be because He is and you abide in Him. Put yourself in Him. Allow Him to fill you and be in you. Don't be an operator. Don't get up in the morning and say, "I prayed to Jesus for three hours this morning. Look how spiritual I am! I kept asking the Lord to do this for me and do that for me, because I read in John 15:7 that I should ask what I wish and it will be done." Yes, but read the first part of the verse about abiding in Him. If you are abiding in Him, you do not even need to ask, because it happens by virtue of what He is in you.

There is an attitude that says, "When I'm really spiritual like Jesus, and when I'm really moving in the gifts of the Spirit, then I am going to raise the dead!" The Pentecostal movement is guilty of this. The Charismatic movement is guilty of this. We are all guilty of this concept that being spiritual is the way to get God to move, and that the works are by virtue of what we are as

---

John 11:41-42 And so they removed the stone. And Jesus raised His eyes, and said, "Father, I thank Thee that Thou heardest Me. [42] And I knew that Thou hearest Me always; but because of the people standing around I said it, that they may believe that Thou didst send Me."

1 John 4:16 And we have come to know and have believed the love which God has for us. God is love, and the one who abides in love abides in God, and God abides in him.

spiritual manipulators of God. We want to be the ones who pray and God does it. If you want an example of someone who prayed and things happened, read about Elijah. When Elijah challenged the prophets of Baal on Mount Carmel, they were crying out and cutting themselves for hours trying to make Baal move. Nothing happened (1 Kings 18:28-29). Then, Elijah asked the Lord one time and fire consumed the altar (1 Kings 18:36-38). That is amazing, but why did it work for Elijah? The answer can be found in the way he identified himself. He said, "I am Elijah who stands in the presence of God" (1 Kings 17:1). That was Elijah's calling card. Elijah was one who knew how to abide in God. He was taken up to God because that was where he was already abiding (2 Kings 2:11).

Get out of your mind that the goal is to grow into being spiritual giants with powerful gifts. Our testimony to the world will not be that we perform miracles and speak the Word of God and do great things. No, that will only create more disciples of man's futile religions, because it demonstrates man's ability to get God to move, apart from Him. That is not what the Lord is looking for. Read in

---

1 Kings 18:28-29 So they cried with a loud voice and cut themselves according to their custom with swords and lances until the blood gushed out on them. [29] And it came about when midday was past, that they raved until the time of the offering of the evening sacrifice; but there was no voice, no one answered, and no one paid attention.

1 Kings 18:36-38 Then it came about at the time of the offering of the evening sacrifice, that Elijah the prophet came near and said, "O LORD, the God of Abraham, Isaac and Israel, today let it be known that Thou art God in Israel, and that I am Thy servant, and that I have done all these things at Thy word. [37] Answer me, O LORD, answer me, that this people may know that Thou, O LORD, art God, and that Thou hast turned their heart back again." [38] Then the fire of the LORD fell, and consumed the burnt offering and the wood and the stones and the dust, and licked up the water that was in the trench.

1 Kings 17:1 Now Elijah the Tishbite, who was of the settlers of Gilead, said to Ahab, "As the LORD, the God of Israel lives, before whom I stand, surely there shall be neither dew nor rain these years, except by my word."

2 Kings 2:11 Then it came about as they were going along and talking, that behold, there appeared a chariot of fire and horses of fire which separated the two of them. And Elijah went up by a whirlwind to heaven.

the Gospels how the works and miracles of Jesus were always a testimony that He was abiding in the Father. Were the works for a proof? Yes, they were for a proof. Were they for a testimony? You bet they were for a testimony—but of what? Were they a testimony that He was God's favorite human being? No, they were a testimony that He abode in the Father and the Father abode in Him. He said, "All things have been handed over to Me by My Father; and no one knows the Son, except the Father; nor does anyone know the Father, except the Son, and anyone to whom the Son wills to reveal Him" (Matthew 11:27). If we come to abide in Christ, then He will introduce us to the Father and we will walk as He walked.

The Lord promised, "My Father and I will come and take up Our abode in you" (John 14:23). Not only will Jesus and the Holy Spirit abide in us, but the Spirit of the Father will come and abide in us also (Romans 8:11). We have to come to the Lord and say, "Lord Jesus, You walked this through. You came into the earth as a man, and as a man You were perfected and You learned by that which You suffered (Hebrews 2:10; 5:8). You were disciplined by the Father that You might become our Savior. You are saving me from being isolated from the Father. Therefore, I come to You that You may be the way. I'm going to abide in You. I am going to abide in Your Word, and as I do that, You are going to teach me. You are going to introduce me to the Father just like You had that introduction to the Father."

Why do we take Communion in the Church? Jesus said, "He who eats My flesh and drinks My blood abides in Me, and I in him" (John 6:56). Communion is about abiding. It is about coming into an abiding relationship with Christ. When we abide in Christ, He is the way to lead us into the Father so that we can abide in the

---

Hebrews 5:8 Although He was a Son, He learned obedience from the things which He suffered.

Father. Then the prayer of Jesus in John 17:20-21 is answered. The Holy Spirit, Jesus, and the Father are abiding in us, and we are abiding in them (John 14:16-17). This is what is pleasing to the Father. You cannot read the Bible without realizing that everything God has done is because He is driven for you to abide in Him. Do you ever feel, "God has given up on me"? No, God will never give up on you. His love is so great that He will not stop until you are abiding in Him (Romans 8:38-39). He is your Creator, and I can guarantee you this: what He wants, He gets. Do you know what He wants? He wants you. He wants you abiding in Him.

John 17:20-21 "I do not ask in behalf of these alone, but for those also who believe in Me through their word; [21] that they may all be one; even as Thou, Father, art in Me, and I in Thee, that they also may be in Us; that the world may believe that Thou didst send Me."

John 14:16-17 "And I will ask the Father, and He will give you another Helper, that He may be with you forever; [17] that is the Spirit of truth, whom the world cannot receive, because it does not behold Him or know Him, but you know Him because He abides with you, and will be in you."

Romans 8:38-39 For I am convinced that neither death, nor life, nor angels, nor principalities, nor things present, nor things to come, nor powers, [39] nor height, nor depth, nor any other created thing, shall be able to separate us from the love of God, which is in Christ Jesus our Lord.

5 | The Spirit Without Measure

I was taught for many years that the Kingdom of God is relationships, and that continues to be more and more of a revelation to me as we go along. In our study of the Lord's Prayer, we find an emphasis that the Kingdom of God is our relationship with the Father. That was very real to Jesus. Speaking of Himself, He said, "No one knows the Father except the Son" (Matthew 11:27). He was aware of the fact that He had something that no one else had in a relationship with the Father. So when one of the disciples asked Him, "Lord, teach us to pray" (Luke 11:1), He took the opportunity to walk them into the revelation of a relationship with the Father. Jesus taught them what is now known as the Lord's Prayer, but the verses that follow the Lord's Prayer in the Gospel of Luke continue to explain this prayer in more detail. These verses focus back on the Lord's Prayer and give us a greater understanding of it.

Matthew 11:27 "All things have been handed over to Me by My Father; and no one knows the Son, except the Father; nor does anyone know the Father, except the Son, and anyone to whom the Son wills to reveal Him."

Luke 11:1 And it came about that while He was praying in a certain place, after He had finished, one of His disciples said to Him, "Lord, teach us to pray just as John also taught his disciples."

It is clear when we read the Lord's Prayer in Luke 11:2-4 that Jesus is drawing us into a relationship with the Father, and the verses that follow continue that focus. Everything about that prayer surrounds the one-on-one relationship that we, as believers, experience with the Father. And this becomes all-important to us because God is moving us into this relationship. Jesus continued His teaching by saying,

> "Suppose one of you shall have a friend, and shall go to him at midnight, and say to him, 'Friend, lend me three loaves; for a friend of mine has come to me from a journey, and I have nothing to set before him'; and from inside he shall answer and say, 'Do not bother me; the door has already been shut and my children and I are in bed; I cannot get up and give you anything.' I tell you, even though he will not get up and give him anything because he is his friend, yet because of his persistence he will get up and give him as much as he needs." (Luke 11:5-8)

Again, He is talking to them about the Father. He is warning them that when they begin to pray as He taught them, when they begin to move into a relationship with the Father, it will not go as easily as they might think. This is something that we often do not understand. When it comes to relating to the Father, will we succumb to being worn out by Him, or will we be absolutely undaunted in our perseverance to wear Him out? This is the Lord teaching us about a relationship with the Father. It has to be very real to us, because it is very evident that some people are worn out, even in worship. They wonder, "Is this going anywhere? How many years do I have to stand and do this?" We need to get past that and understand what Jesus is saying in this parable.

Luke 11:2-4 And He said to them, "When you pray, say: 'Father, hallowed be Thy name. Thy kingdom come. ³ Give us each day our daily bread. ⁴ And forgive us our sins, for we ourselves also forgive everyone who is indebted to us. And lead us not into temptation.'"

The parable in Luke 11:5-8 is in the context of the ancient Middle East, when people understood the importance of hospitality. A man was visited by his friend, and as a friend he was obligated to provide hospitality to him. He had to have something to set before him. Don't forget that the man who knocked on his neighbor's door at midnight had himself just been awakened. He was in bed when his friend showed up, and he had nothing to set before him. If his friend had come earlier in the day, he could have gone to the store and would not have had to go to his neighbor's house. Obviously, his friend showed up banging on his door at midnight saying, "Aren't you glad to see me?" So he had to go to his neighbor's house and start banging on his door.

In this parable, Christ is presenting concepts about God the Father in ways that we can relate to because He is using very natural emotions and terminology. He describes the Father as someone who is saying, "I'm in bed, and My kids are in bed." In other words, He is isolating you from being one of His children. Not only does He seem to ignore you, but then He says, "You're not one of My children. All My children are in bed like they should be. You're bothering Me at midnight, so you're not one of My kids anymore. I can't get up and give you anything." Then Jesus tells us how to relate to the Father at that point: "I tell you, even though he will not get up and give him anything because he is his friend, yet because of his persistence he will get up and give him as much as he needs" (Luke 11:8). This describes the persistence that we need to have.

You have to ask yourself, "Is God really unwilling, or does He just want to see how determined I am to relate to Him?" This is all about a relationship. Jesus explained that the man at the door was the neighbor's friend, but he was not going to give him anything just because they were friends. There are many things that we can point to and say, "We expect God to relate to us. We expect Him to answer us because of our past relationship with Him. He should know by now that we are His friends." We are like those who say, "Haven't we done many mighty works in Your name, Lord?" (Matthew 7:22). Yet God will not move for all of the reasons that we think He should. However, this does not mean that He is rejecting us. God understands human nature. He created us. He understands what is in us. You can read in the Old Testament where God warned Israel, "I tested you in the wilderness, and let you go hungry in order to make sure that you will live with a drive for Me. Now, once you go into the land, and have satisfied your hunger, and have moved into those wonderful houses, after all of these blessings have come upon you, then what will you do?" (Deuteronomy 8:2-3, 11-14).

You have to realize that God lives in this consciousness. He has been relating to mankind for a long time. We may feel, "God is not answering! He is just being cantankerous. He doesn't want to give me anything." That is not the point. God is telling us, "I realize that you're hungry right now, but what about after you eat? Then what happens?" I love the Jewish tradition of blessing meals. I think it is

---

Matthew 7:22   "Many will say to Me on that day, 'Lord, Lord, did we not prophesy in Your name, and in Your name cast out demons, and in Your name perform many miracles?'"

Deuteronomy 8:2-3   "And you shall remember all the way which the LORD your God has led you in the wilderness these forty years, that He might humble you, testing you, to know what was in your heart, whether you would keep His commandments or not. ³ And He humbled you and let you be hungry, and fed you with manna which you did not know, nor did your fathers know, that He might make you understand that man does not live by bread alone, but man lives by everything that proceeds out of the mouth of the LORD."

Deuteronomy 8:11-14   "Beware lest you forget the LORD your God by not keeping His commandments and His ordinances and His statutes which I am commanding you today; ¹² lest, when you have eaten and are satisfied, and have built good houses and lived in them, ¹³ and when your herds and your flocks multiply, and your silver and gold multiply, and all that you have multiplies, ¹⁴ then your heart becomes proud, and you forget the LORD your God who brought you out from the land of Egypt, out of the house of slavery."

significant that they say grace after the meal (Deuteronomy 8:10). We as Christians say grace before meal because who knows if we will still be thankful after we've eaten! The Jews, on the other hand, are very careful that after they have eaten, and are satisfied, they are still thanking God. They are still reaching into a relationship with the Father even though they are no longer doing it out of a drive of hunger.

We have had Words from God for years encouraging us to reach into the Father. This is real to us, but as we pursue a relationship with Him, we will have to face an important issue: at some point, will we tire of pursuing Him? Or if He gives us certain things, will we then be satisfied with a little bit and stop pursuing Him? Part of the danger is that we will be satisfied if God gives us only a small portion. That is why He tested Israel until they came to recognize that man cannot live by bread alone (Deuteronomy 8:3). He tested them so that when they ate and their hunger was satisfied, they realized that, in their pursuit of the Father, there was much more to life than satisfying their hunger. We have to realize that God really understands what He is doing, and He knows that, in our human nature, we are very fickle about pursuing Him and doing His will.

The worst thing that we could do is simply wear out in pursuing the Father. God has to take out of us anything that will cause us to stop our pursuit of Him, anything that can be satisfied and therefore allows us to stop in our tracks. So He uses a seeming unwillingness to test us. And it is a test. God said so Himself, in those exact words, when He spoke to Israel, "I tested you. I tried you to see what was in you" (Deuteronomy 8:2). We are not in a physical wilderness today, but our testing is still about having a relationship with the Father. Jesus explained that the first thing you do when

---

Deuteronomy 8:10 "When you have eaten and are satisfied, you shall bless the Lord your God for the good land which He has given you."

you pray is go into the closet and close the door (Matthew 6:6). You lock yourself in with the Father. You have to stay there and work out your relationship with Him. That is the key, but then Jesus also warned about what you will run into when you do that. Before long, you will get tired and start saying, "I'm ready to get out now! I'm done with my pursuing God." As a result, you leave without really getting what you were asking for.

Jesus continued His teaching by saying, "And I say to you, ask, and it shall be given to you; seek, and you shall find; knock, and it shall be opened to you" (Luke 11:9). This is an amazing promise, because it comes right on the heels of a parable that describes how you will ask and not receive, and request and it will not happen. Immediately after that He said, "If you ask it will be given, and if you seek you will find." In other words, God is not holding out on us. His plan is to give to us, and He will give to us. "For everyone who asks, receives; and he who seeks, finds; and to him who knocks, it shall be opened" (Luke 11:10). The Greek verbs for "ask," "seek," and "knock" in these verses are in the active present imperative tense, which means that you ask and keep on asking, seek and keep on seeking, knock and keep on knocking. It is not when you ask only once that you will receive. He has already told us that if you go and knock once, you won't get what you're asking for. What you will get is a voice behind the door saying, "I'm in bed. My kids are in bed. You should be in bed. You're not even one of My kids. Go away; you're bothering Me." That is the first response you will get.

It is only through persistence that something happens. Even pursuing God until we get what we asked for is not enough of

_____

Matthew 6:6 "But you, when you pray, go into your inner room, and when you have shut your door, pray to your Father who is in secret, and your Father who sees in secret will repay you."

a drive, because He has more for us than what we are asking (Ephesians 3:20). I really don't want what I'm asking for; I want what He has to give me. Do you see the difference? If God just answers my prayers, then I will be satisfied because I received what I asked for. Jesus told the disciples, "God already knows what you need. Don't ask for what you need" (Matthew 6:8). We have to be pursuing God on the basis of what He has for us. That is part of not being satisfied. In His teaching on prayer, Jesus is telling us that if we have the attitude that the Father is looking for, then there is an absolute promise that we will receive. Everyone who asks and keeps on asking will receive. Everyone who seeks and keeps on seeking will find. For everyone who knocks and keeps on knocking, it will be opened to them.

The first question from a human perspective is, "How much asking and knocking is enough? I'm anxious to get to that point." Why? "Because I don't like knocking, and I don't like asking." That brings us right back to God's perspective. He is saying, "You don't really want to pursue Me; you are only looking for a goal." God, however, is not looking for a goal. He is looking for a relationship with you. We are looking to knock until we get. God is looking for the knocking, the seeking, and the asking to be a part of our hungering after Him, which should have no end. There should be nothing that satisfies us. "So how long will it be until I get what I'm asking for?" Until you are no longer worried about how long it takes you to get it. When the object that you are asking for is no longer the goal and nothing is left in your asking except to

---

Ephesians 3:20 Now to Him who is able to do exceeding abundantly beyond all that we ask or think, according to the power that works within us.

Matthew 6:8 "Therefore do not be like them; for your Father knows what you need, before you ask Him."

know Him, then you will receive, because what you receive is Him (Philippians 3:10).

This brings us to Luke 11:11-13:

> "Now suppose one of you fathers is asked by his son for a fish; he will not give him a snake instead of a fish, will he? Or if he is asked for an egg, he will not give him a scorpion, will he? If you then, being evil, know how to give good gifts to your children, how much more shall your heavenly Father give the Holy Spirit to those who ask Him?"

Interestingly, after all of the Lord's teaching on prayer, persistence, and understanding the personality of the Father, we learn that what He gives us is something very specific. The Father gives us the Holy Spirit. Jesus leads us into a relationship with the Father because it is the Father who gives the Holy Spirit to those who ask.

Jesus does not give us the Holy Spirit. He opens the door for the Holy Spirit to be given, but it is the Father who bestows upon us the Holy Spirit. This was the witness that Peter had when he went into the house of Cornelius. The Father showed He had included the Gentiles by pouring out His Spirit upon them. The early Church knew that the Holy Spirit was the seal of the relationship with the Father. Therefore, when the Father wanted to demonstrate that He was including the Gentiles, it was simple; all He had to do was put the Holy Spirit on them. When they began to speak in tongues and prophesy, Peter and the disciples recognized immediately what it meant. They recognized that the Holy Spirit signified that the Gentiles had the same open door to a relationship with the Father

---

Philippians 3:10 That I may know Him, and the power of His resurrection and the fellowship of His sufferings, being conformed to His death.

that they had (Acts 10:44-48). That is still what the Holy Spirit signifies today.

Therefore, we must persistently seek the Father, and continually ask and knock. We have the Holy Spirit, but there is too much satisfaction with the level of the Holy Spirit that we have received. There have been outpourings of the Holy Spirit across the globe, and people have had many experiences in the Holy Spirit, but we need much more than a few gifts and ministries. It is exciting to lay hands on people and see them filled with the Holy Spirit for the first time and move in some of the gifts of the Spirit. As wonderful as that is, I am deeply concerned that those who are receiving Him for the first time do not develop a satisfaction about the Holy Spirit that leads to passivity. This is what the Lord is concerned about when He teaches us about prayer: will we become satisfied? Will we have enough of the Holy Spirit so that we stop asking, knocking, and seeking for something greater? Will we be satisfied to the extent that we actually lose sight of who the Holy Spirit is, why He is given, and what should transpire in our lives because of the Holy Spirit?

We read in John 3:34, "For He whom God has sent speaks the words of God; for He gives the Spirit without measure." This is describing the relationship between Christ and the Father. Christ spoke the Words of the Father because the Father gave Him the Spirit without measure. This Scripture is interesting in the original Greek, because a more literal translation expresses it in the

---

Acts 10:44-48 While Peter was still speaking these words, the Holy Spirit fell upon all those who were listening to the message. [45] And all the circumcised believers who had come with Peter were amazed, because the gift of the Holy Spirit had been poured out upon the Gentiles also. [46] For they were hearing them speaking with tongues and exalting God. Then Peter answered, [47] "Surely no one can refuse the water for these to be baptized who have received the Holy Spirit just as we did, can he?" [48] And he ordered them to be baptized in the name of Jesus Christ. Then they asked him to stay on for a few days.

negative: "He does not give the Spirit by measure." I was struck by this, because we do receive the Spirit by measure. We have a measured-out experience with the Holy Spirit, but that is not how God intended it. Where Christ was concerned, the Father placed the fullness of the Spirit on Him. He had all that there is of the Holy Spirit. This is very important for us to understand. Christ was not superhuman. He was human just like we are; He had to walk with the Father just like we have to walk with the Father. "As He is, so also are we in this world" (1 John 4:17).

To understand how Jesus did what He did and how He functioned, we have to look to what Jesus said about Himself: "I do nothing but what I see the Father do. I speak nothing but what I hear the Father say" (John 5:19; 8:28). We have to recognize that Jesus did all of that through the Holy Spirit. Remember, it is the job of the Holy Spirit to teach you all things, to guide you into all things, to lead you absolutely (John 14:26). All of these are a function of the Holy Spirit, and the reason why Christ was able to see the things the Father was doing was because He had the Holy Spirit without limitation. Jesus did not only function by means of His relationship with the Father; He also functioned through the Holy Spirit resting upon Him, just as we have to.

---

1 John 4:17 By this, love is perfected with us, that we may have confidence in the day of judgment; because as He is, so also are we in this world.

John 5:19 Jesus therefore answered and was saying to them, "Truly, truly, I say to you, the Son can do nothing of Himself, unless it is something He sees the Father doing; for whatever the Father does, these things the Son also does in like manner."

John 8:28 Jesus therefore said, "When you lift up the Son of Man, then you will know that I am He, and I do nothing on My own initiative, but I speak these things as the Father taught Me."

John 14:26 "But the Helper, the Holy Spirit, whom the Father will send in My name, He will teach you all things, and bring to your remembrance all that I said to you."

When Jesus was baptized in the Jordan River by John, He came up out of the water and the Holy Spirit descended upon Him as a dove and never left Him (John 1:32-33). Yet this idea of the Holy Spirit resting upon us without measure, and not in a state of coming and going, is a problem for us. Do you really want to be that driven by the Holy Spirit? A person who has the Spirit without measure lives a life that is totally dedicated to the Lordship of Jesus Christ. This is something we have to come to grips with as humans. When you are knocking and you realize that the Father gives the Holy Spirit to those who ask, and the Holy Spirit comes upon you, do you stop knocking? Or do you stop knocking quite so loudly? Are you seeking just enough to get certain answers, or do you want everything God has to give you?

The Holy Spirit is given to us. We have it, but the measure we have is so limited. We need to go back to the Father. We need to realize what He wants us to ask for, and start pounding on the door again and start asking. He wants us to ask for the Holy Spirit. He wants us to covet a relationship with the Holy Spirit. I want God to restore our drive and our hunger. There is a reason why the Lord is breaking down barriers for us to relate to the Father. It is because there needs to be a greater experience and relationship between us and the Holy Spirit.

The Lord is directing us into a deeper relationship with the Father, and that leads us into a deeper relationship with the Holy Spirit. There is a divine order in God, and there are very specific functions of the Trinity. The Father does specific things as the Father, Christ does specific things as the Son and Savior, and the Holy Spirit has specific functions. They are one, but they have very

---

John 1:32-33   And John bore witness saying, "I have beheld the Spirit descending as a dove out of heaven, and He remained upon Him. [33] And I did not recognize Him, but He who sent me to baptize in water said to me, 'He upon whom you see the Spirit descending and remaining upon Him, this is the one who baptizes in the Holy Spirit.' "

specific expressions within the Godhead. We cannot just look for Jesus to be everything to us. We need Jesus to open the door to the Father so that we can, through a relationship with Him, receive an outpouring of the Holy Spirit. We will not get that by pursuing the Holy Spirit alone. The Holy Spirit does not give the Holy Spirit. The Father gives the Holy Spirit.

Jesus said, "When you lift up the Son of Man, then you will know that I am He, and I do nothing on My own initiative, but I speak these things as the Father taught Me" (John 8:28). What is the teaching method of the Father? The Holy Spirit will teach you all things. That is the anointing of the Holy Spirit (1 John 2:27). How was Jesus taught? He said, "I can do nothing of Myself." We all start in the same place. We also can do nothing of ourselves. We have tried, but there is no power, no authority, no anointing, and no enabling. There is no ability that we have in ourselves, whether it is to perform miracles, heal the sick, raise the dead, or speak the Word of God. Whatever it is, we can do nothing of ourselves. There is nothing within the human flesh that provides anything. The flesh, Jesus said, profits nothing (John 6:63).

The Holy Spirit was given to us so that we would not be orphans (John 14:16-18). Why would we be orphans if we did not have the Holy Spirit? Because the Father and the Son are seated in heaven

---

1 John 2:27 And as for you, the anointing which you received from Him abides in you, and you have no need for anyone to teach you; but as His anointing teaches you about all things, and is true and is not a lie, and just as it has taught you, you abide in Him.

John 6:63 "It is the Spirit who gives life; the flesh profits nothing; the words that I have spoken to you are spirit and are life."

John 14:16-18 "And I will ask the Father, and He will give you another Helper, that He may be with you forever; [17] that is the Spirit of truth, whom the world cannot receive, because it does not behold Him or know Him, but you know Him because He abides with you, and will be in you. [18] I will not leave you as orphans; I will come to you."

but we are on the earth (Mark 16:19). The member of the Godhead who is manifested on this earth right now is the Holy Spirit. He is the one who is sent to be with us so that we are no longer orphans. He is the one who teaches us. Jesus said that the Holy Spirit will teach us **all things**. He will lead us into **all truth**. He will remind us of everything that Jesus said, and that applies to us as well as to the disciples. This means that the understanding of the Scriptures is locked up in a relationship with the Holy Spirit. All of the things that we need and are seeking are within the context of who the Holy Spirit is, what His ministry is, and His relationship to us while we are on this earth.

When Jesus was on the earth in the days of His flesh, He had to have the Holy Spirit without measure. It was the only way that He could do what He did and be who He was, and it is the same with us. We have the same ability in the Holy Spirit to speak what we hear the Father speak. In other words, we can live the life that Jesus lived in the days of His flesh on this earth. You may react to that by saying, "Why aren't we doing that? You tell me that I can, but I don't seem to be able to. I've tried." I know, but it is only with the full measure of the Holy Spirit upon us that we are enabled, taught, and led in how to do the things that God wants.

It is not that we are dense or that we don't care. We need the fullness of the Holy Spirit that teaches us. First of all, you have to erase from your mind the idea that the Holy Spirit is like a lever that you can pull. It will not be effective to say, "Let's try to live according to the fruit of the Spirit," or, "Let's try to move in miracles. I'm going to pull this lever so that I'll be able to heal the sick and raise the dead." People today are really focusing on an attempt to manipulate the Holy Spirit in His moving. The Holy Spirit is not going to do that. The Holy Spirit will teach us and lead us in the same depth to

---

Mark 16:19 So then, when the Lord Jesus had spoken to them, He was received up into heaven, and sat down at the right hand of God.

which we have turned our lives over to Him. In the same way that we have given ourselves to Him, He will give Himself to us.

This is why God tests our persistence. He does not want to simply give us a few gifts. He does not want us in a limited relationship with the Holy Spirit; He is not happy with that. He is concerned that we will be satisfied with a limited relationship, a limited level of anointing, a limited level of the Word, and a limited level of power and authority. God knows what He is doing, because unfortunately I think we would be satisfied. Even if we received a lot, it would still be limited in comparison to the unlimited measure that the Holy Spirit has. We do not fully comprehend what the Holy Spirit is capable of and what He knows. There is nothing that the Holy Spirit does not know. The Holy Spirit was with the Father from the beginning of creation. He knows everything. There is not a single question that you could ask, about anything, to which He does not know the answer. He knows everything, and it is His job to teach that to you. It's not that you are ignorant; it's that you are not hearing what He is saying. Position yourself in a relationship where you can be taught by Him.

The Father will not unfold to us the treasures of the Kingdom if we have no persistence, if we have no drive, or if at some point we will eat and be satisfied. Our focus as humans is so limited! Everyone loses their focus on God so quickly compared to what He really wants from us. He is looking for us to have a fixed focus on Him that never moves and never wavers. As we keep pursuing Him, we discover that He is the issue, and all that we are after anymore is a relationship with Him. Then the Father gives us the Holy Spirit because that is the only way that we can come into the knowledge of Him. The only way that we can have the mind of Christ, and know what we need to know, and move as His sons, is through this relationship.

Now we can understand what God is after. He is saying, "Pursue Me! Come after Me! I am the One who gives you the Holy Spirit. When I give Him to you without measure, you will be unlimited." Jesus was able to do the things that He saw the Father do, and speak the things that He heard the Father speak. The same door is as open to us as it was to Him. Jesus had the same flesh and blood as we have (Hebrews 2:14). "In the days of His flesh, He offered up both prayers and supplications with loud crying and tears to the One able to save Him from death, and He was heard because of His piety" (Hebrews 5:7). He was heard because of His love, His reverence, and His awe for God. Therefore, He received the Spirit without measure. That is what we need. Do not think this is impossible, nor be satisfied with only a small portion of what God wants to do in the earth in this day. God cannot use us if we are complacent and satisfied when He is looking to do something in this generation that eye has not seen, and ear has not heard, and neither has it entered into the heart of man what He has prepared for us (1 Corinthians 2:9).

Hebrews 2:14 Since then the children share in flesh and blood, He Himself likewise also partook of the same, that through death He might render powerless him who had the power of death, that is, the devil.

1 Corinthians 2:9 But just as it is written, "THINGS WHICH EYE HAS NOT SEEN AND EAR HAS NOT HEARD, AND WHICH HAVE NOT ENTERED THE HEART OF MAN, ALL THAT GOD HAS PREPARED FOR THOSE WHO LOVE HIM."

6 | Christ Taught Us to Pray

So far in our study of the Lord's Prayer, we have examined the importance of our relationship with the Father in prayer. The Lord's teaching on prayer begins by explaining very pointedly and clearly who we are addressing when we pray, "Our Father" (Matthew 6:9). When He taught His disciples to pray, Christ did not say, "Pray to Me." He said, "Pray to the Father." You begin prayer by entering into a relationship with the Father. "But you, when you pray, go into your inner room, and when you have shut your door, pray to your Father who is in secret, and your Father who sees in secret will repay you" (Matthew 6:6).

The first step of prayer is to enter into the inner room with the Father. As we learned earlier, Christ is the door (John 10:7). When we pray, we access our relationship with Christ, the open door, to enter into the presence of the Father. Once we are there in that secret place with Him, we shut the door behind us—we are held

---

Matthew 6:9 "Pray, then, in this way: 'Our Father who art in heaven, hallowed be Thy name.'"

John 10:7 Jesus therefore said to them again, "Truly, truly, I say to you, I am the door of the sheep."

in that place with the Father by Christ. He ever lives to make intercession for us so that we can stay in the Father's presence (Hebrews 7:25). It is in that place that we speak with the Father. "Pray, then, in this way: 'Our Father who art in heaven, hallowed be Thy name'" (Matthew 6:9). We worship the Father. We exalt Him. Through Christ, by faith, we enter into the heavenly place with the Father, and there we worship Him. The greatest principle of effective prayer is to start by entering into the Father's presence and worshiping Him. There we find that His presence is the answer to all our needs.

Jesus, speaking about Gentile prayers, said, "Do not be like them; for your Father knows what you need, before you ask Him" (Matthew 6:8). There is nothing we can pray for that the Father is not already aware that we need and that we will ask for. When Christ said, "Do not be like them," He was referring to the kind of prayer described in verse 7: "And when you are praying, do not use meaningless repetition, as the Gentiles do, for they suppose that they will be heard for their many words." When we approach God in prayer, we are not looking to exercise a lot of words or a lot of repetition; we are looking for something to happen.

How do we really see things happen in the earth as a result of our prayers? The first step is Matthew 6:9: "Our Father who art in heaven, hallowed be Thy name." The next step is in verse 10: "Thy kingdom come. Thy will be done, on earth as it is in heaven." After we go in and establish the relationship with the Father, what are we to pray for? Christ did not say, "Now that you are with the Father, just start asking for all kinds of things." Look at Matthew 6:8 again: "Your Father knows what you need." We honestly waste much of our time when we pray because we ask for things that He already knows we need.

Hebrews 7:25 Hence, also, He is able to save forever those who draw near to God through Him, since He always lives to make intercession for them.

Think about your prayers. Write down what you are praying for, then read it back and ask yourself, "Am I praying the way Christ taught His disciples to pray—or am I praying with a lot of repetition, asking for things that God is already aware of?" You can spend all night in prayer asking Him for all kinds of things. To be honest, if you are going to pray like that, you would be better off sleeping. Your sleep could be an expression of faith, as you rest in God knowing that He will take care of everything (Psalm 127:1-2). Instead of praying all night, you could sit at the side of your bed and say one prayer: "Father, You know everything I need; You know everything I am burdened for. You already know everything I would ask You for, so I am going to bed now and I am going to rest. I am not going to keep waking up feeling like something is wrong. I am going to trust that You will provide all that I need. You will bless all those I am burdened for. You will deal with the things that need to be dealt with."

Don't let your prayer be an expression of unbelief. If you feel like you have to stay up all night, does that mean you are worried that you have to take care of something because He won't? If I am going to pray all night, then I want to be effective. I want to pray the way He taught us to pray. Christ was very specific when one of the disciples requested, "Teach us to pray" (Luke 11:1). He said to pray: "Thy Kingdom come! Thy will be done on earth as it is in heaven." Somehow in Christianity we have made the words "prayer" and "asking" to mean the same thing. However, when we read what Christ taught the disciples to pray, we realize

---

Psalm 127:1-2 Unless the LORD builds the house, they labor in vain who build it; unless the LORD guards the city, the watchman keeps awake in vain. [2] It is vain for you to rise up early, to retire late, to eat the bread of painful labors; for He gives to His beloved even in his sleep.

Luke 11:1 And it came about that while He was praying in a certain place, after He had finished, one of His disciples said to Him, "Lord, teach us to pray just as John also taught his disciples."

they weren't asking. "Thy Kingdom come" is not a request. It is a demand. It is a declaration. In that prayer, we are not asking the Father for something; we are enforcing the Kingdom of God in this earth. This is how Christ wants us to pray.

Listen to your prayers and distinguish between asking for something that He already knows you need and proclaiming with faith that the Kingdom of God will come in the earth. There are so many things you can pray for. You can pray for your church; you can pray for your community; you can pray for your country; you can pray for the whole earth. You can pray very specifically for many things. Yet despite all the many ways to pray, there is but one declaration: "Thy Kingdom come." The way the Lord taught us to pray is to enforce His Kingdom in this earth.

The concept of prayer being a declaration of His Kingdom in the earth has always been part of God's plan. Read Genesis 1:26-31. When God created man, he was commissioned over everything in the earth. The authority and dominion over all the earth was given to man. Yet when Adam and Eve fell, they relinquished their commission and their responsibility over the earth. Earth is man's realm, and he was supposed to be fruitful, multiply, and rule over

---

Genesis 1:26-31 Then God said, "Let Us make man in Our image, according to Our likeness; and let them rule over the fish of the sea and over the birds of the sky and over the cattle and over all the earth, and over every creeping thing that creeps on the earth." [27] And God created man in His own image, in the image of God He created him; male and female He created them. [28] And God blessed them; and God said to them, "Be fruitful and multiply, and fill the earth, and subdue it; and rule over the fish of the sea and over the birds of the sky, and over every living thing that moves on the earth." [29] Then God said, "Behold, I have given you every plant yielding seed that is on the surface of all the earth, and every tree which has fruit yielding seed; it shall be food for you; [30] and to every beast of the earth and to every bird of the sky and to every thing that moves on the earth which has life, I have given every green plant for food"; and it was so. [31] And God saw all that He had made, and behold, it was very good. And there was evening and there was morning, the sixth day.

it. When man fell, however, he gave away the blessing and his birthright, just as Esau did (Genesis 25:31-33).

You can take what God has given you, what He has entrusted to you, what He has commissioned you with, and you can give it away. There is nothing that satan can take from you, but you can relinquish it to him. And that is what Adam and Eve did. They relinquished the birthright of mankind over the earth. Now it is in the hands of satan (1 John 5:19). When Christ was tempted in the wilderness, satan took Him up on a high mountain and showed Him all the glories and all the wonders of the earth. Then he said to Him, "If you worship me, I will give this all to you" (Matthew 4:8-9). That means it was satan's to give.

How did the earth, with all its glories and everything that it contains, become satan's to give away? Adam and Eve handed it to him. Now when we look at the prayer that Christ taught man to pray, this should become more significant. There is only one thing man needs to do, and that is to bring this earth back in subjection to the Kingdom of God. In Christ, the Father has provided for us that opportunity. Through the cross, Christ won back man's birthright. Christ's defeat of satan is not a general concept. When Christ defeated satan, it was very specific. He took back man's right to be fruitful and multiply and rule over the earth. Adam and Eve lost it, but now it is back in our hands because Christ won it back.

Genesis 25:31-33 But Jacob said, "First sell me your birthright." [32] And Esau said, "Behold, I am about to die; so of what use then is the birthright to me?" [33] And Jacob said, "First swear to me"; so he swore to him, and sold his birthright to Jacob.

1 John 5:19 We know that we are of God, and the whole world lies in the power of the evil one.

Matthew 4:8-9 Again, the devil took Him to a very high mountain, and showed Him all the kingdoms of the world, and their glory; [9] and he said to Him, "All these things will I give You, if You fall down and worship me."

So when we pray, we pray that this earth is absolutely reaffixed within the Kingdom of God.

The Gospel of Mark is wonderful in the way it presents the stories of Christ. Read chapter 16 and see how it moves through the resurrection up to the ascension in very quick order. It helps your comprehension and understanding of what the Lord was doing with the disciples. The Lord's commission to the disciples is recorded in this chapter:

> And afterward He appeared to the eleven themselves as they were reclining at the table; and He reproached them for their unbelief and hardness of heart, because they had not believed those who had seen Him after He had risen. And He said to them, "Go into all the world and preach the gospel to all creation." (Mark 16:14-15)

This is referred to as the great commission, and it has been a key Scripture to the Church for so long it is difficult to view it in a fresh light. Nevertheless, are we really reading it correctly? Do we truly understand what Christ was saying, or are we missing the point? The great commission is generally interpreted as "Preach the Gospel of salvation to all people." So for 2,000 years, the Church has had a drive to go to mankind, to tell them about Christ, and to get people saved. However, this is not how it is actually stated in Mark 16:15. To help us understand this, first read Romans 8:19-21:

> For the anxious longing of the creation waits eagerly for the revealing of the sons of God. For the creation was subjected to futility, not of its own will, but because of Him who subjected it, in hope that the creation itself also will be set free from its slavery to corruption into the freedom of the glory of the children of God.

The believers in Christ, the children of God, have a commission to all of creation! The souls of men are included in the salvation of all creation, but we have focused on that one aspect exclusively and have missed what Christ told us to do. When Christ appeared to His disciples immediately after the resurrection, He said to them, "Go into **all** the world. Go into all of this world that was originally under the authority of Adam, and preach the Gospel to all creation." Our purpose is to loose creation from futility. We have to bring salvation to creation. That is what the Lord's Prayer is all about: "Thy Kingdom come on this earth." Salvation is God's Kingdom in the earth for all creation.

Oh, Lord, open our eyes! When Christ taught the disciples to pray in Matthew 6, did He tell them to pray for the souls of men to be saved? No. Yet this is what you see manifested most of the time in the Church. You can hear the same thing repeated in church after church: "Jesus died and went to the cross to save you. Come to the Lord." The Church is so convinced that its one purpose is to save souls that it is usually the main topic of preaching. There are hundreds of people who have been saved for years sitting in church, hearing this same message again and again. Believers should be sitting in church to learn one thing: "How do I as a believer bring the Kingdom of God into this earth?" Of course, leading people to accept salvation in Christ is an important part of our purpose. Remember, the Scriptures teach us that the reason people do not believe is because their eyes and their hearts are blinded by the devil (2 Corinthians 4:4). Therefore, if you don't know how to bind the devil, if you don't know how to deal with the realm of spirit, how will you bring mankind to salvation?

---

2 Corinthians 4:4 In whose case the god of this world has blinded the minds of the unbelieving, that they might not see the light of the gospel of the glory of Christ, who is the image of God.

You have to bind the strong man in order to plunder his house (Matthew 12:29). This earth has been satan's house. We are the plunderers of his house because Christ gave it back to us. Christ returned the keys of the house to us and said, "Whatever you shall bind on earth shall have been bound in heaven, and whatever you shall loose on earth shall have been loosed in heaven" (Matthew 16:19, NASB 1995). Now, what will you do with the keys the Lord has given you? The reality is that He would not have to give you the keys if you were in the house already. Now that you have the keys, you have to plunder the house. Someone stole your house, but the Lord has given you the keys. Go take your house back! Plunder it!

When Christ was resurrected and ascended to the right hand of the Father, all of heaven was cleared of everything that was against Him. At that point satan lost all the access that he had. Revelation 12:7-9 tells us that there was no longer a place found for satan in heaven and he was cast out. Christ's responsibility was to bring the Kingdom of God to heaven. Then He gave us the commission to bring the Kingdom of heaven into the earth. This earth is man's responsibility, as it was from the beginning of creation. This is why there really is only one prayer: "Father, bring Your Kingdom into this earth." To do that, we must rid the earth of everything that is against the Kingdom. We read in Mark 16:17-19,

> "And these signs will accompany those who have believed: in My name they will cast out demons, they will

---

Matthew 12:29 "Or how can anyone enter the strong man's house and carry off his property, unless he first binds the strong man? And then he will plunder his house."

Revelation 12:7-9 And there was war in heaven, Michael and his angels waging war with the dragon. And the dragon and his angels waged war, [8] and they were not strong enough, and there was no longer a place found for them in heaven. [9] And the great dragon was thrown down, the serpent of old who is called the devil and Satan, who deceives the whole world; he was thrown down to the earth, and his angels were thrown down with him.

speak with new tongues; they will pick up serpents, and if they drink any deadly poison, it shall not hurt them; they will lay hands on the sick, and they will recover." So then, when the Lord Jesus had spoken to them, He was received up into heaven, and sat down at the right hand of God.

When Christ described the signs that follow those who believe, did He say, "Those who believe will be able to save souls"? No, He said, "In My name they will cast out demons." When we read that passage, we imagine little demons that are in people or running around like goblins, but the word "demon" in the Scriptures has a deeper meaning. It is dealing with the spirit realm, with spiritual forces of evil, with powers and principalities (Ephesians 6:12). The authority we have in Christ has a far greater purpose than a limited focus on demons. The first sign that Christ said would follow those who believe is the ability to bring down satan's realm. The first result of being a believer is that we have authority to cast out satan from this earth. Christ did not go into heaven and just throw out a few demons; He threw satan out of heaven. Satan was cast out of heaven and there was no longer a place found for him there. Likewise, we also must do more than just cast out demons. We must cast out satan from the earth and bring down the powers of the satanic realm. We cast out all of satan's government and all of his hordes.

The burden to save souls is very real, but we understand, as the Scripture says, that the whole earth is under the power of the wicked one (1 John 5:19). The hearts of men—the souls of men—are held in bondage under the satanic restraint and government that reigns in this earth. If the Church exercises its authority to

---

Ephesians 6:12 For our struggle is not against flesh and blood, but against the rulers, against the powers, against the world forces of this darkness, against the spiritual forces of wickedness in the heavenly places.

cast out the prince of this world and his government (John 12:31), then the simplest thing will be to save souls. If you get rid of the blindness and the unbelief and the bondage that covers people, they will believe.

We spend so much time trying to talk people into things. Christ never did that. Read the Gospels about Christ's ministry. He did not focus on trying to convince people that He was right. He did not sit for hours arguing with the Pharisees to try to show them that He was right and they were missing it. He did not even try to persuade them that their minds were clouded by deception and satan. He knew He had to do one thing: He needed to go to the cross and take authority and dominion over satan's realm and cast him out. Once the strong man is bound, plundering his house is easy.

We could spend the next 2,000 years trying to evangelize the world, or we could see the Body of Christ move in authority to bring the Kingdom of God in the earth. Then, believe me, people will come and ask us to pray for them, to minister Christ to them. Their hearts will be able to see. Man is not innately evil and against God. Man is a creation of God. There is something in the hearts of people that when God is manifested, they will open up. There is a famous line from a movie: "If you build it, they will come." If we bring the Kingdom into the earth, people will come. Their hearts will be changed because they will no longer be controlled by the satanic forces.

The Scriptures do not teach you to go out and argue with people to persuade them to receive Christ, or to rail against their doctrines, or to confront them about their sins and their problems. Nowhere

---

John 12:31 "Now judgment is upon this world; now the ruler of this world shall be cast out."

in the Bible does it command you to point your finger at people and say, "That's wrong, wrong, wrong! You're bad! You need Jesus." On the contrary, it says that our fight is not against flesh and blood (Ephesians 6:12). We are not at war with man until he gives up his evil ways and accepts Christ. The Kingdom of God is not God's fight against man and his sin. God so loved the world that He gave His Son that everyone might be saved (John 3:16). Then, what is wrong with man? His mind and his heart are held in bondage to the prince of the power of this world (Ephesians 2:2). Our fight is not against people; it is against principalities and powers, the authorities of wickedness that exist in the spirit realm, which have continued to hold this planet in bondage.

Christ went into heaven and created the prototype of what this earth will be like. The Kingdom of God already exists. It has already been accomplished, but it is up to us to grab it and bring it into this earth. We are to manifest it in this realm. This earth is our responsibility. The Lord taught us to pray, "On earth as it is in heaven." Whatever exists in heaven, we are to bring here on earth. Is there sickness in heaven? No. Then we should end sickness here. Does the devil have any authority in heaven? No. Then why do we give him authority here? We should take it away from him. Is there backbiting in heaven? Is there hatred there? No. Then we should end those things here on earth.

Some might say, "I understand all that, but I'm just waiting for Jesus to come and deal with it." Well, He is waiting until His enemies are

---

John 3:16 "For God so loved the world, that He gave His only begotten Son, that whoever believes in Him should not perish, but have eternal life."

Ephesians 2:2 In which you formerly walked according to the course of this world, according to the prince of the power of the air, of the spirit that is now working in the sons of disobedience.

made a footstool for His feet, and we are the ones who do that (Hebrews 10:13). Christ did not command His disciples to pray, "Father, we are waiting for the 'rapture.' We are sitting and waiting for You to come and make everything good." He told them to proclaim the Kingdom into being; to pray, "Thy Kingdom come." We have a very simple application. Whenever we see something on earth that is not the way it is in heaven, then we take our key and we bind it. The things that we bind on earth, we see that He has already bound in heaven. Likewise, the qualities that we see in the Kingdom, we loose in our community, in our city, in our country, and on this earth. We loose them because we see that Christ has already done it. Whatever He has done in heaven, we will do on earth. It is the time and it is our responsibility. We turn loose the cry of our hearts for all of creation. We pray, "Lord, bring Your Kingdom. Bring Your dominion as it is right now in heaven."

Hebrews 10:13   Waiting from that time onward UNTIL HIS ENEMIES BE MADE A FOOTSTOOL FOR HIS FEET.

7 | On Earth, As It Is in Heaven

As we study the Lord's Prayer, we are looking to apply it in real and practical ways. When we pray, "Thy kingdom come. Thy will be done, on earth as it is in heaven" (Matthew 6:10), we are believing to see His Kingdom and His will, which is established in heaven, actually come here on this earth. We are believing for it to be a tangible experience in our personal lives. We are determined to see this simple prayer become something so powerful in our lives and in our church that we begin to bring this world into subjection to His Kingdom.

When you are in spiritual battle and surrounded by circumstances, you tend to become very focused on the natural level. The circumstances surrounding daily life take a great deal of energy, and you can find yourself feeling hemmed in and not able to break free. You can't seem to get the money you need. You can't seem to get out of the negative situations you are in. You begin to feel as if you are trapped in a bubble and you can't do anything about it. In response, you try, on a very natural level, to solve all of your problems. Your efforts become very concentrated, on a physical, mental, and emotional level, trying to deal with everything you are facing. On that level, it is very easy to get frustrated and become defeated in your emotions. You begin to think, "There is no way out! I can't change anything. I have tried so many times."

When you are young, you have more physical energy, and it is easy to rely on your own strength for answers. We all do that, and the more we do, the more we lock ourselves into the physical level. It is difficult for us to imagine that there is any other way to deal with our circumstances, because the issues we face seem so physical. We deal with our health; we deal with our finances. Everything about our personal circumstances seems physical.

Satan is very happy when he can keep you hemmed in by your circumstances, because you have no power when you approach things purely on a natural level. But there is something else that we can do. There is a different approach that we can take. We do not want to be like a dog chasing its tail that expends a great deal of energy running around and around but still never catches its tail. People are facing many difficult circumstances, and we need to be much more effective in dealing with those needs. So let's look at the Lord's Prayer and see how we can apply it specifically.

Jesus began His teaching on prayer by saying, "Your Father knows what you need, before you ask Him" (Matthew 6:8). That is something you must keep uppermost in your mind. God knows your situation. He knows your circumstances, and He is very aware of what you are facing. It is easy to say, "Well then, why should we pray?" God is always trying to get us to be His instruments in the earth. He always moves through human vessels. Therefore, He tries to get us to the place where we can be His expression.

The next verse reads, "Pray, then, in this way: 'Our Father who art in heaven, hallowed be Thy name'" (Matthew 6:9). God is holy. The first thing you do in prayer is recognize Him; you honor and worship Him. Realize, first of all, that He is there. Hebrews 11:6 teaches that if you are going to come to God, you have to believe that He is. That may sound silly, especially for believers, but there are varying degrees to which we recognize that. Is He really in charge? Is He really all-powerful? Is He really engaged in our lives? Your awareness has to be more than saying, "God is out there somewhere." No, you have to believe that God is right here. He is in you. He is working with you. His presence surrounds you. By your worship, you make Him a force that is surrounding you and is engaged with you. In your awareness of Him, you make God alive to you.

After we come into this awareness of Him, we make a demand: "Thy kingdom come. Thy will be done, on earth as it is in heaven" (Matthew 6:10). This is by no means an inordinate demand on God. We are not approaching Him with a bad attitude. Instead, we recognize that He knows what we need, and His purpose is to bring His will here on earth as it is in heaven. The heavenly, or spiritual, reality is the world where He rules and reigns. His will already exists there, but He wants His will to be here also. Jesus told the disciples to be His instruments, to be those who pray, "Father, all of the elements that are in place in the heavens—the same control and the same freedom—let them be here on earth." When you get that concept, you really begin to understand what God is doing, and you begin to understand why you are here and what your purpose is.

More than just praying a prayer, you have to see yourself literally as the enforcer who declares, "It will be this way." The Lord's Prayer is not a general prayer. It applies specifically to your circumstances and the things you need, like health or finances. You have to confront these areas directly and say, "Lord, Thy Kingdom come.

Hebrews 11:6 And without faith it is impossible to please Him, for he who comes to God must believe that He is, and that He is a rewarder of those who seek Him.

This circumstance needs to conform to Your will in the earth. It needs to bow to Your Kingdom." All things need to be brought into subjection to the way God wants them to be. Refuse to allow your circumstances to become so huge that they are bigger to you than He is. Look at them and declare, "Come into subjection to Christ's authority!"

"Thy Kingdom come" is a declaration that you make with intensity and persistence. You do not just say it once and walk away. It is something that you become convinced of. The Lord's Prayer is an unending prayer. The Bible teaches us to "pray without ceasing" (1 Thessalonians 5:17). This is not vain repetition (Matthew 6:7). You are declaring His Kingdom to be the reality. It is something you are saying with every breath. As you walk through your day, your spirit declares, "Thy Kingdom come on this earth!" What do you do with your finances? You command them to bow to the will of God. What do you do about your physical health? You tell your body to bow to the Kingdom of God. Whatever His will is for us physically and financially, that is what we expect to see manifested. We expect that whatever we own or manage will be in the will of God. We expect it to have the blessings of God, because everything we are about is bringing heaven into the earth.

That is what this prayer is really all about: "God, let heaven be manifested on this earth. Let it be here just as it is now there." The Lord's Prayer is not weak in any respect. It is saying, "Everything about my life and my circumstances, line up to the Kingdom of God!" What is the Kingdom of God? It is a kingdom. A kingdom means there is a king, a ruler who is all-powerful, who determines everything that happens. He determines how it happens, when it happens, and where it happens. In the Kingdom of God, God is the King. He is the One who determines what happens. The Kingdom

---

Matthew 6:7 "And when you are praying, do not use meaningless repetition, as the Gentiles do, for they suppose that they will be heard for their many words."

of God is not a democracy. The government of the Kingdom of God is not something we vote on. If you are disappointed that you do not get a vote, just remember that the devil does not get a vote either! It is God who makes up His mind. What is in His heart and what is in His will is what will be. He is the determining factor. We, in turn, become the enforcers of His will in the earth.

The Kingdom of God begins within us (Luke 17:21). We cannot scream at our circumstances and say, "I want you to line up to the will of God, but when it comes to me, I want to do whatever I want." It does not work that way! The Kingdom gets applied to you first, and then to everything around you. One of the greatest ways to align yourself with His will is to start praying this prayer, because when you do, God will start dealing with everything in you that is not in line. He will start putting His finger on things and say, "How do you expect Me to make this circumstance line up to My will when you are not aligned with My will?" That is what a walk with God is all about. It is, first, about us becoming the Kingdom. We are the house of the Lord, the sanctuary, the dwelling place of God (1 Corinthians 3:16). He is making us that.

Continuing in the Lord's Prayer, we read, "Give us this day our daily bread" (Matthew 6:11). This verse is literally translated, "Give us this day our bread for tomorrow." It is about providing for our needs. This verse repeats what Jesus said before He started His teaching on prayer: "Your Father knows what you need" (Matthew 6:8). We can do nothing in ourselves about our needs; the Father provides for us. It must be deeply rooted in our hearts and minds that the Lord honestly will provide for us. The Lord, according to His will, provides the necessities while we are

---

Luke 17:21 "Nor will they say, 'Look, here it is!' or, 'There it is!' For behold, the kingdom of God is in your midst."

1 Corinthians 3:16 Do you not know that you are a temple of God, and that the Spirit of God dwells in you?

declaring His will in the earth. We need to change our negative thought patterns: "I prayed and the Lord did not do anything about it." That is an outgrowth of our mindset, that we have to provide for ourselves. We tend to think, "Yes, the Lord is there, but I have to take care of everything because He won't do it if I don't."

It is contradictory to say, "The Lord is the King and He is in charge, but I had better take care of this." Something has to be settled in your heart so that you pray, "Lord, You know what my needs are, and I am expecting that You will provide for my needs. Give me today my daily bread. Give me what I need for tomorrow." This prayer means that today, before your foot sets down in tomorrow, the Father will provide for your needs. This prayer literally becomes a covenant with God where you say, "You are going to provide for me, and I will trust You." Trusting the Lord for our needs is extremely important because this is an area where we experience a gradual erosion of our relationship with Him. Everything seems to come in and tell us, "Did the Lord say that? That's not going to work." Do not buy into the serpent's lie (Genesis 3:1). Keep yourself positioned in the Father.

Jesus continued teaching about prayer, saying, "And forgive us our debts, as we also have forgiven our debtors. And do not lead us into temptation, but deliver us from evil" (Matthew 6:12-13). It is a spiritual principle that the Lord will act toward us as we act toward one another. If we are not acting toward others with a right spirit, then the Lord cannot move. He is always waiting for us to come into an attitude of spirit in which He can act. You see this happen with married couples who come for marriage counseling. Sometimes both come with such bad spirits that God cannot intervene in their situation. They won't find an answer until they

---

Genesis 3:1 Now the serpent was more crafty than any beast of the field which the LORD God had made. And he said to the woman, "Indeed, has God said, 'You shall not eat from any tree of the garden'?"

are right in their spirits toward the Lord. We have to be positioned in such a way that He can move. We do not want our own actions and attitudes to literally be blocking His will. We do not want to be an impasse that stops Him from being able to move. We want to make sure that the switch is on and the power can flow into our circumstances. The Kingdom of God is connected to our relationships. What is going on in our midst? How am I relating to you? Am I loving you? Am I forgiving you? Am I holding things against you? We need our relationships to literally be the atmosphere in which God moves.

We read in the Book of Hebrews: "Thou hast made him [speaking of Christ] for a little while lower than the angels; Thou hast crowned him with glory and honor, and hast appointed him over the works of Thy hands" (Hebrews 2:7). When Christ was resurrected, God handed everything over to Him. God appointed Him over all the works of His hands, which is everything that exists. "Thou hast put all things in subjection under his feet" (Hebrews 2:8). That is the heavenly position; all things are in subjection under Christ's feet. "For in subjecting all things to him, He left nothing that is not subject to him. But now we do not yet see all things subjected to him" (Hebrews 2:8).

From where we are here on this earth, we do not yet see all things subjected to Christ. When we look around at our circumstances, our relationships, our finances, whatever we are in the midst of, we do not yet see the Kingdom of God on earth as it is in heaven. This is where the Lord's Prayer comes in, because we must bring these areas into subjection to Him. We see that all things are not yet in subjection here on the earth, but we know that all things have been brought into subjection in the heavenly places. Therefore, we enforce the subjugation of all things in this earth unto Christ. That is the role that we play. We should not be deceived by the fact that we do not see everything in subjection. That is not a reason to give up and simply accept things the way they are. It may be the way things are, but those are the very things we are supposed to deal with. We are in a relationship with God to change this age.

The way of prayer that Jesus taught His disciples shows us how we can change all of these areas, and we need to go about doing just that. There may be a different application for each individual, but everyone can apply this prayer to their situation. Some people are under a weight of problems that they need to break out of. Some are influenced by circumstances from the past that have conditioned them to think that there is nothing they can do. Others are under a heavy financial burden that they feel is impossible to change. The truth is, there is a way to change everything. That is what the family of God is about; there is a way to do it. Ask God to make everything in your life align to His Kingdom and His will. Bring every area of your life into subjection to Him.

8 | Heaven Is Moving to Earth

Christ taught the disciples how to pray, saying, "Pray, then, in this way: 'Our Father who art in heaven, hallowed be Thy name'" (Matthew 6:9). We always begin with worship and adoration of the Lord. Then He said, "Thy kingdom come. Thy will be done, on earth as it is in heaven" (Matthew 6:10). This is a command. It is a prophecy. We proclaim, "Let Thy Kingdom come in this earth right now." This is how the Lord taught us to pray. We pray for His Kingdom to manifest here on earth as it already exists in heaven. This means that for us in the Body of Christ, heaven is our example. Heaven is not some place way out there that we cannot see. On the contrary, we can see into heaven by the Word of God, and it is our example of the way it should be here on earth.

We think, "Heaven has been perfect for thousands and thousands of years. Heaven is a wonderful place." Heaven has not always been a wonderful place. Ask Job how wonderful it was when satan had access to heaven. When the sons of God appeared before the Lord, satan was there in heaven at the throne of God (Job 1:6; 2:1). Read the third chapter of Zechariah. Ask Joshua the high priest, "How wonderful was it to stand before the angel of the Lord in heaven?" He will tell you, "It wasn't wonderful! Satan was there at my right hand accusing me!" (Zechariah 3:1). One of the key aspects of being sons of God is that we must stand before the Father. However, there is a new aspect to heaven since those Scriptures were written, since the time when Christ entered heaven and satan was thrown down (Luke 10:18).

We read about this event in the 12th chapter of Revelation:

> And there was war in heaven, Michael and his angels waging war with the dragon. And the dragon and his angels waged war, and they were not strong enough. [Get that—they were not strong enough!] And there was no longer a place found for them in heaven. And the great dragon was thrown down, the serpent of old who is called the devil and Satan, who deceives the whole world; he was thrown down to the earth, and his angels were thrown down with him. And I heard a loud voice in heaven, saying, "Now the salvation, and the power, and the kingdom of our God and the authority of His Christ have come, for the accuser of our brethren has been thrown down, who accuses them before our God day and night." (Revelation 12:7-10)

Job 1:6 Now there was a day when the sons of God came to present themselves before the LORD, and Satan also came among them.

Job 2:1 Again there was a day when the sons of God came to present themselves before the LORD, and Satan also came among them to present himself before the LORD.

Zechariah 3:1 Then he showed me Joshua the high priest standing before the angel of the LORD, and Satan standing at his right hand to accuse him.

Luke 10:18 And He said to them, "I was watching Satan fall from heaven like lightning."

When satan was thrown down to earth, the angel said, "Now!" A new state of heaven was established immediately. The salvation, the power, the Kingdom of God and the authority of His Christ were established in heaven. Why? All these now exist because the accuser of the brethren has been cast down.

Now when we stand in the presence of God, the accuser is not there. In fact, it is the only safe place to be. Christ said, "Where I am, you shall be also" (John 14:3). Why is that? It is because the accuser was thrown out of heaven to the earth. That is why we pray, "Thy Kingdom come on earth as it is in heaven." In heaven, the accuser has been cast out, but on earth he still has access to us. When the accuser was no longer in heaven, the voice proclaimed, "Now is the salvation. Now is the power. Now is the Kingdom. Now is the authority" (Revelation 12:10). That is the way it is in heaven, and we are to make it be the same way here on earth. It should be of great concern to us that the power and authority of the Kingdom do not yet exist in the Church. We still do not have salvation in all of its aspects. You can say, "I have salvation. I believe on the Lord Jesus Christ. I know my sins are washed away." Yes, that is all true; but that is just the first step in a salvation that is so vast. Our salvation includes the transformation of our minds into the mind of Christ (Romans 12:2; 1 Corinthians 2:16). It includes the end of disease and sickness and oppression. It includes the end of poverty. It includes the end of ignorance. It includes the end of the oppression of our children in every country of the world. We have a great God with an eternal and unlimited salvation. In

---

John 14:3 "And if I go and prepare a place for you, I will come again, and receive you to Myself; that where I am, there you may be also."

Romans 12:2 And do not be conformed to this world, but be transformed by the renewing of your mind, that you may prove what the will of God is, that which is good and acceptable and perfect.

1 Corinthians 2:16 For WHO HAS KNOWN THE MIND OF THE LORD, THAT HE SHOULD INSTRUCT HIM? But we have the mind of Christ.

comparison, the Church's vision in its preaching and appropriation of salvation is quite small and limited.

We read in the Book of Malachi that we will be able to distinguish between those who serve God and those who do not serve Him (Malachi 3:18). Yet if you were to take a large group of Christians and unbelievers, and mix them all together in a crowd, I believe that you would have a difficult time finding any difference between those who are Christians and those who are not. Why isn't the difference evident? The reason is because there is still a level of salvation that we do not have. Perhaps you believe that your experience of salvation is already perfect, and you do not need anything more. Okay, then read the next result mentioned in Revelation 12:10—power. Is there power in the Word? Is there power in the Body of Christ? We are to have power "to the pulling down of strong holds" (2 Corinthians 10:4, KJV). What about the next result—the Kingdom? Is the Kingdom existing in the Church, in our midst on this earth? Theologians are arguing whether or not it is even the time of the Kingdom. I do not want to argue theology. I want to pray what Christ taught us to pray: "Thy Kingdom come in this earth." If it is not time for the Kingdom, then why did Jesus tell us to pray for it? We loose the Kingdom of God on the earth. Let the Church be swallowed up by the Kingdom of God and His presence. These are to be the results of our salvation.

It is time for the King to reign over His Church. There are too many activities that go on in the Church that have nothing to do with the Lordship of Jesus Christ over His Body. We need His authority now. When Jesus was on the earth, people marveled at

---

Malachi 3:18 So you will again distinguish between the righteous and the wicked, between one who serves God and one who does not serve Him.

2 Corinthians 10:4, KJV For the weapons of our warfare are not carnal, but mighty through God to the pulling down of strong holds.

His authority (Mark 1:22). He rebuked the storm and the disciples said, "What kind of man is this? Even the wind and the rain obey Him" (Luke 8:25). Jesus had authority over the realm of the natural. That is the same authority that the Church should have today. So what happened to these things? Why do we not see them in operation in the Church? What is blocking the salvation and the power that we should have? What is blocking the manifestation of the Kingdom of Christ and His Lordship over His Body? Why isn't the authority of Christ flowing through the Church as it should? The reason is because the accuser of the brethren has been thrown down to the earth and has access here.

The things manifested in heaven are what should be manifested on the earth. Satan is no longer in heaven, so he should be removed from our midst in the earth. When we pray, "Thy kingdom come. Thy will be done, on earth as it is in heaven" (Matthew 6:10), we want something to happen. Whatever has been done in heaven must now be accomplished in the earth. Prayer is all about tying together what is in heaven and what is on earth, and making them one. The Kingdom of God is the merging together of the spiritual level and the natural level. You can find references to spiritual things in the Hebrew Scriptures, but for the most part, the Old Testament stories and prophecies pertain to what was happening on a physical level. The Greek Scriptures of the New Testament, on the other hand, are more focused on a spiritual manifestation. Paul wrote that the natural is first, and then the spiritual follows afterwards. The first man, Adam,

---

Mark 1:22   And they were amazed at His teaching; for He was teaching them as one having authority, and not as the scribes.

Luke 8:25   And He said to them, "Where is your faith?" And they were fearful and amazed, saying to one another, "Who then is this, that He commands even the winds and the water, and they obey Him?"

was a natural man; the second man, Christ, was a spiritual man (1 Corinthians 15:45-46). However, as we get into the time of the Kingdom, what we actually see happening is both of these realms coming together, being knit together (1 Corinthians 15:49, 53).

Many Christians are critical of the Jews, saying, "They missed Jesus. They did not recognize that He was the Messiah." However, the concept of "Messiah" in the Hebrew Scriptures is very clear that He must be a ruler in the earth (Isaiah 9:6-7; Daniel 7:13-14; Jeremiah 23:5-6). So there is a sense in which we could say, "Yes, at this moment, Jesus may be the Messiah to the Christians; but

---

1 Corinthians 15:45-46 So also it is written, "The first MAN, Adam, BECAME A LIVING SOUL." The last Adam became a life-giving spirit. [46] However, the spiritual is not first, but the natural; then the spiritual.

1 Corinthians 15:49 And just as we have borne the image of the earthy, we shall also bear the image of the heavenly.

1 Corinthians 15:53 For this perishable must put on the imperishable, and this mortal must put on immortality.

Isaiah 9:6-7 For a child will be born to us, a son will be given to us; and the government will rest on His shoulders; and His name will be called Wonderful Counselor, Mighty God, Eternal Father, Prince of Peace. [7] There will be no end to the increase of His government or of peace, on the throne of David and over his kingdom, to establish it and to uphold it with justice and righteousness from then on and forevermore. The zeal of the LORD of hosts will accomplish this.

Daniel 7:13-14 "I kept looking in the night visions, and behold, with the clouds of heaven one like a Son of Man was coming, and He came up to the Ancient of Days and was presented before Him. [14] And to Him was given dominion, glory and a kingdom, that all the peoples, nations, and men of every language might serve Him. His dominion is an everlasting dominion which will not pass away; and His kingdom is one which will not be destroyed."

Jeremiah 23:5-6 "Behold, the days are coming," declares the LORD, "When I shall raise up for David a righteous Branch; and He will reign as king and act wisely and do justice and righteousness in the land. [6] In His days Judah will be saved, and Israel will dwell securely; and this is His name by which He will be called, 'The LORD our righteousness.'"

another step is required for Him to be the Messiah fulfilling the Hebrew Scriptures and the Jewish hope." As much as it seems that Christians and Jews are going in two different directions, I believe that God is looking to knit these two faiths together. Look at the question the disciples asked Jesus at His ascension: "Is it at this time You are restoring the kingdom to Israel?" (Acts 1:6). The disciples, being Jewish, were looking for Christ to bring about a natural kingdom in the earth. People criticize, saying, "See, the Jews missed it. Didn't they understand that what Christ was doing was spiritual?" We must realize that today Christianity is also missing it, because Christ's purpose is to establish His Kingdom on the earth. The disciples had a valid question. The question was not, "**Will** You establish Your Kingdom on the earth?" The question was, "**When** will You establish Your Kingdom on the earth? Is this the time?" Jesus' disciples were looking for Him to fulfill **all** the prophecies of the Messiah. They wanted to know if it was at that time that the physical aspect of the Kingdom would be manifested.

Ask Jews today, "When you talk about the Messiah, what are you looking for?" They will probably tell you, "We are looking for a leader to emerge who will bring peace and who will bring the earth under the dominion of God." It sounds to me like we, as Christians, are believing for the same thing. We are believing that Christ is coming forth on this earth. When Jesus taught His disciples to pray, He said, "Pray, then, in this way: . . . 'Thy kingdom come. Thy will be done, on earth as it is in heaven'" (Matthew 6:9-10). Whatever has taken place through Christ and the sacrifice of His blood must be manifested on earth, as it is now in heaven.

Both the heavenly and the earthly manifestations are aspects of Christ's ministry. He is a spiritual being who took dominion in the spirit realm. He went into the abyss and took captive a host of captives, and He was exalted and is seated at the right hand of the

Father (Ephesians 4:8-10; 1:20). Yet Christ Himself is waiting until His enemies are made the footstool for His feet (Hebrews 10:12-13). We cannot be disengaged from the idea of the physical realm. We know that all is accomplished in Christ, who is seated at the right hand of God, but it is not enough that our walk with God is based solely on the spiritual aspect. When we take that approach, we completely miss the meaning of the prayer, "Thy kingdom come. Thy will be done"—finished, completed—"on earth as it is in heaven" (Matthew 6:10). Like the Jewish faith, we too have the messianic hope of Him who comes to rule and reign on earth. Whatever Christ has done spiritually must manifest physically on the earth.

When Peter had the revelation of who Christ was, Jesus said to him, "Blessed are you, Simon Barjona, because flesh and blood did not reveal this to you, but My Father who is in heaven. And I also say to you that you are Peter, and upon this rock I will build My church; and the gates of Hades shall not overpower it" (Matthew 16:17-18). What is the rock that Christ was talking about? It is the rock of revelation. Peter heard from the Father who Jesus was, and that was a very spiritual manifestation of Christ. What did Jesus say next? "I will give you the keys of the kingdom of heaven; and whatever you shall bind on earth shall be bound in heaven, and whatever you shall loose on earth shall be loosed in

---

Ephesians 4:8-10 Therefore it says, "WHEN HE ASCENDED ON HIGH, HE LED CAPTIVE A HOST OF CAPTIVES, AND HE GAVE GIFTS TO MEN." 9 (Now this expression, "He ascended," what does it mean except that He also had descended into the lower parts of the earth? 10 He who descended is Himself also He who ascended far above all the heavens, that He might fill all things.)

Ephesians 1:20 Which He brought about in Christ, when He raised Him from the dead, and seated Him at His right hand in the heavenly places.

Hebrews 10:12-13 But He, having offered one sacrifice for sins for all time, SAT DOWN AT THE RIGHT HAND OF GOD, 13 waiting from that time onward UNTIL HIS ENEMIES BE MADE A FOOTSTOOL FOR HIS FEET.

heaven" (Matthew 16:19). Christ gave us the keys to bring what is spiritual, what is in heaven, to the earth.

We often pray, "We bind this in the name of the Lord," but I do not think we completely understand what we are talking about. When we say "we bind" and "we loose," we need to understand what we are really doing. One beautiful translation of the Greek word for "bind" is "knit."[5] Whatever you knit on earth is knit in heaven. This conveys the idea that what we do as believers is tie together heaven and earth. Whatever we loose, whatever we cut free or dislodge on earth has already been cut free or dislodged in heaven. There are things that need to be dislodged on earth. The entire satanic kingdom, the wickedness on the earth that is drawing its power from that which is spiritual, needs to be dislodged (Ephesians 6:12).

What we need in order to manifest this on earth is spiritual; it is in heaven. We need the authority that comes only from God (Romans 13:1). If we can move in authority, things change. Therefore we look to knit what we are doing on earth with the authority that is in heaven. We also look to cut loose everything on this earth that feeds on the power of wickedness that is drawn from satan. It is a spiritual force, a living power, and we look to see that cut off. The prayer, "Lord, Thy Kingdom come on earth," also includes the prayer, "Lord, cut off the power of satan that wicked men draw from."

Ephesians 6:12 For our struggle is not against flesh and blood, but against the rulers, against the powers, against the world forces of this darkness, against the spiritual forces of wickedness in the heavenly places.

Romans 13:1 Let every person be in subjection to the governing authorities. For there is no authority except from God, and those which exist are established by God.

[5.] James Strong, *A Concise Dictionary of the Words in the Greek Testament and the Hebrew Bible* (Bellingham, WA: Logos Bible Software, 2009), 21.

Even though Christ has all authority, which was given to Him by God, satan tries to usurp that authority; and he does so by moving in power, or force. What we look to do in prayer is to cut off the wickedness. There are wicked men throughout the earth; we do not want them to have a power behind what they are doing that is fed from the realm of spirit. So in our prayer we cut them off. Satan being thrown down to earth is representative of this fact. Satan has no more connection with heaven. For satan, the knitting together between heaven and earth has ended and all he has is an earthly ability to move. He has been cut off from heaven. We are looking for the opposite to happen for us. We are looking to knit ourselves with heaven to have the power and authority behind what we are doing in the earth. What we bind on this earth will be bound in heaven. Alternate translations of Matthew 16:19 actually put it in the past tense: "Whatever you bind in earth shall have been bound in heaven" (Matthew 16:19, NASB 1995). We are literally drawing together two realms that have been isolated in a way that can no longer be; for the Kingdom of God must now manifest on this earth.

In a sense, heaven is moving to earth, and we are the movers. We must bring into manifestation in the earth the things that are necessary for this time. We need to go in and get what is in heaven, bring it here, and set it up in this realm. We need to recognize the impact of time and delay on the natural world, and see the importance of not letting our efforts languish on a physical level. When that happens, we lose things that we should have. When Jesus spoke of the end time, He said that the time must be cut short (Matthew 24:22). Therefore, we cannot stress enough the importance of impacting the earth in prayer, prophecy, and speaking creatively. Our prayer becomes a prophetic proclamation

---

Matthew 24:22 "And unless those days had been cut short, no life would have been saved; but for the sake of the elect those days shall be cut short."

whereby we create in the earth that which is in the heavens. Our prayer creates what needs to be manifested in the natural realm in order for the Kingdom of God to flow freely. Do not say, "This is too much for me to believe. I can believe that events were that important in the time of Jesus, but what is happening in the natural circumstances surrounding me today are certainly not that important." Don't think that way! What is happening in your life is just as important, because Christ is coming to the earth again.

From the Scriptures, we recognize how important it is for everything to be in place on the natural level in order for certain spiritual events to happen. There is a timeframe involved. The first time that Christ came to the earth, it was absolutely essential that many things on the physical level be in place for His coming. For Christ to be born of Mary, she had to be old enough to have a child (Galatians 4:4). Elizabeth had to be pregnant for six months prior to Mary's conception (Luke 1:31, 36). According to the prophecy, Christ's birth was to be after Elizabeth's pregnancy (John 1:15). His birth was literally triggered by the natural unfolding of events as they were taking place. It was important that once Christ grew up and was ready to gather the disciples, that they were not three years old. It would not have worked if Jesus had to start a nursery school rather than discipleship! John the Baptist had to be a young man, ready to go out into the world, before Jesus came into His ministry. Can you imagine John the Baptist as a ten-year-old kid running around in the wilderness saying in a high voice, "Repent

---

Galatians 4:4 But when the fulness of the time came, God sent forth His Son, born of a woman, born under the Law.

Luke 1:31 "And behold, you will conceive in your womb, and bear a son, and you shall name Him Jesus."

Luke 1:36 "And behold, even your relative Elizabeth has also conceived a son in her old age; and she who was called barren is now in her sixth month."

John 1:15 John bore witness of Him, and cried out, saying, "This was He of whom I said, 'He who comes after me has a higher rank than I, for He existed before me.'"

of your sin"? It certainly would have drawn attention, but no one would have been drawn to hear him. It was the very fact of who he was on a natural level that was interesting to people. Here was the son of a priest, who should have been in the Temple, but he, instead, was in the wilderness preaching something different; that was what caught everyone's attention. People went to listen to John, wondering, "What is this guy talking about?" and soon they were being baptized by him (Matthew 3:1-6; Luke 3:2-3, 7).

History is tremendously important and influential with regard to the unfolding of the Kingdom. The children of Israel could not go into the land that God had promised them until the wickedness of the Amorites had come to the full (Genesis 15:16). They had to wait until everything was prepared within a specific historical timeframe. Yet today, when we as Christians relate to the Kingdom of God, we have become focused on the spiritual, almost to the exclusion of the physical, as if nothing on the natural level matters. We essentially throw all of that reality out the window in our

---

Matthew 3:1-6 Now in those days John the Baptist came, preaching in the wilderness of Judea, saying, ² "Repent, for the kingdom of heaven is at hand." ³ For this is the one referred to by Isaiah the prophet, saying, "THE VOICE OF ONE CRYING IN THE WILDERNESS, 'MAKE READY THE WAY OF THE LORD, MAKE HIS PATHS STRAIGHT!' " ⁴ Now John himself had a garment of camel's hair, and a leather belt about his waist; and his food was locusts and wild honey. ⁵ Then Jerusalem was going out to him, and all Judea, and all the district around the Jordan; ⁶ and they were being baptized by him in the Jordan River, as they confessed their sins.

Luke 3:2-3 In the high priesthood of Annas and Caiaphas, the word of God came to John, the son of Zacharias, in the wilderness. ³ And he came into all the district around the Jordan, preaching a baptism of repentance for the forgiveness of sins.

Luke 3:7 He therefore began saying to the multitudes who were going out to be baptized by him, "You brood of vipers, who warned you to flee from the wrath to come?"

Genesis 15:16 "Then in the fourth generation they shall return here, for the iniquity of the Amorite is not yet complete."

prayers and in our spiritual life. We cannot continue to do that. The physical events and histories surrounding us individually and globally are as important today as they were in biblical times. Things must be positioned and things must be in place. When we pray, we are not just biding our time, waiting for something to happen. We are actually the crew that is setting the stage, hanging the lighting, putting everything out for the next scene that has to take place for the show to go on. More than we know, we are what God is staging. What God is creating us into is a big part of it. How fast can we grow into the place where we can move in authority, where we can move in this kind of prayer and intercession? How effective are we being? We had better not be slowing things down, because everything has to be in place.

The Book of Daniel describes a time when Daniel was praying for an answer. When the answer finally came, the angel who brought the message said, "From the first day you started praying, I tried to come to you, but the prince of the kingdom of Persia was restraining me. At last, Michael the archangel helped me until I was free to come and deliver the answer" (Daniel 10:12-13). How does that apply? Prayer and intercession are absolutely about ending delay. Prayer is about removing what is trying to stop the physical manifestation of what we are looking to see happen. For example, your spiritual body is in heaven; don't you think it is about time you had it on the earth? Our spiritual bodies are

---

Daniel 10:12-13 Then he said to me, "Do not be afraid, Daniel, for from the first day that you set your heart on understanding this and on humbling yourself before your God, your words were heard, and I have come in response to your words. [13] But the prince of the kingdom of Persia was withstanding me for twenty-one days; then behold, Michael, one of the chief princes, came to help me, for I had been left there with the kings of Persia."

waiting for us (2 Corinthians 5:1-4). They exist and are manifested in heaven. So why do we put up with these carcasses that we have on earth? There are many things that Christ has won that are all there in heaven, but how much good does that do for us here? Not very much, unless we do something about it. If we sit here and do nothing, then we will start singing songs like, "On Jordan's stormy banks I stand and cast a wistful eye," or, "I have a mansion just over the hilltop." We sing those songs when we believe that it is all out there, far away from us, somewhere in the future. But these things that we are looking for are not luxuries. Healings are not luxuries. We need them now. Until we have healings, we will keep losing people.

Our prayer is, "Do it here, Lord, as it is in heaven." Heaven and earth have to be knit together. Bless one another and say, "I bind you over to that which is in heaven. May it be here for you in the earth." Find your voice of prayer and intercession that declares, "Your will is going to be in this earth!" It does not happen by saying, "It is already done in heaven, so let's just wait until the Lord comes. Who are we to think that we can initiate the coming of the Lord? We're not important enough to do that." That should not be our attitude. Christ said the end time will be like the days of Noah (Matthew 24:37-38). God said that He would bring a flood,

---

2 Corinthians 5:1-4 For we know that if the earthly tent which is our house is torn down, we have a building from God, a house not made with hands, eternal in the heavens. ² For indeed in this house we groan, longing to be clothed with our dwelling from heaven; ³ inasmuch as we, having put it on, shall not be found naked. ⁴ For indeed while we are in this tent, we groan, being burdened, because we do not want to be unclothed, but to be clothed, in order that what is mortal may be swallowed up by life.

Matthew 24:37-38 "For the coming of the Son of Man will be just like the days of Noah. ³⁸ For as in those days which were before the flood they were eating and drinking, they were marrying and giving in marriage, until the day that Noah entered the ark."

but He waited 120 years until Noah built the ark (1 Peter 3:20, Genesis 6:3). There was not a single drop of rain until there was a boat prepared to do what God wanted done in the earth. If the days of the coming of the Lord are like the days of Noah, then that means we cannot be an ignorant, unprepared people who are just waiting for someone else to do something. It means that we will be an aggressive company of people who get the plans and blueprints for what God is directing us to do and make it happen. After Noah built the ark, it did not start raining until the very moment when all the animals were in and the doors were closed (Genesis 7:16-17). That is a great picture of the Kingdom of God: as soon as we can get the will of God on earth as it is in heaven, as soon as it is completed right here and we get the door closed, it will start raining. The Kingdom of God will come.

We have to get out of our minds years of church teaching that says, "Fulfillment comes when we die and go to heaven." My Bible does not read that way. According to what I read, we are to bring heaven into this earth. Now. Christ taught about the link and interdependency between heaven and earth, and we are the ones who must knit that energy together. We must tie these realms together until what is in heaven happens on earth. Let our intercession, prophecy, and prayer be with the understanding of what we are doing and how we are doing it. We expect to see things happen on the physical plane. We expect to see healings

---

1 Peter 3:20 Who once were disobedient, when the patience of God kept waiting in the days of Noah, during the construction of the ark, in which a few, that is, eight persons, were brought safely through the water.

Genesis 6:3 Then the LORD said, "My Spirit shall not strive with man forever, because he also is flesh; nevertheless his days shall be one hundred and twenty years."

Genesis 7:16-17 And those that entered, male and female of all flesh, entered as God had commanded him; and the LORD closed it behind him. [17] Then the flood came upon the earth for forty days; and the water increased and lifted up the ark, so that it rose above the earth.

:ssings. If we sit around and wait for God to drop
of the sky, we will be waiting a long time—and
ity is a very long time. The Kingdom of God does
he sky; we are the ones who bring it. We make
things happen. We set the stage. That is what we are all about.

Lord, knit us to the power of God. Knit us to the authority of God
so that we are not doing anything on our own, but we have an
enabling to create in this earth on a physical plane. Lord, do not
let us languish, whether we are raising up and maturing people,
building physical facilities, or creating whatever needs to be in
place for Your coming. We are going to do it. We are going to make
it happen, in the name of the Lord.

9 | Our Daily Bread

In this book, we are studying the Lord's Prayer, verse by verse. Earlier, we expounded Matthew 6:9: "Pray, then, in this way: 'Our Father who art in heaven, hallowed be Thy name.'" Our prayer is to the Father. We come into the presence of the Father and we bless Him. We enter into the secret place with Him through Christ the door (Matthew 6:6; John 10:7). We are not throwing our prayers up to God in heaven; we are right there with Him. We also studied what Christ commands us to pray from this position in His presence: "Thy kingdom come. Thy will be done, on earth as it is in heaven" (Matthew 6:10). As His people, we must have a cry and a demand for the Kingdom of God to be here in this earth. We then discussed the spiritual warfare and the casting out of satan from this earth. Our prayer is, "On earth as it is in heaven." How are things in heaven? Satan has been cast out of heaven, and so it is to be the same on this earth. We simply duplicate on earth the

---

Matthew 6:6   "But you, when you pray, go into your inner room, and when you have shut your door, pray to your Father who is in secret, and your Father who sees in secret will repay you."

John 10:7   Jesus therefore said to them again, "Truly, truly, I say to you, I am the door of the sheep."

way it is in heaven. We therefore cast him out of the earth. We do not want satan to be confused about what he is supposed to do. He is to be cast out.

In this section, we will look at Matthew 6:11: "Give us this day our daily bread." After we enter into the Father's presence and worship Him, we proclaim His Kingdom in the earth. What is the next thing Christ taught us to pray? "Give us our daily bread." In the Greek language, this verse uses the aorist imperative tense of the verb. That means this is a demand: "Give me!" It is not a request. You do not pray, "Oh, please, I wish I had some bread." No, you demand, "Give me this day my daily bread!" This is almost scary for us to think of doing in the presence of the Father. It is difficult to conceive of humbly standing before the face of God and demanding, "Give me!" According to the Scripture, however, we are to "come boldly unto the throne of grace" (Hebrews 4:16, KJV). It is only because of Christ that we can enter boldly into the presence of the Father. We have no standing in ourselves. We have no worthiness. There is no reason why He would listen to us or give us anything. But in Christ we can come boldly before the throne of grace and demand our daily bread.

I do not think Christ was talking about physical bread. In the first two sections, we discussed how Jesus said, "Your Father knows what you need" (Matthew 6:8). God already knows we need food, but He is relating the concept of bread to something greater. What is it that we need so dearly that Christ would tell us to come with such a demand? It is Christ Himself. We read in John chapter 6,

> They said therefore to Him, "What then do You do for a sign, that we may see, and believe You? What work do You perform? Our fathers ate the manna in the wilderness; as

---

Matthew 6:8 "Therefore do not be like them; for your Father knows what you need, before you ask Him."

it is written, 'HE GAVE THEM BREAD OUT OF HEAVEN TO EAT.'" Jesus therefore said to them, "Truly, truly, I say to you, it is not Moses who has given you the bread out of heaven, but it is My Father who gives you the true bread out of heaven." (John 6:30-32)

Christ was saying, "Moses did not give your fathers bread. My Father who is in heaven gave the bread." Man cannot do anything of himself. Christ was firm on that point. "With men this is impossible, but with God all things are possible" (Matthew 19:26). So He said to them, "It is not Moses who has given you the bread out of heaven, but it is My Father who gives you the true bread out of heaven. For the bread of God is that which comes down out of heaven, and gives life to the world" (John 6:32-33).

It is God who gives this bread out of heaven, which is life to the world. Therefore, this request for bread is truly a request based on life or death. You either have life by virtue of the bread of heaven, or you have death because you are without this bread. "They said therefore to Him, 'Lord, evermore give us this bread'" (John 6:34). They asked Him, "Give us this bread," which is what we read in Matthew 6:11. In response to their request, Christ identifies for us exactly what we are looking for. "Jesus said to them, 'I am the bread of life'" (John 6:35). This passage defines what it is that Christ taught us to demand from the Father. He did not make it a mystery. Christ says to us, "What is it you are asking for?" He said, "I am the bread of life; he who comes to Me shall not hunger, and he who believes in Me shall never thirst" (John 6:35).

The reason we ask for bread is because we are hungry. We must hunger after Christ; and the Lord's Prayer, or the prayer of the disciples, is addressing this hunger. When you stop being hungry, you stop asking. One of the last things people experience when dying from starvation is that they stop being hungry. I am afraid that this is the picture of the Church in this generation. Too many people have stopped being hungry. When you really die from starvation, you do not know that you are starving. Your body stops asking for food. When it comes to our need for the bread from heaven, Christ is saying, "Never stop asking. Do not lose your hunger. Come before the Father every day and demand Christ in your life." We could respond to that by saying, "Well, I've received Christ. I believe. I ate of the bread of heaven and I am saved." I think He must be talking about something more than that. If He were talking about the salvation experience, why would He say that we need to come daily and demand this bread? There is a presence of Christ that we must have in our life daily. We are not talking about salvation. We are talking about the daily partaking of Christ, a daily filling of His presence, and He teaches us to cry out for that filling: "Father, give me Christ today. Let me partake. Let me eat of Him and His presence today."

I wish we would roll out of bed every day voicing that prayer. Probably the first awareness you have in the morning is your hunger. The first thing you do after you wake up is eat breakfast, so don't forget that you also have a spiritual hunger that must be satisfied as well. Our spiritual hunger must be satisfied daily, the same as our physical hunger. When you talk to people who have walked with God for many years, they will often tell you about their past experiences. "Let me tell you about my meeting with the Lord. Let me tell you about when I was saved. It was such a wonderful experience." Is there some reason why we always relate to the things of God in the past tense? What about today? Do you talk about your wonderful Thanksgiving dinner in 2002? Do you remember that? Can you still taste it? Not likely. Yet we continually talk about the things of God that happened years ago. It does not matter what I ate a year ago. It was good. I ate it; I digested it. I lived that day in the energy of that food.

Something is missing in our walk with the Lord if we keep trying to live and walk every day in the energy of a meal that happened years ago. Why is it that we attend worship services? We know that we have a hunger for Christ that must be satisfied, and according to Matthew 6:11 we must partake of Him daily. It is not enough that you worshiped last night. You need to worship today, because you need to partake of Him every day. What do you normally do after a Sunday morning service? There is a good possibility you go to a restaurant and eat. Before you go, do you say, "Oh, I ate lunch yesterday. Why should I eat today?" There is a reason we keep eating meals again and again. We eat because we have to in order to live. Why don't we have this same concept with regard to our walk with God? In the Lord's Prayer, He teaches us to have that concept: "Give us this day our daily bread" (Matthew 6:11). It doesn't matter how awesome the previous worship service might have been. It is not enough for today. It was the strength and the food you needed yesterday. Now you need something for today.

One of the reasons many churches get stuck and cannot move on with God is because they are always talking about the same meal—the same old revelation that came to someone in the past. You need to have a new meal every day. When you ask God for your daily bread, you are saying, "This is what I need today." There is bread that the Body of Christ needs for what we are going to face in our generation. If you are going to have strength to live as a believer, you need feeding every day. It is wonderful that you had a salvation experience 20 years ago. Maybe you had dreams or revelations, and the Lord spoke to you in the past. But are you hearing what He is saying today? It is a daily walk and relationship with Christ, and every day we must partake of Him.

We read in John chapter 6 that the people were asking Christ, "Give us a sign. Moses gave our fathers the bread" (John 6:30-31). They were talking about the time in the wilderness after the children of Israel left Egypt. What they experienced is summarized in Deuteronomy 8:1-3:

> "All the commandments that I am commanding you today you shall be careful to do, that you may live and multiply, and go in and possess the land which the LORD swore to give to your forefathers. And you shall remember all the way which the LORD your God has led you in the wilderness these forty years, that He might humble you, testing you, to know what was in your heart, whether you would keep His commandments or not. And He humbled you and let you be hungry, and fed you with manna which you did not know, nor did your fathers know, that He might make you understand that man does not live by bread alone, but man lives by everything that proceeds out of the mouth of the LORD."

God humbled the children of Israel and let them be hungry. Hunger is humbling because it causes you to know that you have nothing in yourself. You are reminded many times during the day that you have no life in yourself (John 6:53). When you pray, "Give us our daily bread," you have to admit that you have no life in yourself. You have no strength for the day. Lord, we humble ourselves before You today. By our very request for bread, we confess that we have nothing, that we are nothing, that no matter how many meetings with God we have had, today we have no strength. Today we need Your life. We need to partake of Christ in our hearts in a new way. There are depths to His life. There are realities in Christ that we have never seen. We have never known all that He is and all that He has for us in this generation. We come before the Lord very humbly, but with the demand, "Give us today our daily bread. Shock us, Lord, with what You have for us today."

John 6:53 Jesus therefore said to them, "Truly, truly, I say to you, unless you eat the flesh of the Son of Man and drink His blood, you have no life in yourselves."

Deuteronomy 8:3 describes how God fed them with manna. The Hebrew word for manna means "what."[6] The people saw it lying on the ground and they said, "What?" (Exodus 16:15). They did not know how to identify it so they called it "manna" (Exodus 16:31). When God feeds you daily, you should have that same response: "What is this?" It is something new. Eye has not seen it; ear has not heard it; neither is it anything our hearts have even thought to ask for (1 Corinthians 2:9). Remember, Jesus said, "Don't ask for the things your Father already knows you need" (Matthew 6:8). When you ask the Father for bread, you have no idea what you are asking for. "Lord, I don't even know what I need, but I know that You will feed me exactly what I need. You have got something that is so new, so real! It is not the same old stuff." When God feeds you, it will be impossible to say, "Oh, I was expecting that." No, you will always have the same response as the Israelites did in the wilderness: "What is this that You are giving me?" He always does something beyond your mind, beyond your imagination, but it is the food that you need.

We see the same principle at work when Christ responded to those who were essentially baiting Him, saying, "What sign do You do? Moses fed our fathers manna in the wilderness. What are You going to do for us?" Just as God gave their ancestors manna— something they never knew—that day Christ gave the people

---

Exodus 16:15 When the sons of Israel saw it, they said to one another, "What is it?" For they did not know what it was. And Moses said to them, "It is the bread which the LORD has given you to eat."

Exodus 16:31 And the house of Israel named it manna, and it was like coriander seed, white; and its taste was like wafers with honey.

1 Corinthians 2:9 But just as it is written, "THINGS WHICH EYE HAS NOT SEEN AND EAR HAS NOT HEARD, AND which HAVE NOT ENTERED THE HEART OF MAN, ALL THAT GOD HAS PREPARED FOR THOSE WHO LOVE HIM."

[6.] William Lee Holladay and Ludwig Köhler, *A Concise Hebrew and Aramaic Lexicon of the Old Testament* (Leiden: Brill, 2000), 200.

something they never knew when He told them that He was the bread of life (John 6:30-35).

You cannot re-digest yesterday's food. Read the instructions Moses gave concerning manna. There were specific rules about how to gather it and eat it. They had to go out every day and collect only a certain amount (Exodus 16:16). This presents a beautiful picture of our walk with the Lord. Every day there is something you need, something that you have to appropriate from Him, and you have to eat it that day. If you try to save it until tomorrow, it will breed worms (Exodus 16:19-20). Don't try to eat tomorrow what God is speaking today. That manna will have worms in it. You better get it right now and eat it today. Take it, digest it, and live in it now. Tomorrow you will have to go get something more, because what you received today will not take care of you tomorrow. Tomorrow you should be hungry again. If you are not hungry, be careful; you may be starving to death and not know it.

So what should we do? We should get up every morning and say, " 'Give us this day our daily bread' (Matthew 6:11). Feed us Christ, our bread from heaven, who gives us the strength that we need today." Feed us what we need, lest we die. We either die daily or we live in the life that comes from Him daily. Wake up and pray, "Let me partake of Christ today. I'm hungry, Lord." Give us this day, Lord, our daily bread. Feed us Christ in a new way. If we are walking in God's will, we are facing things every day that we have never faced before, and we need the strength from that which we have never known.

Exodus 16:16 "This is what the LORD has commanded, 'Gather of it every man as much as he should eat; you shall take an omer apiece according to the number of persons each of you has in his tent.' "

Exodus 16:19-20 And Moses said to them, "Let no man leave any of it until morning." [20] But they did not listen to Moses, and some left part of it until morning, and it bred worms and became foul; and Moses was angry with them.

In our generation, we do not even know what we need to do, what we need to be, or how we should be walking in this time. We are in one of the most tremendous times in the history of mankind, and we do not know how to deal with it. What is the answer to these days in which we live? First of all, the answer is, "Thy Kingdom come." This prayer is a key for us in these political times. It becomes a prophetic proclamation—an anointed, authoritative declaration from God's people that His Kingdom will come forth in the world around us. Secondly, the answer is, "Father, give us today our daily bread."

When we need answers, we seek God for a Word, for a vision, for a revelation. Wouldn't it be fantastic if the church leadership got together praying for answers and said, "God spoke to us and here is a Word from God. Here is what God wants us to do." In a sense, God does that, but not in the way we would expect. He simply says, "I am going to feed you every day with daily bread." It is about having a relationship with the Father and having a Living Word from God every day. The Living Word is not a doctrine; it is the daily bread that we need. We need it as much as if we were Israel in the wilderness, when having daily bread was a matter of life or death.

How do you get a Living Word? You cannot make it up. It doesn't come because you are a good speaker. There is nothing you can do to produce a Living Word from yourself. It is something that God has to grant. He has to give it to us, just as He gave the manna to the children of Israel in the wilderness. Imagine the feeling of living in the wilderness. How many times did they wake up in the morning wondering if the manna would be there? How many times, before they opened the door to their tent, did a little question run through their minds: "I know that the manna has always been there, but I wonder if it will be there this morning?"

We could easily say, "Will we have a Living Word this morning? Is this the day the Living Word stops, or will it be there today?" How many little areas of mistrust do we have when we wake up in the morning? We cannot let go of the faith and trust in the Father that is required. Of course the Living Word will be there, because He is good; His lovingkindness endures forever (Psalm 106:1). Having that manna appear every morning required a relationship with the Father. There has to be something of knowing Him. There has to be something of trusting His very person and nature that begins to release all that He is in manifestation for us. What He is really trying to do is to bring us into a connection with Himself.

I wonder if that moment of trust is really what brought the manna in the wilderness. I wonder if that connection with the Lord, whereby they knew His nature, knew His provision, and knew His promise, was the reason the manna began raining down. I do not know if that is what did it then, but I do know that is what triggers a Living Word today. If God would give us one big solution, one great revelation, I think we all know what would happen. We would not get up every morning asking for our daily bread. That is the reality of a walk with God. Every day when we get up we have to walk with Him. We have to know that whatever problems we face, whatever situations we run into in our lives, there will be daily bread. Jesus said, "I am the bread that came down out of heaven" (John 6:41). We are going to believe that the Father will give us His Son daily as the bread that comes down out of heaven for us. So daily we must eat His flesh and drink His blood.

These days that we are living through and getting ready to live through are not easy, but I truly believe that our daily bread will always be there. I do not think the Living Word will ever stop, because I know that God is bringing us into a relationship with Himself that will trigger that Living Word forever. He is the King

---

Psalm 106:1 Praise the Lord! Oh give thanks to the Lord, for He is good; for His lovingkindness is everlasting.

of the universe, and that is for all eternity. His lovingkindness endures forever.

The answer for our needs every day is that God gives us a Living Word. And what is a Living Word? It is Christ, the Word made flesh. It is the bread that the Father gives from heaven, which is Christ in our lives on a daily basis. How do we get a Living Word? We walk with the Lord every day and trust Him. I don't want to wake up in a cold sweat, saying, "Will the manna be there?" I want us to be able to rest in the Lord because we know Him; we know that the manna will be there. As we wake up and open the doors of our tents to look out, not only do we see God's presence over the tabernacle, we also have our daily bread that has been delivered right to the doorstep of our hearts (Exodus 40:34; 16:13-15). So wake up in the morning and open your heart to Him, just like opening a tent door. Let Him in. View His presence and receive your daily bread. Receive the Living Word, but more than that, become a vessel of the Living Word. Let us speak the Living Word and live the Living Word, because that is an expression of how the Body of Christ is moving in the earth today. We know what we are doing in this day. We are absolutely taking dominion over this age. We are not getting caught up in the things of this world, but we are speaking into existence the Kingdom of God in the earth, and we are receiving, every day, Christ our daily bread. We eat Him, we digest Him, and we manifest Him.

Exodus 40:34   Then the cloud covered the tent of meeting, and the glory of the LORD filled the tabernacle.

Exodus 16:13-15   So it came about at evening that the quails came up and covered the camp, and in the morning there was a layer of dew around the camp. [14] When the layer of dew evaporated, behold, on the surface of the wilderness there was a fine flake-like thing, fine as the frost on the ground. [15] When the sons of Israel saw it, they said to one another, "What is it?" For they did not know what it was. And Moses said to them, "It is the bread which the LORD has given you to eat."

10 | Hunger That Bypasses Our Understanding

Earlier, we continued our study of the Lord's Prayer with an exposition of Matthew 6:11: "Give us this day our daily bread." This verse is an expression of our cry to the Lord. It is not a request for physical bread; it is a demand that we partake of Christ who is the bread of life (John 6:35). It is a hunger that we cannot let go of. In this chapter, we want to take another step in understanding what this hunger means and how we appropriate Christ in our lives on a daily basis. We know that having hunger is also about having faith. It is a level of faith that is beyond what we have touched, and it demands something on our part to lay hold of Him in a way we have not yet done. We must get ahold of this principle, because there is a life in Christ that we have yet to obtain. To pray, "Give us this day our daily bread," is to ask for an experience beyond what Christianity has had since the time of the early Church. There is a life; there is an effect; there is something that was completed in Christ that we are not yet demanding.

John 6:35 Jesus said to them, "I am the bread of life; he who comes to Me shall not hunger, and he who believes in Me shall never thirst."

When you read the sixth chapter of John, you realize that Christ was provoking the people to believe, to receive, to accept what He was doing and what He had become, in order that they might appropriate Him. "They said therefore to Him, 'Lord, evermore give us this bread.' Jesus said to them, 'I am the bread of life; he who comes to Me shall not hunger, and he who believes in Me shall never thirst'" (John 6:34-35). This is the same prayer as in Matthew 6:11. When we pray, "Give us this day our daily bread," we understand that what we are focused on is Christ. He is the bread of life, and He said that if we come to Him we will never hunger, and if we believe in Him we will never thirst. We have to say, then, "Lord, there must be more. Give us this day all of our bread, the complete provision of that bread, because we are still hungry. We are still thirsty."

Christ told them, "But I said to you, that you have seen Me, and yet do not believe" (John 6:36). This statement deals with how much we really believe in what Christ said. It applies to us today as much as it applied to those Christ was addressing. Today we have seen Him, but we still do not believe all that He is and all that He has for us. This is what we must get ahold of. When we pray, "Give us this day our daily bread," it is to be an appropriation of all that Christ is.

The truth is that we have not appropriated Christ in His totality. There is so much more of His fullness that we have yet to obtain (Ephesians 3:17-19; Philippians 3:12-14). Therefore, we are still

---

Ephesians 3:17-19 So that Christ may dwell in your hearts through faith; and that you, being rooted and grounded in love, [18] may be able to comprehend with all the saints what is the breadth and length and height and depth, [19] and to know the love of Christ which surpasses knowledge, that you may be filled up to all the fulness of God.

Philippians 3:12-14 Not that I have already obtained it, or have already become perfect, but I press on in order that I may lay hold of that for which also I was laid hold of by Christ Jesus. [13] Brethren, I do not regard myself as having laid hold of it yet; but one thing I do: forgetting what lies behind and reaching forward to what lies ahead, [14] I press on toward the goal for the prize of the upward call of God in Christ Jesus.

hungry and still thirsty. What God has done for us up to now is not enough if we are not walking in His fullness. We have to reject any satisfaction with what we have appropriated from Him so far (Philippians 3:8). If you go to a store and put your money down on the counter to buy something and then receive half of what you paid for, do you walk away saying, "I am so happy! I'm satisfied with what I got"? Yet this is a picture of how the Church is walking today. What the Church is happy with today is not enough (Revelation 3:17-20). It cannot be that a Church filled with limitations represents what Christ died for. I refuse to believe that He suffered everything He suffered in order for us to have what the Church has today, and then say, "That's it; that's all of it." No, the price He paid is much greater than what we are walking in. We do not have it yet, so we cry for our daily bread. We are hungry and we are thirsty because what we bought in Christ, we are only receiving in part.

> "All that the Father gives Me shall come to Me, and the one who comes to Me I will certainly not cast out. For I have come down from heaven, not to do My own will, but to the will of Him who sent Me. And this is the will of Him who sent Me, that of all that He has given Me I lose nothing, but raise it up on the last day. For this is the will of My Father, that everyone who beholds the Son and

---

Philippians 3:8 More than that, I count all things to be loss in view of the surpassing value of knowing Christ Jesus my Lord, for whom I have suffered the loss of all things, and count them but rubbish in order that I may gain Christ.

Revelation 3:17-20 "Because you say, 'I am rich, and have become wealthy, and have need of nothing,' and you do not know that you are wretched and miserable and poor and blind and naked, [18] I advise you to buy from Me gold refined by fire, that you may become rich, and white garments, that you may clothe yourself, and that the shame of your nakedness may not be revealed; and eye salve to anoint your eyes, that you may see. [19] Those whom I love, I reprove and discipline; be zealous therefore, and repent. [20] Behold, I stand at the door and knock; if anyone hears My voice and opens the door, I will come in to him, and will dine with him, and he with Me."

believes in Him, may have eternal life; and I Myself will raise him up on the last day." The Jews therefore were grumbling about Him, because He said, "I am the bread that came down out of heaven." And they were saying, "Is not this Jesus, the son of Joseph, whose father and mother we know? How does He now say, 'I have come down out of heaven'?" Jesus answered and said to them, "Do not grumble among yourselves. No one can come to Me, unless the Father who sent Me draws him; and I will raise him up on the last day. It is written in the prophets, 'AND THEY SHALL ALL BE TAUGHT OF GOD.' Everyone who has heard and learned from the Father, comes to Me. Not that any man has seen the Father, except the One who is from God; He has seen the Father. Truly, truly, I say to you, he who believes has eternal life. I am the bread of life. Your fathers ate the manna in the wilderness, and they died. This is the bread which comes down out of heaven, so that one may eat of it and not die." (John 6:37-50)

Our appropriation of His life is still too limited. We miss the point when we think only in terms of life after death. Christ said, "Your fathers ate the manna in the wilderness, and they died" (John 6:49). Do you believe that the fathers in the wilderness had no life after death? I do not think they died eternally; they did not perish without partaking of eternal life. I believe that they were raised up with Christ. When Christ was raised, those fathers were also raised (Ephesians 4:8; Matthew 27:52-53). Christ was talking about their physical death, not eternal death. Their fathers, even

---

Ephesians 4:8 Therefore it says, "WHEN HE ASCENDED ON HIGH, HE LED CAPTIVE A HOST OF CAPTIVES, AND HE GAVE GIFTS TO MEN."

Matthew 27:52-53 And the tombs were opened; and many bodies of the saints who had fallen asleep were raised; [53] and coming out of the tombs after His resurrection they entered the holy city and appeared to many.

though they had this bread from heaven, died physically. "This is the bread which comes down out of heaven, so that one may eat of it and not die" (John 6:50). Is He just saying that He will give us life after death? No, this is about what physically happened to the fathers, and it is also about what physically happens for us.

When we pray, "Give us this day our daily bread," we are asking for life; we are asking to be filled with the life of Christ. He died for it. He paid the price (1 Corinthians 6:20). If He paid the price, who are we to say, "Oh, we don't believe that. We don't want that"? I honestly believe there is so much life in Christ that we should not die. We should have life (Romans 8:11). We should have health. We should break out of physical limitations. We should not say, "Well, we're used to death. We're used to sickness. We're used to all of these things happening to our bodies, so we just let them happen." How much life is in Christ? Is there a limit to how much life we can have now? The limitations of your thinking should not dictate how much life you can have. He is life (John 14:6). He is the bread that came down from heaven, which we eat so that we can have life.

> "I am the living bread that came down out of heaven; if anyone eats of this bread, he shall live forever; and the bread also which I shall give for the life of the world is My flesh." The Jews therefore began to argue with one another, saying, "How can this man give us His flesh to eat?" (John 6:51-52)

---

1 Corinthians 6:20 For you have been bought with a price: therefore glorify God in your body.

Romans 8:11 But if the Spirit of Him who raised Jesus from the dead dwells in you, He who raised Christ Jesus from the dead will also give life to your mortal bodies through His Spirit who indwells you.

John 14:6 Jesus said to him, "I am the way, and the truth, and the life; no one comes to the Father, but through Me."

When we use the term "bread," we have a concept of something that we like, or something that we are used to eating. However, as we just read in this Scripture, when they asked for bread, He offered them His flesh to eat; but when He offered it, they rejected it. Have you ever watched people eat something that they don't understand? They can have very strong reactions to it. They might gag, because their brain does not accept what they are eating. There are types of food that provide good nourishment for our bodies, but many of us will not eat those things because the thought is repulsive to us. Our minds dictate what we can eat, and if it does not make sense to our brains, we will reject it. It is the same with our faith. Christ was feeding them the bread of life and they were rejecting it. They did not have the ability to eat what they could not understand. That is a problem.

Nothing God does makes sense to the human mind. We need a deeper level of faith when we ask for our daily bread, because what we receive will be beyond our ability to comprehend. Our tendency as humans is to reject what our mind cannot comprehend. We tend to reject what we do not understand. The reason the Israelites called the bread that came out of heaven "manna" was because they did not understand what it was (Exodus 16:15, 31). The meaning of the word "manna" is literally "what." We must have a faith that pushes through our tendency to reject what God wants to give us. You do not have to eat with your brain. You can eat that which you do not understand, and spiritually you can do the same. There is a way that we can receive beyond our understanding. This is an important aspect of the prayer, "Give us this day our daily

---

Exodus 16:15 When the sons of Israel saw it, they said to one another, "What is it?" For they did not know what it was. And Moses said to them, "It is the bread which the Lord has given you to eat."

Exodus 16:31 And the house of Israel named it manna, and it was like coriander seed, white; and its taste was like wafers with honey.

bread" (Matthew 6:11). We may be saying, "What? I don't know what this is," but we have to reach in to eat it and partake of His life.

We read in 1 Corinthians that He will do that which eye has not seen and ear has not heard, neither has it entered into our hearts what God has prepared (1 Corinthians 2:9). How do we receive that? Here comes God with the wonderful meal He has prepared for us, filled with all these things that our eyes have not seen and our ears have not heard. We look at it and we do not know what any of it is. In fact, something in there looks like it is still moving! So instead of demanding the bread, as Christ said to do, we ask very squeamishly, "Give us this day our daily bread, but just give us something that we can identify—something that we are used to. Give us something we like, something that we want. Ice cream would be good!" Consequently, we find ourselves unprepared for what He wants to give us.

> The Jews therefore began to argue with one another, saying, "How can this man give us His flesh to eat?" Jesus therefore said to them, "Truly, truly, I say to you, unless you eat the flesh of the Son of Man and drink His blood, you have no life in yourselves. He who eats My flesh and drinks My blood has eternal life, and I will raise him up on the last day. For My flesh is true food, and My blood is true drink. He who eats My flesh and drinks My blood abides in Me, and I in him." (John 6:52-56)

---

1 **Corinthians 2:9** But just as it is written, "THINGS WHICH EYE HAS NOT SEEN AND EAR HAS NOT HEARD, AND WHICH HAVE NOT ENTERED THE HEART OF MAN, ALL THAT GOD HAS PREPARED FOR THOSE WHO LOVE HIM."

The people rejected what Christ was speaking. To them what He was saying could not be food. They had laws that prohibited drinking blood, and yet He said to them, "You must drink My blood" (Leviticus 17:10-11). It did not even seem to go along with the Scriptures, but it was the plan of God. It was the food from heaven.

What Christ spoke was beyond their ability to grasp. Do you think it is any easier for us today? To the human mind God is unacceptable, so there has to be enough hunger to drive us beyond our rejection of Him. We must be hungry enough to eat what our mind rejects. People who are lost in the wilderness eventually become hungry enough to eat just about anything they find. They will turn over rocks and hunt through bushes to find food. We have to apply this idea of desperate hunger to receiving something from God. If you want something from God, you need to be hungry. Do you feel, "We're always praying and seeking the Lord. It seems like He doesn't bring us an answer"? He is making you hungry. He is making you ask, "Lord, we don't know what that is, but make us hungry until we eat the bread of heaven, until we eat what You provide."

The teaching about the Lord's Prayer in the Gospel of Luke provides an important key. Here we find the parable of the man asking for food from a friend who is in bed. The man was desperate for food, but his friend would not get out of bed. Finally, his friend responded, not because he was a friend, but because the man

---

Leviticus 17:10-11   "And any man from the house of Israel, or from the aliens who sojourn among them, who eats any blood, I will set My face against that person who eats blood, and will cut him off from among his people. [11] For the life of the flesh is in the blood, and I have given it to you on the altar to make atonement for your souls; for it is the blood by reason of the life that makes atonement."

would not quit pounding on his door (Luke 11:5-8). Christ used this parable to illustrate how to pray to the Father. He said that when you pray, you should relate to God as someone who does not want to give you anything and who only responds when you irritate Him enough. Again, this is a concept that our minds have difficulty accepting. It is contrary to our idea of how to approach God. God does not want us to be satisfied; He wants us to be hungry for Him.

If we are hungry enough, we will say, "We're not satisfied. What we have so far is not enough." If we are hungry enough, we will not give Him any rest (Isaiah 62:7). If we are hungry enough, we will relate to God as the friend who is asleep. He thinks He can ignore us because He is comfortable in His house. He has His children all tucked in bed. But we need bread, so we are going to knock and keep on knocking, seek and keep on seeking! We are going to irritate Him until He gives us bread! If He thinks we are going away, He will learn differently. This is the kind of hunger and faith that pushes through the human rejection.

Lord, we want to stop rejecting You. Christ, You are the bread of heaven. Give us enough hunger to free us from our response of rejecting what You bring to us. Lord, forbid that we be so conditioned to what we know and to what we like and to what is

---

Luke 11:5-8   And He said to them, "Suppose one of you shall have a friend, and shall go to him at midnight, and say to him, 'Friend, lend me three loaves; [6] for a friend of mine has come to me from a journey, and I have nothing to set before him'; [7] and from inside he shall answer and say, 'Do not bother me; the door has already been shut and my children and I are in bed; I cannot get up and give you anything.' [8] I tell you, even though he will not get up and give him anything because he is his friend, yet because of his persistence he will get up and give him as much as he needs."

Isaiah 62:7   And give Him no rest until He establishes and makes Jerusalem a praise in the earth.

acceptable to us that we instantly reject Your moving. Lord, we lift our hearts to You. Rid us of that which rejects the bread of heaven. We are praying for our daily bread, so give us the ability and the hunger to partake of what You give us.

11 | Forgive and Be Forgiven

Each verse we have studied in the Lord's Prayer has given us a key to more effective prayer, and each chapter has challenged us to reach into the Lord's presence in a deeper way to execute His will in the earth. This chapter will be no exception. In this chapter, we are studying Matthew 6:12: "And forgive us our debts, as we also have forgiven our debtors." We must be able to implement this verse. As we covered earlier, it is one thing to talk about casting satan out of the earth, but we are still limited if we do not learn to forgive. This is perhaps the most important verse on prayer that there is in the Bible. If we do not walk in this verse about forgiving others, nothing else we have learned about prayer will work.

How do we understand forgiveness? We could get into a very complicated study about the mysteries of God concerning forgiveness and sanctification. We could expound the scriptural passages in Genesis and Leviticus about the sacrifices. We could dig into the meanings of the Hebrew and Greek words in Old and New Testament verses that give us insight into the principle of transference. However, all we need to do is focus on the simplicity of what Matthew 6:12 is saying. Forgiveness is one of the most mystical concepts in the Bible, but it functions with tremendous simplicity. When we pray, "Forgive us our debts," we are asking God to forgive the debt that we have to Him because of our sin. The wages—the cost—of sin is death (Romans 6:23), and because we have sinned, we owe God our lives. It is the price we must pay. One way or another, you give your life to God, either voluntarily in salvation, or when He takes your life as a debt in death.

The concept of forgiving debt is very simple and easy to understand. Little children understand it. If someone owes you money and that person comes to you and says, "Forgive me the debt," you understand exactly what that means. If you forgive the debt, it means that person owes you nothing. Likewise, if God forgives your debt to Him, it means that you no longer owe Him your life. Simply read Matthew 6:12 literally and accept that it means exactly what it says. When we do this, we are confronted by something. The Lord said to pray, "Forgive us our debts as we forgive our debtors." In the same way that God forgives our debts, we must forgive our debtors. Suddenly this concept is not so easy anymore. Forgiving others in the same way that God forgives us is a hard concept, not to understand, but to live.

Who are our debtors? Our debtors are those who owe us because they have sinned against us or taken from us. This debt that is owed to us is that which we hold in our own minds against people. We build up and hold on to reasons why others owe us for what they do or what they have done. We are the ones who make people indebted to us because of their actions. Clearly, the debt we feel others owe us is not on the same level as the debt we owe God, and Christ gave a parable to make this point.

Romans 6:23 For the wages of sin is death, but the free gift of God is eternal life in Christ Jesus our Lord.

Then Peter came and said to Him, "Lord, how often shall my brother sin against me and I forgive him? Up to seven times?" Jesus said to him, "I do not say to you, up to seven times, but up to seventy times seven. For this reason the kingdom of heaven may be compared to a certain king who wished to settle accounts with his slaves." (Matthew 18:21-23)

Who do you suppose He was referring to when He said "a certain king"? He is the King of kings and Lord of lords (Revelation 19:16). He is the King who wants to settle accounts with his slaves—that's us. It is clear that the Lord is talking about us and our relationship with Him.

"And when he had begun to settle them, there was brought to him one who owed him ten thousand talents. But since he did not have the means to repay, his lord commanded him to be sold, along with his wife and his children and all that he had, and repayment to be made." (Matthew 18:24-25)

This slave owed the king a very large debt. How could he ever repay a debt like that? The debt was so great that the slave, his wife and children, his house, and everything he owned would have to be sold in order to repay it. Our debt of sin is also very great. Just as it was with that slave, our debt not only affects us; it affects everyone we are around—the entire family of God.

"The slave therefore falling down, prostrated himself before him, saying, 'Have patience with me, and I will repay you everything.' And the lord of that slave felt compassion and released him and forgave him the debt" (Matthew 18:26-27). This is a picture of

---

Revelation 19:16 And on His robe and on His thigh He has a name written, "KING OF KINGS, AND LORD OF LORDS."

our salvation. The Lord felt compassion for us. He forgave our debt completely. It is not merely a matter of being patient with us and saying, "You can pay it over time." He says it is completely forgiven. There is no debt anymore. It is a complete release. "But that slave went out and found one of his fellow slaves who owed him a hundred denarii; and he seized him and began to choke him, saying, 'Pay back what you owe'" (Matthew 18:28). His master had forgiven his very large debt, but this slave refused to forgive his fellow slave's small debt. He screamed at him, "Pay me what you owe! Pay me back!"

> "So his fellow slave fell down and began to entreat him, saying, 'Have patience with me and I will repay you.' He was unwilling however, but went and threw him in prison until he should pay back what was owed. So when his fellow slaves saw what had happened, they were deeply grieved and came and reported to their lord all that had happened. Then summoning him, his lord said to him, 'You wicked slave, I forgave you all that debt because you entreated me. Should you not also have had mercy on your fellow slave, even as I had mercy on you?' And his lord, moved with anger, handed him over to the torturers until he should repay all that was owed him." (Matthew 18:29-34)

This time the punishment was much worse. Originally he was going to sell him; now he turned him over to the torturers until he repaid all that was owed him. "So shall My heavenly Father also do to you, if each of you does not forgive his brother from your heart" (Matthew 18:35).

One of the great doctrinal questions about salvation is: if you are saved once, are you saved forever? Can you lose your salvation? What I read from these verses is that it is possible for God to restore our original debt. We have received forgiveness for our debts, but do not think those debts cannot come back on us if we do not forgive. Christ said to pray, "Heavenly Father, forgive us our debts while we are forgiving those who owe a debt to us." Then at the end of His teaching on prayer, He said, "For if you forgive men for their transgressions, your heavenly Father will also forgive you. But if you do not forgive men, then your Father will not forgive your transgressions" (Matthew 6:14-15). Of the entire Lord's Prayer, this is the only part that Christ commented on when He finished His teaching. Of all the things He could have talked about, of all the concepts in the Lord's Prayer that He could have taught more about, the only thing Jesus emphasized is our requirement to forgive others. That is because everything depends on it—everything. If we stand before God to pray, we are wasting our time if we do not forgive. According to Mark 11:25, when we stand to pray, the first thing we do is forgive. If we do not, the rest of it is a waste of time, because our debt is put back on us, and God does not hear us.

As we studied earlier in this book, we begin our prayer by entering into the Father's presence (Matthew 6:6). Everything about prayer is absolutely dependent upon our access to the presence of the Father, to stand before His face, to boldly come into His presence (Hebrews 4:16). Christ is the door, but with no forgiveness there is no way to enter in. The only way we come into the Father's presence is through the forgiveness of our debt. If that debt comes back, we are excluded from His presence. There is no way to begin to pray if we cannot enter into the presence of the Father; so whenever

---

Mark 11:25 "And whenever you stand praying, forgive, if you have anything against anyone; so that your Father also who is in heaven may forgive you your transgressions."

Matthew 6:6 "But you, when you pray, go into your inner room, and when you have shut your door, pray to your Father who is in secret, and your Father who sees in secret will repay you."

Hebrews 4:16 Let us therefore draw near with confidence to the throne of grace, that we may receive mercy and may find grace to help in time of need.

you pray, you must begin with forgiveness. Forgive those that owe you so that your Father will forgive you. Only then will you have access. Only then can you enter His presence. Only then can you come before Him and begin to contend with Him.

Forgiveness is not necessarily easy. It certainly was not easy for Christ to forgive while He was on the cross.

> And when they came to the place called The Skull, there they crucified Him and the criminals, one on the right and the other on the left. But Jesus was saying, "Father, forgive them; for they do not know what they are doing." And they cast lots, dividing up His garments among themselves. And the people stood by, looking on. And even the rulers were sneering at Him, saying, "He saved others; let Him save Himself if this is the Christ of God, His Chosen One." And the soldiers also mocked Him, coming up to Him, offering Him sour wine, and saying, "If You are the King of the Jews, save Yourself!" (Luke 23:33-37)

It was not easy for Him to utter the words, "Father, forgive them." Imagine what it was like for Him on the cross observing all that was going on around Him. People were mocking Him and jeering Him. There were those who were stealing His belongings. They took His clothes, which in those days were very valuable. People ridiculed everything about Him, saying, "Oh, so You're the Savior! If You're the King, then save Yourself. Come down off the cross." His response to all of this was, "Father, forgive them," and those words triggered our salvation.

Can we come to the place where we forgive others just as God forgives us? We know we cannot do it in ourselves, but we know that He did it and that He is able to do it. Christ forgave when He was in an impossible situation. The need to forgive never arises when you are alone in meditation, resting in a place of perfect peace. The need to forgive comes during a time when people are stealing your garments, mocking you and accusing you. It is not something you can fake. You don't just say, "Okay, Lord, I forgive everybody," and then start praying. Remember what He said: You must forgive from your heart (Matthew 18:35). It is not just words; forgiveness has to come from your heart. When God forgives our sin, He forgets it (Jeremiah 31:34). You have not forgiven if you have just buried it in your subconscious and still hold the offense in your memory. Forgive for real, until you have forgotten.

This is not a philosophy. Debt is a real thing. Your sin does not just evaporate. It has to go somewhere. In accounting, you cannot just throw numbers away. Those numbers have to go somewhere, and the debt you are holding against people has to go somewhere. It has to leave. You have to find the way to let go of it. You have to put it on the Lord. You have to bring it to the cross. Your heart has to let go of it, and it has to go onto Christ. Only He can get rid of it. "How blessed is he whose transgression is forgiven, whose sin is covered!" (Psalm 32:1). Do you wonder sometimes, "Where did my blessing go?" Are you as blessed as you should be? Is there a sense of blessing in your life? Is the presence of God in your life? Have you sought for His presence many times, only to ask, "Where is His presence?" His presence dwells in the place of forgiveness.

The tabernacle in the wilderness was the place where the sacrifices were made and God's forgiveness was administered. It is also where the column of smoke and fire appeared. It appeared above the

---

Jeremiah 31:34 "And they shall not teach again, each man his neighbor and each man his brother, saying, 'Know the LORD,' for they shall all know Me, from the least of them to the greatest of them," declares the LORD, "for I will forgive their iniquity, and their sin I will remember no more."

tabernacle (Numbers 9:15-16). His presence did not just randomly dwell over the whole camp; it rested over the place of forgiveness. The Holy of Holies was where the forgiveness took place, and that is where His presence dwelt (Hebrews 9:2-3; 6-7; Leviticus 16:2). His presence with us will always dwell at our place of forgiveness. When we are forgiving, then His presence will dwell with us. Where is our blessing? Where is the anointing in our lives? The blessing is His presence. "How blessed is he whose transgression is forgiven" (Psalm 32:1). If my debt is gone, I should be blessed. I should live in blessing. I should live in His presence. Our lives should be blessed because we have become a place of forgiveness.

Psalm 32:3 says, "When I kept silent about my sin, my body wasted away through my groaning all day long." Do you wonder sometimes, "Where is my health? Where is my strength?" Why is it that we as the Body of Christ are not seeing the release, the freedom, the healings, and the health that we should have? "For day and night Thy hand was heavy upon me; my vitality was drained away as with the fever heat of summer" (Psalm 32:4). Now this is something we can relate to: experiencing our energy being sapped away like a fever, like the heat of summer.

Numbers 9:15-16   Now on the day that the tabernacle was erected the cloud covered the tabernacle, the tent of the testimony, and in the evening it was like the appearance of fire over the tabernacle, until morning. [16] So it was continuously; the cloud would cover it by day, and the appearance of fire by night.

Hebrews 9:2-3   For there was a tabernacle prepared, the outer one, in which were the lampstand and the table and the sacred bread; this is called the holy place. [3] And behind the second veil, there was a tabernacle which is called the Holy of Holies.

Hebrews 9:6-7   Now when these things have been thus prepared, the priests are continually entering the outer tabernacle, performing the divine worship, [7] but into the second only the high priest enters, once a year, not without taking blood, which he offers for himself and for the sins of the people committed in ignorance.

Leviticus 16:2   And the LORD said to Moses, "Tell your brother Aaron that he shall not enter at any time into the holy place inside the veil, before the mercy seat which is on the ark, lest he die; for I will appear in the cloud over the mercy seat."

> I acknowledged my sin to Thee, and my iniquity I did not hide; I said, "I will confess my transgressions to the LORD"; and Thou didst forgive the guilt of my sin. Selah. Therefore, let everyone who is godly pray to Thee in a time when Thou mayest be found. (Psalm 32:5-6)

When we pray, we will find Him if we forgive. Therefore, we refuse to keep silent about our sin. We refuse to harbor any longer the debts that we have determined against others.

"For if you forgive men for their transgressions, your heavenly Father will also forgive you. But if you do not forgive men, then your Father will not forgive your transgressions" (Matthew 6:14-15). This is a hard saying. If we accept this statement literally, then we are in trouble, because to some degree our debt is coming back upon us unless we can forgive. We must forgive. There must be a way to let go of every debt that we are holding in our minds and in our hearts against others. The Word of God says to forgive men. Forgive everybody. It has to be total. We must get out of our hearts anything we are holding against others. Lord, help us. Teach us to forgive. Show us where we are holding on to the things that are our destruction.

Do you say, "I don't know if I can do this"? You can do this. Christ did it; therefore the door is open for you. Get rid of the debt that you are holding against others. Nothing is worth the debt that you are holding on to. It cannot have value when compared to God's presence, when compared to His blessing in your life. What value can exist for that which you hold against people? Is it worth losing His presence and His blessing, or worse, having your debt to Him come back on you? "How blessed is he whose transgression is forgiven, whose sin is covered! How blessed is the man to whom the LORD does not impute iniquity, and in whose spirit there is no deceit!" (Psalm 32:1-2). Don't deceive yourself. Forgive! Don't just say, "Oh, I let go. Oh, I'm not holding on to anything." Don't deceive yourself. Don't be a person of deceit. Forgive in truth, with your heart. Lord, deliver us from the deception where we say we have forgiven but we have not.

Lord, by Your blood, we can forgive. This forgiveness courses as power in Your blood. As we partake of Your blood, we partake of the ability to forgive just as You forgave. Father, forgive us; we let go of the debts of others. Lord, Your body was broken for us and Your blood was given to us, and in them is the power to forgive. Lord, we let go of the debts completely, thoroughly, until our hearts, our minds, and our subconscious forget the debts completely. Let the debts of others be obliterated from our being, in the name of the Lord. We forgive from our hearts. Today we let go. We position ourselves as those whose prayers will be heard and answered because we are in a place of forgiveness. Let Your blessing rest upon us as it did upon the Holy of Holies, because we constantly exercise the release of debt to all men.

12 | Want to Live? Forgive!

We come to God often asking Him to forgive us. We know that we need forgiveness, because we want to be rid of the things in our nature that are an offense to God and to others. I was thinking, "We have been praying for months now; why are we not being more effective?" Then the Lord spoke to my heart: "Why don't you try something different? Try forgiving. Learn what forgiveness is and enter into it." When Jesus taught His disciples to pray, He told them to ask the Father for forgiveness in this way: "And forgive us our debts, as we also have forgiven our debtors" (Matthew 6:12). In other words, God will forgive you in the same way that you have already forgiven others.

To understand this, we must have a deeper understanding of what God means by forgiveness. We often forget what really went into God's forgiveness of us. In our minds, forgiving someone is almost a passive act. Someone says to us, "I did this; I'm sorry." Then we say, "I forgive you." There is something detached and even insipid about that. However, when God set about to forgive us, He took His Son, stripped Him of His divinity, and placed Him in human form, because it is the flesh that is the nature of sin (Philippians 2:6-8). God is not simply focused on our deeds; He is focused on the nature itself. Therefore, He took away Christ's divinity and put Him in the likeness of those He was going to forgive (Romans 8:3). Now that is proactive!

What God does in forgiveness is intense. When you ask God for forgiveness, it is far more than you saying, "God, I did this and I'm sorry," and then God saying, "Okay, I forgive you." Forgiveness is a principle that was created by God at great personal expense. It required a tremendous amount of intensity on His part and on the part of His Son, who was willing to become the sacrifice for our sin. He volunteered for the job (John 10:17-18). He was literally immersed into sin because He was placed in the flesh, and it is the flesh that is the issue. Christ lived on this earth in the flesh and went through all the experiences of being in the flesh. Then He suffered humiliation and beating, and He was executed on the cross (Mark 15:15-20, 24). He literally died, which was the

---

Philippians 2:6-8 Who, although He existed in the form of God, did not regard equality with God a thing to be grasped, 7 but emptied Himself, taking the form of a bond-servant, and being made in the likeness of men. 8 And being found in appearance as a man, He humbled Himself by becoming obedient to the point of death, even death on a cross.

Romans 8:3 For what the Law could not do, weak as it was through the flesh, God did: sending His own Son in the likeness of sinful flesh and as an offering for sin, He condemned sin in the flesh.

John 10:17-18 "For this reason the Father loves Me, because I lay down My life that I may take it again. 18 No one has taken it away from Me, but I lay it down on My own initiative. I have authority to lay it down, and I have authority to take it up again. This commandment I received from My Father."

Mark 15:15-20 And wishing to satisfy the multitude, Pilate released Barabbas for them, and after having Jesus scourged, he delivered Him to be crucified. 16 And the soldiers took Him away into the palace (that is, the Praetorium), and they called together the whole Roman cohort. 17 And they dressed Him up in purple, and after weaving a crown of thorns, they put it on Him; 18 and they began to acclaim Him, "Hail, King of the Jews!" 19 And they kept beating His head with a reed, and spitting at Him, and kneeling and bowing before Him. 20 And after they had mocked Him, they took the purple off Him, and put His garments on Him. And they led Him out to crucify Him.

Mark 15:24 And they crucified Him, and divided up His garments among themselves, casting lots for them, to decide what each should take.

price for our sin (Romans 6:23; 1 Corinthians 6:20). There are consequences to our sin, and Christ paid the price. Then, after He was buried, the Father reached down into Sheol and pulled Him back to life (Ephesians 1:19-20; 4:9-10). Therefore, when God says, "I forgive you," He is applying all of that intensity.

In the mind of God, He relates to forgiveness and applies forgiveness as something that He has already done. In fact, it was done in the heart of God before He sent His Son to the cross 2,000 years ago, because Christ was the Lamb slain from the foundation of the world (Revelation 13:8, KJV). This is a tremendous principle. We need to get into our own hearts and minds what God's mindset is about forgiveness. God did it and He did it very, very aggressively.

It has become so real to me just how much Christ came down to our level. He literally got into the mire of sin with us, and that is honestly what He is all about. We have a vision of Christ as the exalted Lord adorned in fine raiment, and that is true (Philippians 2:9-11). However, we forget that Christ's mission was to come down into the flesh along with each one of us on an

---

Romans 6:23   For the wages of sin is death, but the free gift of God is eternal life in Christ Jesus our Lord.

1 Corinthians 6:20   For you have been bought with a price: therefore glorify God in your body.

Ephesians 1:19-20   And what is the surpassing greatness of His power toward us who believe. These are in accordance with the working of the strength of His might [20] which He brought about in Christ, when He raised Him from the dead, and seated Him at His right hand in the heavenly places.

Ephesians 4:9-10   Now this expression, "He ascended," what does it mean except that He also had descended into the lower parts of the earth? [10] He who descended is Himself also He who ascended far above all the heavens, that He might fill all things.

Revelation 13:8, KJV   And all that dwell upon the earth shall worship him, whose names are not written in the book of life of the Lamb slain from the foundation of the world.

Philippians 2:9-11   Therefore also God highly exalted Him, and bestowed on Him the name which is above every name, [10] that at the name of Jesus EVERY KNEE SHOULD BOW, of those who are in heaven, and on earth, and under the earth, [11] and that every tongue should confess that Jesus Christ is Lord, to the glory of God the Father.

individual basis. He knew what each of us was going to do, and He, personally, already took care of it Himself.

Every time we sin, God's response comes from His proactive determination to forgive the entire world (John 3:16-17). Christ's sacrifice is not merely a historical event that somehow gets generally applied to the world. Through Christ, God dealt with every single one of your mistakes and every single one of your sins. It has already been done. Whatever happens to you, moment by moment, Christ is right there with you in it. He knew what you were going to do when He was on the cross. He literally became the forgiveness of the Father to us.

We have lost the perspective of what is really behind forgiveness. There is a predetermination in the heart of God that nothing will ever happen for which there is no forgiveness. He has already made the provision; He has already forgiven the offense. When Jesus said, "This is how you pray," we do not fully understand what He was trying to tell us. When it comes to forgiveness, He wants us to be like God. He said, "And forgive us our debts, as we also have forgiven our debtors" (Matthew 6:12). Notice it is in the past tense: "Forgive me, Father, as I have already forgiven those who trespass against me."

Forgiveness is God's state of spirit, and He is looking for us to live in that same state. He wants to see the same quality in us, where we have already done the forgiving. We still relate to this too passively. We wait for someone to say, "I'm sorry I thought this," or, "I'm sorry I did this." Then we say, "I forgive you"; but that is not God's forgiveness. God's forgiveness is intense; it is proactive, and it has already been provided for the violator. He does not say, "I forgive

---

John 3:16-17 "For God so loved the world, that He gave His only begotten Son, that whoever believes in Him should not perish, but have eternal life. [17] For God did not send the Son into the world to judge the world, but that the world should be saved through Him."

you"; He has already provided the forgiveness for the violation. In Matthew 6:12 Jesus was saying that we must have the same quality that God has, having already provided forgiveness for one another. Forgiveness is a provision; it is not just saying, "I forgive you." There is still something very important that we are missing regarding forgiveness.

At the end of the Lord's Prayer is an amazing statement: "For if you forgive men for their transgressions, your heavenly Father will also forgive you. But if you do not forgive men, then your Father will not forgive your transgressions" (Matthew 6:14-15). If we cannot forgive, we cannot be forgiven. That is almost scary to think about. How can God relate that way? Is there really a catch to salvation? As determined as God is to forgive, you have to be willing to come and receive it from Him; but in order to receive His forgiveness, there is this little catch that you must have already forgiven those who sinned against you. Repentance only works if you have already forgiven. That involves more than being poised somehow to forgive people when they violate you. God is looking for you to take on the same quality of spirit that He has. You literally have to live in a state of pre-prepared, pre-executed release and deliverance for people. This is how we become a house of deliverance (Joel 2:32).

What is proactive forgiveness? How do we get into this state where we have already forgiven no matter what happens? For the most part, we are still in a state of deciding whether we will forgive or not. If someone asks us for forgiveness, we think, "Tell me what you did, and I will see how bad it is and decide if I can forgive you." That is how we tend to relate to forgiving others. But God says to us, "If I am going to forgive you, I have to know that you have already

---

Joel 2:32 "And it will come about that whoever calls on the name of the LORD will be delivered; for on Mount Zion and in Jerusalem there will be those who escape, as the LORD has said, even among the survivors whom the LORD calls."

forgiven those who sinned against you. How can I permanently forgive you if you do not permanently forgive others?"

Let's look at another Scripture on forgiveness:

> Then Peter came and said to Him, "Lord, how often shall my brother sin against me and I forgive him? Up to seven times?" Jesus said to him, "I do not say to you, up to seven times, but up to seventy times seven. For this reason the kingdom of heaven may be compared to a certain king who wished to settle accounts with his slaves." (Matthew 18:21-23)

Jesus explained the concept of unlimited forgiveness to Peter, and then went into this parable about a king and his slaves to illustrate that we are to live in a state of forgiving others. "And when he had begun to settle them, there was brought to him one who owed him ten thousand talents" (Matthew 18:24). The king forgave this slave of his debt of ten thousand talents. Then the slave went out and found a fellow slave who owed him a hundred denarii, and began to choke him by the throat saying, "Pay back what you owe" (Matthew 18:25-28).

The man who was choking his fellow slave was the same person who had been before the king crying, "Please forgive me! Don't sell my wife and children into slavery!" It touched the king's heart so much that he forgave him. Yet immediately after this, the slave was literally choking another slave to death, demanding, "Give me my money!" Why wasn't he after his money from the other slave

---

Matthew 18:25-28 "But since he did not have the means to repay, his lord commanded him to be sold, along with his wife and children and all that he had, and repayment to be made. 26 The slave therefore falling down, prostrated himself before him, saying, 'Have patience with me, and I will repay you everything.' 27 And the lord of that slave felt compassion and released him and forgave him the debt. 28 But that slave went out and found one of his fellow slaves who owed him a hundred denarii; and he seized him and began to choke him, saying, 'Pay back what you owe.' "

before? Because he knew he would have to give it to the king, so why bother? But now that he could keep it, he wanted the money. Finally, the king found out about this, and was not very happy about it. "And his lord, moved with anger, handed him over to the torturers." He didn't just go to jail; he was tortured "until he should repay all that was owed him. So shall My heavenly Father also do to you, if each of you does not forgive his brother from your heart" (Matthew 18:34-35).

How could God act that way toward us? He can act that way because He put so much energy into forgiving us. Forgiveness is no small matter to Him. When God says, "I forgive you of your sins," it is something very serious to Him, because He allowed His own Son to be crucified to provide that forgiveness. God gave His dear Son and saw Him beaten, bruised, crucified, and buried. If He was willing to do that, then He is also expecting something from us. When we receive salvation, we may say that it is free, but it was not free to God. God gave everything He had for us. He gave the one person He cared most about. Therefore, God is not happy if we do not make provision in our own hearts beforehand to forgive those who sin against us.

You must understand the heart of God when you come to Him asking for forgiveness. The truth is, if you do not know this principle, you could get yourself into more trouble. According to this parable, you could literally find yourself being tormented if you ask the Father for forgiveness but you have not predetermined to forgive others. Do not ask God for forgiveness without having something in your spirit that is predetermined to forgive those who sin against you. What they might do to you is nothing in comparison to what might happen if you have not already forgiven them. When it comes to forgiveness, God is requiring that we be like Him. That means that when someone offends us, we must have already forgiven that person, and then God will forgive us.

We read more about forgiveness in Luke chapter 17: "Be on your guard! If your brother sins, rebuke him" (Luke 17:3). In other words, stop him. Tell him to go a different direction than the way he is going. "'And if he repents, forgive him. And if he sins against you seven times a day, and returns to you seven times, saying, "I repent," forgive him.' And the apostles said to the Lord, 'Increase our faith!'" (Luke 17:3-5). This is not a simple thing. There are many difficult sayings of the Lord that would be easier to walk in. For example, Jesus said that if you look at a woman with lust you have already committed adultery, or if someone slaps you on one cheek, you should give them your other cheek (Matthew 5:28, 39). It would be easier to follow one of those commandments first, and then try to work up to forgiving someone who sins against you multiple times a day but repents each time. I love the apostles' response: "Increase our faith!" The Lord's reply is interesting: "And the Lord said, 'If you had faith like a mustard seed, you would say to this mulberry tree, "Be uprooted and be planted in the sea"; and it would obey you'" (Luke 17:6). Jesus agreed with the apostles that forgiveness is an operation of faith, yet what He said about faith uprooting a mulberry tree almost seems disconnected. However, if you consider that your brother's sin is like the mulberry tree, then the two thoughts come together. If you have faith to forgive, then that faith can literally uproot the tree of sin that is in your brother's life and plant it in the sea!

God is requiring that we have a provision for people who sin against us because that is what God did. Forgiveness is His provision for our sins. What does God do with our sins? He throws them into

---

Matthew 5:28 "But I say to you, that everyone who looks on a woman to lust for her has committed adultery with her already in his heart."

Matthew 5:39 "But I say to you, do not resist him who is evil; but whoever slaps you on your right cheek, turn to him the other also."

the sea of His forgetfulness (Micah 7:19; Isaiah 43:25). I do not want my sins only forgiven; I want them forgiven and forgotten. I want them taken away from me as far as they possibly can be taken away (Psalm 103:12). It is like dealing with nuclear waste—how do you get rid of it? You have to put it some place where it cannot be dredged up and found, where it cannot be remembered, where nothing can be done with it.

Jesus said that if your brother is sinning, the first thing you should do is stop him. Do not simply let him continue without doing something about it. That is your first responsibility. Then, once someone has sinned against you, forgive that person; but make sure your forgiveness is effective. We must have a forgiveness that reaches in with faith on a prophetic level, with a drive that pulls the tree of sin out of that person's life and plants it in the sea!

This means that we must be like God, who has a proactive predetermination that when someone approaches Him with sin, He has already dealt with it. Do more than pray, "O Lord, forgive me of my sins." Let each of us resolve, "Number one, I will not let sin go on anymore; I will attempt to prevent it. Number two, when there is sin, I predetermine that with prophetic authority I will pray, I will prophesy, and I will do whatever I have to do to see that sin rooted out of the person's life and cast into the sea, never to be found again. That is my determination beforehand."

Micah 7:19 He will again have compassion on us; He will tread our iniquities under foot. Yes, Thou wilt cast all their sins into the depths of the sea.

Isaiah 43:25 "I, even I, am the one who wipes out your transgressions for My own sake; and I will not remember your sins."

Psalm 103:12 As far as the east is from the west, so far has He removed our transgressions from us.

One of the great cries of this restoration is that there will be deliverance in the remnant whom the Lord God calls (Joel 2:32, KJV). There must be deliverance and forgiveness, but that will not happen if we have not predetermined to be the provision for one another's sins. This means that, as the remnant, we are in the position of ministering the saving grace of God to people. I do not ever again want to say, "I forgive you," as an ineffective, halfhearted expression. I want there to be something in my heart that goes into prayer for someone who has sinned and sees that person delivered from what caused the sin. My prayer is, "Lord, extract this tree of sin from that person's life. Take it out."

I know how badly I want sin taken out of me. When I forgive someone, I do not want to have to think about the offense, to pray about it, or to analyze it. I do not expect God to do that when I go to Him and say, "I repent of this; I just want it removed!" I know that He will take it away. God does not pull out a calculator to try to figure out whether I should be forgiven or not. He has already figured that out and taken care of it. I want to be that way with others. I want to have a predetermined plan of forgiveness for those who ask.

Now we can pray, "Forgive us our sins as we forgive those who sin against us." We have predetermined in our spirits to move in faith to forgive our brother up to seventy times seven if necessary. Whether we are forgiving alone in our prayer closet or face-to-face with someone, their sin will be rooted out. It will take a great deal of faith if we are trying to uproot a sin that keeps happening seven times a day, but uproot it we will. We take this very seriously because, as we are coming to the Father, asking, seeking and knocking, we do not want to leave any open door for Him to deny

---

Joel 2:32, KJV And it shall come to pass, that whosoever shall call on the name of the Lord shall be delivered: for in mount Zion and in Jerusalem shall be deliverance, as the Lord hath said, and in the remnant whom the Lord shall call.

us. I believe that this revelation of forgiveness closes that open door in a greater way than we have ever seen before.

Lord, we are set on meeting You, and our hearts are fixed on deliverance and forgiveness. Let us stand before Your face. Let us see You as You are. Purify the sons of Levi; smelt away the sin of Your people (Malachi 3:3). We ask it in Jesus' name. Amen.

Malachi 3:3 "And He will sit as a smelter and purifier of silver, and He will purify the sons of Levi and refine them like gold and silver, so that they may present to the LORD offerings in righteousness."

13 | Don't Waste Your Time Repenting

In this chapter, we will continue our study of forgiveness, as Jesus emphasized in His teaching on prayer. We read in Matthew 6:12, "And forgive us our debts [or, forgive us our sins], as we also have forgiven our debtors." Notice how these words are in the past tense: "as we also have forgiven." The Lord will forgive you your sin as you have already forgiven the sins of others. Then we read in Matthew 6:14-15, "For if you forgive men for their transgressions, your heavenly Father will also forgive you. But if you do not forgive men, then your Father will not forgive your transgressions." There is not a lot of wiggle room in that, is there? God is bound by His own righteousness. He cannot forgive us, He cannot release us, if we are constantly stuck on what everyone has done against us.

We know that there is no one who has not sinned. "For all have sinned and fall short of the glory of God" (Romans 3:23). What is sin? The greatest definition of sin is this: sin is failing to be like God. He wants us to be just as He is. God created us in His image; and when we fall short of being like Him, we violate our relationship with Him (Genesis 1:27). This means much more than trying to follow a religious code of ethics, or obeying religious laws and moral rules. We want to have a closeness with the Lord, and the only way we can have that is by getting rid of everything that separates us from Him. When these violations exist, the Lord is obligated to respond to the sin. He cannot deny it, and He cannot ignore it. He cannot simply pretend that we have not done these things.

The things that get between us and God are destructive; they are detrimental to our relationship with Him. God has spent years emphasizing that His Kingdom is relationships, and the most important relationship is between **you and Him**. The relationship between **us and Him** comes second to that. The only reason there is an "**us and Him**" is because there is a personal relationship between you and God. There are many ways that each one of us has violated that simple relationship with Him. These are the sins and the ways that we have fallen short. In repentance, you must literally experience being freed from these violations of the relationship, the things that get between you and God.

As I was seeking the Lord about this, I prayed, "Lord, I want the relationship with You! I want to be forgiven, because I want to have the closeness with You. Whatever I have done, whatever offenses that have happened in my life, I want to be free of them. I want the relationship between You and me, Lord." Then the Lord spoke to me, "That's good, but don't waste your time in repentance." I thought, "What do You mean, don't waste my time in repentance?" Suddenly, a flood of revelation came from the Lord, and it was all about this fact: if I do not forgive, then I cannot be forgiven.

Genesis 1:27 And God created man in His own image, in the image of God He created him; male and female He created them.

What the Lord was saying to me was, "If you are holding back from forgiving others who have sinned against you, then you are wasting your time repenting. I cannot forgive you if you are not forgiving others." Why spend any more time in repentance if you hold things in your heart against others? However, if you really have an experience of forgiving others, then right from the beginning of your repentance, from the very moment you go before Him asking for His forgiveness, you will be effective in finding His forgiveness for you.

Do not say, "I've heard this before. This is a waste of time!" However long it takes for God to work His Word in you, it is not a waste of time. When God is trying to do something in our hearts, it takes walking us through it, level by level, before we really get what He is after. I do not want this to be just another teaching about forgiveness. I want you to be able to reach into your being, and uproot the last remnants of those things which are not forgiven. The new thing that He wants to do for us is absolutely dependent on this forgiveness.

We read in the Scriptures that we cannot mix the old and the new, but this is exactly what we do in our hearts when we allow the new things of God to become cluttered with our old bitterness, lack of forgiveness, and grudges (Matthew 9:16-17). We truly are mixing the old and the new when we receive the anointing that God is imparting to us, but at the same time, we keep those things that we have somehow been unable to uproot. The fact is, forgiveness is not easy. The offenses that we have not forgiven are usually the ones that have caused us deep hurts. There are deep wounds created by

---

Matthew 9:16-17 "But no one puts a patch of unshrunk cloth on an old garment; for the patch pulls away from the garment, and a worse tear results. [17] Nor do men put new wine into old wineskins; otherwise the wineskins burst, and the wine pours out, and the wineskins are ruined; but they put new wine into fresh wineskins, and both are preserved."

offenses that people did to us, or through events that happened in our lives, and we do not drop those things very quickly.

God has been working with us for such a long time, saying over and over, "You have to forgive!" The reason this is so important is because God wants to do something miraculously new, something that has never happened before (Isaiah 43:19). It will not simply be chronologically new, or a logical outgrowth of where we have been so far. God is looking to miraculously intervene in our lives and do something that eye has not seen, ear has not heard, and neither has it entered into our hearts what He has prepared for us as His people (1 Corinthians 2:9). According to Jeremiah 31:31, God will make a new covenant with His people. This is the same promise referred to in Luke 22:20, where Christ proclaimed the new covenant in His blood. The Greek word for "new" used by Christ expresses the thought of being "miraculously new."[7] It is not a natural outgrowth of an old covenant; it is God doing something completely new.

The heart of this new covenant is expressed in Jeremiah 31:34: "'And they shall not teach again, each man his neighbor and each man his brother, saying, "Know the LORD," for they shall all know

---

Isaiah 43:19 "Behold, I will do something new, now it will spring forth; will you not be aware of it? I will even make a roadway in the wilderness, rivers in the desert."

1 Corinthians 2:9 But just as it is written, "THINGS WHICH EYE HAS NOT SEEN AND EAR HAS NOT HEARD, AND which HAVE NOT ENTERED THE HEART OF MAN, ALL THAT GOD HAS PREPARED FOR THOSE WHO LOVE HIM."

Jeremiah 31:31 "Behold, days are coming," declares the LORD, "when I will make a new covenant with the house of Israel and with the house of Judah."

Luke 22:20 And in the same way He took the cup after they had eaten, saying, "This cup which is poured out for you is the new covenant in My blood."

[7.] Gerhard Kittel, Geoffrey W. Bromiley, and Gerhard Friedrich, eds., *Theological Dictionary of the New Testament* (Grand Rapids, MI: Eerdmans, 1964–.), 449-450.

Me, from the least of them to the greatest of them,' declares the LORD." This new covenant is about knowing Him. Earlier in this book, we spoke about the end of illusion, coming to know the Father, and coming into a new relationship with Him. The new, miraculous thing that God is doing is a provision to know the Father. When Christ came, He said, "You do not know the Father. Only I know the Father" (Matthew 11:27). Yet the promise that we read in Jeremiah 31:34 is that "they shall all know Me, from the least of them to the greatest of them." The fact that we will all know the Father and come into a relationship with Him is very much the new thing.

Jeremiah 31:34 continues with the reason that we will know Him: "For I will forgive their iniquity." In Hebrew, the words "for" and "because" are the same word, so let's look at this verse again with that understanding. "'They shall all know Me, from the least of them to the greatest of them,' declares the LORD, '[because] I will forgive their iniquity, and their sin I will remember no more.'" God has been working with us to bring us into something miraculously new, and it is so alive to me that what triggers the "new" is the forgiveness of our sin until it is remembered no more.

You cannot read the New Testament without realizing the impact of everything being new. Everything is different from what it was in the past. It is not the same old experience. There is something absolutely new, but walking in it takes faith. Somehow we have to position our lives around the appropriation of the new thing, which is triggered by forgiveness. God said, "You will all know Me, **because** I have forgiven your sin." You can call it deliverance if you want to, but it is a forgiveness in which we experience the removal

---

Matthew 11:27 "All things have been handed over to Me by My Father; and no one knows the Son, except the Father; nor does anyone know the Father, except the Son, and anyone to whom the Son wills to reveal Him."

of those things that cause the illusion of who God is, until we come into a true knowledge of Him. This happens because of His Word: "I will forgive their iniquity, and their sin I will remember no more" (Jeremiah 31:34). There is a thorough and complete letting go of our sin on God's part.

When our own offenses and sins are not being wiped away, we are not made new. There is something innately in us that is a constant reminder of our sin, our downfalls, our failures and all that our flesh is. It is like waking up to a drumbeat every day that is continually bringing all those things to our remembrance. However, the promise is that there will be a forgiveness that literally wipes away even the memory of the sin. God Himself will not remember. This level of forgiveness will do something completely life-changing for us. There is a new level of repentance and forgiveness, even greater than what we have experienced before. I do not want to just repent; I want God's total response to my repentance. I want to be completely forgiven.

This takes us back to the most simple salvation experience that we know in Christianity. This is a principle that is so simple, yet so deep. Someone invented the "sinner's prayer" for people who first come to Christ. I wonder if we should include a prayer of forgiveness in that initial salvation experience. If we want people to have a revelation of Christ, it would be good to expand that prayer: "Lord Jesus, I open my heart to You. I receive You as my Savior. I believe that Your sacrifice on the cross was for the forgiveness and the washing away of my sin. And now, Lord, like You, I forgive all who have offended me. Now I am able to receive Your forgiveness of my sin." Without this simple truth, we miss the true progression of salvation in our lives. Without this truth, we have not appropriated forgiveness to the depth that we need to.

When we come to the Communion table, the Scriptures teach us, "Let a man examine himself" (1 Corinthians 11:28). Let us examine our lack of forgiveness. Let us examine those things that we are still holding against someone because of their actions against us. When we come to the Communion, we should say, "Lord, I let go of those things; and not only do I forgive them, I forget their sins against me. I let go of them" (Matthew 5:23-24). Reach into your heart by faith and begin to pluck out those weeds that are there. There is nothing greater than to be forgiven in this way: "I will forgive their iniquity, and their sin I will remember no more" (Jeremiah 31:34). Don't you want that? There is something in our hearts that cries for that experience.

2 Corinthians 5:17 says, "Therefore if any man is in Christ, he is a new creature; the old things passed away; behold, new things have come." How much do we believe that we can change, that the old can really pass away? How much have we accepted, as part of our Christian experience, that we have to keep dealing with the old? How many times have you repented of a certain sin? How many times have you crucified your flesh? Yet the Scripture says that when any man comes to Christ, he is a new creature; the old things pass away, and new things have come. I believe that is part of the salvation experience. However, that experience is not possible as long as I am retaining and remembering the offenses of others against me, as long as my own bitterness, refusal, or inability to let go of those things exists. We must get to the root of our lack of forgiveness, because we are dealing with the laws of God.

---

1 Corinthians 11:28 But let a man examine himself, and so let him eat of the bread and drink of the cup.

Matthew 5:23-24 "If therefore you are presenting your offering at the altar, and there remember that your brother has something against you, [24] leave your offering there before the altar, and go your way; first be reconciled to your brother, and then come and present your offering."

Lord, give us a miracle. We do not want our repentance to be a waste of time. We want to begin our repentance with the fact that we have already forgiven others (Matthew 6:12). There is a beautiful Jewish tradition during the celebration of Rosh Hashanah (the Jewish New Year). They call the tradition *tashlich*,[8] which is born out of a Scripture in Micah 7:

> Who is a God like Thee, who pardons iniquity and passes over the rebellious act of the remnant of His possession? He does not retain His anger forever, because He delights in unchanging love. He will again have compassion on us; He will tread our iniquities under foot. Yes, Thou wilt cast all their sins into the depths of the sea. (Micah 7:18-19)

The word *tashlich*[9] means "you throw," based on the Hebrew word for "cast" in this Scripture from the Book of Micah. During Rosh Hashanah, the Jews who follow this tradition take a rock, which represents their sin, and they throw that rock into a river, lake, or ocean. It is an expression of this idea that God casts our sins into the sea, and He remembers them no more. I like this tradition. We need to have an expression that is even more than throwing away our sin; it is throwing away our lack of forgiveness. We need to throw away all those things that we are holding on to.

Reach into your heart to find a way to express this. Do something about it. Find some way to give expression to removing what has come between you and God. It does not have to be throwing a stone in the ocean, but find some expression of getting rid of

---

Matthew 6:12 "And forgive us our debts, as we also have forgiven our debtors."

[8.] Rabbi Joseph Telushkin, *Jewish Literacy: The Most Important Things to Know about the Jewish Religion, Its People, and Its History.* (New York: William Morrow and Company, Inc., 1991), 566-567.

[9.] W. E. Vine, Merrill F. Unger, and William White Jr., *Vine's Complete Expository Dictionary of Old and New Testament Words* (Nashville, TN: T. Nelson, 1996), 32.

your lack of forgiveness toward specific individuals. You need to honestly know in your mind what you are getting rid of. You need to think of the specific people, places, and events that were the causes of offense. Where family is concerned, there are many offenses, agitations and irritations that we generate out of our humanity. Whatever the source, be serious about taking action, because God is driven to forgive you. He is saying, "Get rid of the things that stop Me from forgiving you! Get rid of your lack of forgiveness toward others."

The Lord has been working with us to free us from whatever has blocked us in our walk with God. He is opening a door for us so that we can get out of situations that are binding us. There is an experience we can have that comes because He is able to forgive us; however, He cannot forgive us if we do not forgive others. There are things deep in our minds and in our hearts that we hold on to. It is essential that we find those things and get rid of them! We cannot pretend that they are not there. Ask the Holy Spirit to convict you of sin (John 16:8). There is no greater sin than your lack of forgiveness, because that literally blocks God's forgiveness of anything else within you that is wrong. You have to forgive. Isn't that what you want from God? Break out of your inability to forgive and come to the place where your forgiveness is just like God's forgiveness, and you literally tread the offense underfoot until it is gone from your memory.

Lord, restore to us the joy of Your salvation (Psalm 51:12). Let us be a people who deeply know, understand, and experience forgiveness. Let this Scripture be our experience: "They shall all know Me because I will forgive their iniquity; their sin I will remember no more" (Jeremiah 31:34).

John 16:8 "And He, when He comes, will convict the world concerning sin, and righteousness, and judgment."

Psalm 51:12 Restore to me the joy of Thy salvation, and sustain me with a willing spirit.

14 | The Laws of the Spirit

We have been studying the important principles that Jesus taught in the Lord's Prayer. In this chapter, we want to continue our study of forgiveness and look at how the principle of forgiveness functions in the realm of spirit. In Matthew 6:11-15 we read,

> "'Give us this day our daily bread. And forgive us our debts, as we also have forgiven our debtors. And do not lead us into temptation, but deliver us from evil. For Thine is the kingdom, and the power, and the glory, forever. Amen.' For if you forgive men for their transgressions, your heavenly Father will also forgive you. But if you do not forgive men, then your Father will not forgive your transgressions."

Forgiveness is not simply a teaching; it is a law in the realm of spirit. That is why, throughout this entire prayer, Jesus came back to one point. He said to His disciples, "I want to call your attention to something, because you need to get this: as you forgive, you will be forgiven." It is very important for us to understand that forgiveness truly is a law in the spirit realm that impacts your life just as if it were a law in the natural realm.

There is a danger of becoming so spiritual in our own thinking that we actually miss what the spirit realm is all about. There is a concept in Christian thought that when you are spiritual you are not bound or limited by anything. Paul wrote that "if you are led by the Spirit, you are not under the Law" (Galatians 5:18), and people develop a concept from this that when you are spiritual you can bypass laws. However, being spiritual does not mean that you are suddenly free from everything pertaining to laws and principles that the Lord has set in motion.

We have a great deal of teaching about becoming spiritual, about moving into a life in the Spirit. Yet as you watch people try to walk in the spirit realm, they appear lost. The spirit world seems completely nebulous; there does not appear to be anything there that we can relate to. We cannot understand it; we cannot come to grips with how to function in it, and so walking in the Spirit seems impossible. Obviously no one can function in a world that is a vacuum, in which nothing exists. This idea of having no law and no requirements gives a false impression of the realm of spirit.

The truth is that the world of spirit is very much bound by laws. You have to remember that the same God created the natural world and the spirit world. God did not create a natural world that is bound by laws and principles, and then create a completely separate spirit world in which there are no laws or principles. If you want to walk in the realm of spirit, one of the first things that you need to grasp is the idea that there are rules and laws which apply in that realm.

We read in Romans, "There is therefore now no condemnation for those who are in Christ Jesus. For the law of the Spirit of life in Christ Jesus has set you free from the law of sin and of death" (Romans 8:1-2). There it is. When you receive Christ and begin to walk in the Spirit, you exchange one set of laws for another. In Christ, you are now governed by the laws of the Spirit; those are the laws that are now functioning in your life. We are becoming a spiritual people, but we cannot enter into the realm of spirit without recognizing that it is a realm of laws. When Paul wrote that by walking in the Spirit you are free from the Law, he was referring to the Law of Moses (Galatians 5:18). You are free from that law, but you are bound by the law of the Spirit. If you walk in the Law of Moses, then you are bound by the Law of Moses; but if you want to move in the Spirit, then you will be bound by the laws of the Spirit.

People have said, "I don't understand why we have all of these great words, but they do not seem to have a fulfillment in my life in a practical way." We are all looking for real, practical fulfillments by virtue of the Words that we have. So why are things not working? It is because we try to move in the realm of spirit without exercising the principles of the realm of spirit. Spiritual principles are like levers. This means that when you do certain actions, just like pulling a lever, you will get automatic reactions. We all understand how that works in the natural realm when it comes to the laws of physics or chemistry. It is the same in the spirit realm. God is saying, "Do you want things to work? Then start applying the laws of the Spirit in such a way that they will work for you."

We continually grapple with the lie that we can somehow transcend the laws of the Spirit. We have been taught that authority is the most important thing in the spirit realm. Authority does not transcend laws. If the President of the United States, who has a great deal of authority, was to drive his car off of a cliff, the law of gravity would pull his car down just as fast as it would pull anyone else's car down. Of course, we do not have to drive a car off of a cliff to know what will happen; we already know. We should have the same type of awareness when we are moving in the Spirit. In the realm of spirit, there are many things we should not have to try because we already know what will take place.

The laws of nature work whether you know about them or not. Gravity does not wait to start working until you understand it. Your third grade teacher does not have to teach you about the law of gravity before it suddenly starts working in your life. Before you learned about gravity, you could not jump off a building and hang in midair. The laws of nature affect us from the time we are born, even though we are born completely ignorant of the laws of this world. Part of the process of raising children is to train them about the physical realm as quickly as possible, because until they learn those laws, they are in constant danger.

You always have to watch your children because you know that if they do certain things, they will reap the reality of natural laws. You teach them not to put their hands on the stove. You tell them, "Don't run out into the street." Even before they can really grasp the concept, you teach them to simply be obedient to your voice. If they start to run out in the street, you want them to stop when you tell them to—whether or not they understand the significance of a moving car. We train our children in order to prevent them from getting hurt until they come to a place of understanding.

We have a very similar experience when it comes to spiritual laws. When we are born of the Spirit, we are born as children. And as newborn children, we should long for the milk of the Word, that by it we may grow and mature (John 3:5; 1 Peter 2:2). As children, we do not necessarily understand, nor can we necessarily obey, all of the laws in the realm of spirit. But it does not matter whether we understand them or not; they still operate in our lives. The spirit world is just like the natural world. Once you are born of

---

John 3:5 Jesus answered, "Truly, truly, I say to you, unless one is born of water and the Spirit, he cannot enter into the kingdom of God."

1 Peter 2:2 Like newborn babes, long for the pure milk of the word, that by it you may grow in respect to salvation.

the Spirit, the laws of the Spirit apply to your life, and they will function regardless of whether or not you know them or believe in them.

In Christianity we are very focused on faith, but the laws of the Spirit, just like natural laws, operate whether we have faith in them or not. We do not say, "I don't believe in gravity; that is not part of my doctrine." We do not have to pray about gravity for it to work. Some ideas in Christian thought are actually senseless when we overlay them on the principles of God in His creation. The point is not to have a theological debate about gravity. The issue is to learn about it as fast as we can because it is already working in our lives. We do not need as much faith as we think we need. What we need is the ability to execute the laws of the Spirit, and if we can execute them, certain things will simply happen.

Of great importance, especially in the realm of spirit, are the things that do not happen. In your daily life, there are many actions that you do not do so that negative results will not occur. These things can have the greatest impact on your life. For example, when you are driving your car, you do not drive into any of the trees along the road. You do not drive into those trees because you understand the laws of nature. You probably do not think, "I wonder what will happen if I run into that tree?" Without really thinking about it, your whole day is spent making decisions based on what you know about natural laws.

There are many things that we do not do because it is ingrained in our minds what will happen if we do them. This applies to our relationships. There are ways in which we relate to others, and also ways in which we do not relate. For example, we learn not to relate in anger to our family because it will reap a certain result. There are many things that we do not do because of the negative ramifications of those actions. In the spirit realm it is the same way. There are many things that we simply should not do, because doing those things sets in motion specific results that we do not want (Galatians 6:7).

We need to repent of spiritual pride. We feel that we are not bound by some of these spiritual laws. When people say, "I do not understand why certain things are not happening in my life," one of the best answers I can give is this: it is because of what you are creating in the realm of spirit by what you are doing. These things are real. There needs to be a calculated effort on our part to reverse the consequences of what we have created, turn them around, and erase them out of the spirit realm. That may sound hard to do, but it is not, because that is what Christ is all about. The whole concept of salvation is that He erases, by His blood, what should happen to us because of what we have done. By His sacrifice on the cross He took away the consequences of our life and our nature (John 1:29). Repentance and honestly seeking the Lord can completely change and reverse the consequences that we have set in motion in our lives.

When I receive the Lord Jesus Christ, He takes away my sin and the judgment that is written against me (Colossians 2:13-14). Do we really see this as a law, just as real as any law we deal with in the natural realm? Are there any consequences if we do not obey this law? Jesus said, "If you forgive others, your Father in heaven will forgive you" (Matthew 6:14). Is it really true that God

---

Galatians 6:7 Do not be deceived, God is not mocked; for whatever a man sows, this he will also reap.

John 1:29 The next day he saw Jesus coming to him, and said, "Behold, the Lamb of God who takes away the sin of the world!"

Colossians 2:13-14 And when you were dead in your transgressions and the uncircumcision of your flesh, He made you alive together with Him, having forgiven us all our transgressions, [14] having canceled out the certificate of debt consisting of decrees against us and which was hostile to us; and He has taken it out of the way, having nailed it to the cross.

can only forgive us when we forgive others? Visualize a ledger in heaven that has your name at the top of it. All of your sins and the negative things that you set in motion are written on this ledger, so you come to the Lord and ask for forgiveness. Then the angel of the Lord erases everything written on your ledger. Now it is completely blank and you walk away rejoicing in your salvation experience. After this, someone does something horrible to you, and you think, "I am so mad at that person! God judge them for this offense against me!" Then the angel has to take out his pencil and begin writing your sins on that ledger again.

We have the reality of our salvation and forgiveness from God intact, and we can walk through life with our ledger erased. However, when we stop forgiving, it is not long before our sins are written again on that ledger. Personally, I want God to forgive me of everything. There is no offense of mine that I do not want God to forgive, but I have to give that same forgiveness to others or it does not work for me. Without forgiveness, we go back to living in the sin of whatever we did, and God stops covering the nature of our flesh.

Realize that we walk under the blood of Christ. We have a protection around us by the blood and forgiveness of Christ. Therefore we have access to boldly go into the presence of the Father (Hebrews 10:19, KJV). However, when that protection is gone, we are in trouble, because the sin nature is still there. We are in the process of the crucifixion and removal of the sin nature. Yet until that is absolutely gone, we live under the blood of Christ that covers and constrains the results of this nature within us. Sin is not just individual actions: "I did this, and I did that." It is the entire nature. So when grace is gone from us, we stand accused

---

Hebrews 10:19, KJV Having therefore, brethren, boldness to enter into the holiest by the blood of Jesus.

before God because of the nature that is within us. As soon as we stop forgiving, we are exposed again, standing in our old nature.

Many of us have heard this teaching for such a long time that it really does not have the impact on us that it should. That is why I am stressing the comparison with natural laws. Once you understand a natural law, you do not play around with it. You do not say, "I have a feeling that gravity will be different today, so I'm going to jump off a building." No, gravity will not be different, and there is no way to not be affected by the law of gravity.

The same is true of the laws of the Spirit. If we truly understand that God's forgiveness of us only happens when we forgive others, then we do not want to stop forgiving people. Knowing how much we want to be forgiven, there must be something in us that is forgiving of others. We know the commandment in the Scriptures: love your neighbor as yourself (Leviticus 19:18; Matthew 19:19). How badly do you want forgiveness? Then you must want your neighbor to have forgiveness as much as you want it for yourself.

Matthew 18:21-35 is an important passage of Scripture dealing with the spiritual law of forgiveness. This is the story about the slave who was forgiven by his master but would not forgive his fellow slave. Read this story with the intent of allowing the directness of the Lord to get to your spirit.

> Then Peter came and said to Him, "Lord, how often shall my brother sin against me and I forgive him? Up to seven times?" Jesus said to him, "I do not say to you, up to seven times, but up to seventy times seven. For

---

Leviticus 19:18 "You shall not take vengeance, nor bear any grudge against the sons of your people, but you shall love your neighbor as yourself; I am the Lord."

Matthew 19:19 "HONOR YOUR FATHER AND MOTHER; and YOU SHALL LOVE YOUR NEIGHBOR AS YOURSELF."

this reason the kingdom of heaven may be compared to a certain king who wished to settle accounts with his slaves." (Matthew 18:21-23)

Jesus is trying to get something through to His disciples in response to Peter's question. Essentially He is saying, "I don't care how many times you have to forgive your brother for sinning against you; forgive him each time. Whatever he did to you is unimportant compared to the consequence of not forgiving him." Near the end of the story the master said to his servant, "Should you not also have had mercy on your fellow slave, even as I had mercy on you?" (Matthew 18:33). That is us; we are all fellow slaves. We are all serving the Lord.

"And his lord, moved with anger, handed him over to the torturers until he should repay all that was owed him. So shall My heavenly Father also do to you, if each of you does not forgive his brother from your heart" (Matthew 18:34-35). The point of the story is this: God will be angry with you if you do not forgive your brother from your heart. This answers the question, "Why don't things always go the way we think they should?" In our minds, we are executing what we understand are the principles of the Kingdom. We pray in the name of the Lord (John 14:14). We get together with two or three and agree on what we are praying for (Matthew 18:19-20). However, we are forgetting the principle of forgiveness. We cannot execute certain spiritual principles, but in the process ignore the foundational laws of the Kingdom. Every other principle begins to operate after these laws. In a sense, violating these laws can erase every other principle, because they deal with our grace and forgiveness toward others. So when you say, "I prayed, and God

---

John 14:14 "If you ask Me anything in My name, I will do it."

Matthew 18:19-20 "Again I say to you, that if two of you agree on earth about anything that they may ask, it shall be done for them by My Father who is in heaven. [20] For where two or three have gathered together in My name, there I am in their midst."

did not answer my prayer," are you considering the possibility that He is mad at you? No one else answers your prayers except God. So when you pray and nothing happens, look and see if He is angry with you, and take care of it as quickly as you can. "Our God is a consuming fire" (Hebrews 12:29), and you do not want Him to stay mad at you for very long.

Do not think that you can violate the law of forgiveness, and then be disgusted because God is not answering your prayer. He is not going to answer your prayer when He is mad at you. Go back and get your relationship with God straightened out, and then try voicing your prayer again. Get back into the grace of God through Jesus Christ, and search your heart until you find the deep things that are there. Do not just go over situations in your mind and say, "Yeah, I know I was mad at that person. I'm sorry." You have to dig down into your heart because areas where you have not forgiven people are buried deep in your spirit, and many times your mind does not even remember them.

You will have to work at this. You need to throw a bucket way down into the well of salvation and start pulling up more grace in your life (Isaiah 12:3). You have to sweep out those areas in your heart where you have violated major principles and laws of the Spirit (1 Corinthians 5:7-8). You cannot be unforgiving, because if you are, God will be angry with you. If He is angry with you, there should be no question as to why things are not going exactly the way you want them to go. This should be enough of an answer: "So shall My heavenly Father also do to you, if each of you does not forgive his brother from your heart" (Matthew 18:35).

Isaiah 12:3 Therefore you will joyously draw water from the springs of salvation.

1 Corinthians 5:7-8 Clean out the old leaven, that you may be a new lump, just as you are in fact unleavened. For Christ our Passover also has been sacrificed. [8] Let us therefore celebrate the feast, not with old leaven, nor with the leaven of malice and wickedness, but with the unleavened bread of sincerity and truth.

Forgiveness has to come from your heart. It has to honestly be forgiveness. It is not really forgiveness when you say, "I forgive them, Lord," and then walk away with your mind going right back to the offense that happened. When God forgives you, He forgets (Isaiah 43:25). God's forgiveness includes His forgetting; and your forgiveness will have to include your forgetting about the incident. Consciously and subconsciously, you will have to forget it. That is the only depth of forgiveness that works in the realm of spirit.

Let's read another Scripture about our responsibility in forgiveness. When Jesus gave His disciples the Holy Spirit, He said to them, "If you forgive the sins of any, their sins have been forgiven them; if you retain the sins of any, they have been retained" (John 20:23). Can you conceive of the power that God has put in our hands when it comes to forgiveness? It is one thing to say, "If you forgive people, their sins are forgiven." That is wonderful. But He also said, "If you retain people's sins, their sins are retained." My reaction to that is to say, "God, don't give me that kind of power yet!"

The whole reality of God sending His Son to the earth to die for us was to achieve the forgiveness of the world. Then He turns to us and says, "I sent My Son. He suffered; He went to the cross and died for the sins of mankind. But in spite of all that, if you retain people's sins they are retained." Think about the judgment that we face from this reality on a daily basis. God is saying, "I forgave you, and I have already forgiven that person who offended you. Are you not going to forgive him?" We are called into account more than we realize.

What we sow, we reap (Galatians 6:7). This is a law of the Spirit that goes hand in hand with forgiveness. Look at the example of sowing seeds in the natural realm. Those seeds grow into plants,

---

Isaiah 43:25 "I, even I, am the one who wipes out your transgressions for My own sake; and I will not remember your sins."

and after the plants mature, their fruit ripens and is harvested. It happens very much the same way in the realm of spirit. More than we understand, things that we have sown are continually becoming ripe and coming to fruition in our lives. As we go through life, we tend to plant violations, like seeds, almost every day. Those violations, at some point, become ripe and then we reap the results. We could be affected today by something that we did twenty years ago, and tomorrow we could plant a seed that we will reap in the future.

Whenever we do not forgive someone, we are sowing a seed in the realm of spirit, and we eventually will reap the results. You can go along in your day and think, "I don't get it. I did all of these wonderful things today but the day just seems to be an absolute disaster." You have to ask yourself what you sowed that you are now reaping. You have to burn those crops before they become ripe. That is part of salvation. That is why Jesus said, "Pick up your cross daily and follow Me" (Luke 9:23). Why do you have to pick up your cross daily? Something has to happen for you in salvation every day to release you from all those things that you have planted.

In Matthew we read about another law of the Spirit: "Do not judge lest you be judged. For in the way you judge, you will be judged; and by your standard of measure, it will be measured to you" (Matthew 7:1-2). This Scripture does not tell you when your own judgment will come back on you. Generally, God will surprise you. It will happen at the most inopportune time in your life. Just when you are really reaching into God for something, suddenly God will say, "Today is a good day; let's have that judgment come back to you as you have judged." By our standard of measure is exactly

---

Luke 9:23 And He was saying to them all, "If anyone wishes to come after Me, let him deny himself, and take up his cross daily, and follow Me."

how we will be measured. We continually have little criticisms of people: "You could have done that a little better!" The list goes on of all of the ways that we judge one another.

The Lord has given us Words about exercising judgment, and we have sought to move in judgment. However, the way we have done it is incorrect, because the key to judgment is that it cannot be ours. You are not being a pure channel of judgment if your own personal motives and will are involved. To visualize how your personal motives affect judgment, compare it to playing pinball. You can use your body to move the pinball machine just a little to change the direction that the ball is going. Suddenly, the sign flashes "Tilt!" and the game is over. That is the way judgment is. When God is getting ready to judge a situation, you get your own motives involved and try to change the direction a little bit. Suddenly God says, "Tilt! Game over!"

As you judge, so shall you be judged. I believe that the sons of God will move in judgment (1 Corinthians 6:2-3). But Christ said, "Even if I do judge, My judgment is true" (John 8:16). He also said, "I did not come to judge the world; I came to save the world" (John 3:17). We know that the judgments of God will happen, but we also know that the judgments of God are true and that His purpose is salvation. When the judgments happen, they will be absolutely God and not man. Whatever attempts that we have made to move in judgment have resulted in a backlash against us, because our motivations were not pure and our own judgments came into play. We need to repent and start expunging what has

---

1 Corinthians 6:2-3 Or do you not know that the saints will judge the world? And if the world is judged by you, are you not competent to constitute the smallest law courts? ³ Do you not know that we shall judge angels? How much more, matters of this life?

John 3:17 "For God did not send the Son into the world to judge the world, but that the world should be saved through Him."

resulted from our own judgments. Pray, "Lord, the judgment is Yours; I repent for my judgments." We should especially repent of the judgments we make on a daily basis within the Body of Christ and within the home. Judgment happens so quickly. Something comes up and immediately our response is to judge how someone did something, or what they should have done.

Lord, loose us from these things. As we have learned, the spirit realm is not a spooky place that we cannot relate to. It is very much like the natural realm, which has laws that we can follow. If you want to be blessed in the realm of spirit, then follow the laws. Forgive others. Do not judge. Sow what you want to reap. Do unto others as you would have them do unto you (Matthew 7:12). These are not childish ideas that we learned in Sunday school. You cannot say, "I've outgrown those things being necessary in my life." No, you never grow beyond them being necessary. For those who are in Christ, these are the fundamental laws of the Spirit that literally control everything else that happens in the realm of spirit.

Repent for how you have violated these fundamental laws. As you repent, start with the fact that there is no condemnation in Christ. Do not be condemned about what you have done; just stop doing those things. Get rid of everything that you have done wrong. The blood of Christ can cleanse us of all of our sins (1 John 1:7, 9). So you do not need to be morbid in your repentance, but also, do not take it lightly. A cursory repentance for five minutes will not take care of it. Remember that the heart is desperately wicked; who can

---

Matthew 7:12 "Therefore, however you want people to treat you, so treat them, for this is the Law and the Prophets."

1 John 1:7 But if we walk in the light as He Himself is in the light, we have fellowship with one another, and the blood of Jesus His Son cleanses us from all sin.

1 John 1:9 If we confess our sins, He is faithful and righteous to forgive us our sins and to cleanse us from all unrighteousness.

know it (Jeremiah 17:9)? There are deep things in our conscious and subconscious minds that need to be uprooted. Become so sensitive to what you are doing that you can stop the violation the moment it appears. You learn that sensitivity by dealing with the past, by digging into where and how the violation happens. Get to the root, because it is from the roots in our spirits that come judgment, lack of forgiveness, and the sowing of what we do not want to reap.

Part of the problem is that we believe that we are basically good, and we miss the reality of the Adamic nature. When a certain ruler came to Jesus and said, "Good Teacher," He turned around and said, "What do you mean, 'good'? There is no one good but the Father" (Luke 18:18-19). Even Jesus did not refer to Himself as good, because He was still in the flesh. Paul said, "In me, that is in this flesh, there is no good thing" (Romans 7:18). We also need to rid our minds of this idea that we are basically good, and that we have lived good lives. We have continually violated these spiritual laws, not as unbelievers and sinners, but as Christians— as believers. We cannot violate the laws of the Spirit and then expect everything to go our way. To really change things, we need to stop the train we are currently on, turn it around, and put it on a completely different track.

Jeremiah 17:9 "The heart is more deceitful than all else and is desperately sick; who can understand it?"

Luke 18:18-19 And a certain ruler questioned Him, saying, "Good Teacher, what shall I do to inherit eternal life?" [19] And Jesus said to him, "Why do you call Me good? No one is good except God alone."

Romans 7:18 For I know that nothing good dwells in me, that is, in my flesh; for the wishing is present in me, but the doing of the good is not.

We can find passages in the Bible directing us to correct our brother (Matthew 18:15-17; Luke 17:3), but I am concerned about first dealing with the depths of our individual hearts. We can read about this in Matthew 7:3-4:

> "And why do you look at the speck that is in your brother's eye, but do not notice the log that is in your own eye? Or how can you say to your brother, 'Let me take the speck out of your eye,' and behold, the log is in your own eye? You hypocrite, first take the log out of your own eye, and then you will see clearly to take the speck out of your brother's eye."

The problem with trying to talk to your brother about his problems comes when you have not dealt with your problems first. We change our own circumstances when we truly deal with the roots of our own spirit and not necessarily when we attempt to correct our brother. Make your own heart your focus. Say, "At this point, I do not care if my brother has not forgiven me. I am going to deal with it right here in my own heart. I am going to find out what is there, and I am going to deal with it. I will not open my mouth until I know that my violation is dealt with in my own heart and spirit. Then the Lord can lead me as to whether anything needs to be spoken to my brother or not."

Jesus said, "Do not judge and you will not be judged; and do not condemn, and you will not be condemned; pardon, and you will be pardoned" (Luke 6:37). Isn't it interesting how difficult it is for

---

Matthew 18:15-17   "And if your brother sins, go and reprove him in private; if he listens to you, you have won your brother. [16] But if he does not listen to you, take one or two more with you, so that BY THE MOUTH OF TWO OR THREE WITNESSES EVERY FACT MAY BE CONFIRMED. [17] And if he refuses to listen to them, tell it to the church; and if he refuses to listen even to the church, let him be to you as a Gentile and a tax-gatherer."

Luke 17:3   "Be on your guard! If your brother sins, rebuke him; and if he repents, forgive him."

people to overcome condemnation? People struggle with a sense of condemnation all the time. They say, "I don't understand where my condemnation is coming from." It is actually simple. It is a law of the Spirit. If you are wrestling with condemnation, search your heart and determine whom you have condemned, because what may be happening is that your own condemnation is coming back on you. You are reaping it. You did not do anything to be condemned; you are simply reaping what you have done in condemning others. It is a fundamental law of the Spirit: "Give, and it will be given to you; good measure, pressed down, shaken together, running over, they will pour into your lap. For by your standard of measure it will be measured to you in return" (Luke 6:38). The way that we measure out will be measured back to us.

Do you feel like you want to forgive everyone really fast? You think, "I don't want to wait another minute. I want to go into my prayer closet right now and start forgiving people." That is good, but we need these keys to be really effective. These laws are some of the greatest keys to being blessed; they are some of the greatest answers to the questions, "Why do things not work? Where is the blessing? Where are the answers to my prayers?" We can literally turn our lives around if we enter into repentance for how we have related in the past, and stop doing those things as we go forward. The Lord said, "Why do you call Me, 'Lord, Lord,' and do not do what I say?" (Luke 6:46). That certainly applies to us right now concerning these laws of the Spirit. Let's take what we have learned about forgiving and not judging, and honestly practice them.

Our lack of forgiveness changes today. We are going to begin forgiving. We will change. When we give ourselves to the Lord to change our hearts, His grace and His blood and His forgiveness is there for us. We will be changed, we will be forgiven, and we will be freed. All of these consequences that we are ready to reap will be done away with, and we will stand clean before the Lord. The blessings will begin to come, and we will reap the blessings that we sow from this day forward (Galatians 6:8-9).

Galatians 6:8-9   For the one who sows to his own flesh shall from the flesh reap corruption, but the one who sows to the Spirit shall from the Spirit reap eternal life. [9] And let us not lose heart in doing good, for in due time we shall reap if we do not grow weary.

15 | Deliver Us From Evil!

In this book, we have studied the Lord's Prayer as it is recorded in the sixth chapter of Matthew. In summary, the Lord's Prayer, or more correctly the Disciples' Prayer, is about us and our walk with the Lord right now. "Pray, then, in this way: 'Our Father who art in heaven, hallowed be Thy name. Thy kingdom come. Thy will be done, on earth as it is in heaven'" (Matthew 6:9-10). This prayer is about the Kingdom of God, and it is about our involvement in seeing that the Kingdom of God is established on this earth. Our cry has to be, "Thy Kingdom come on earth as it is in heaven." We must appropriate Him in our lives on a daily basis: "Give us this day our daily bread" (Matthew 6:11). We have to be filled with His life. "And forgive us our debts, as we also have forgiven our debtors" (Matthew 6:12). To be able to stand in His presence, we have to let go of every debt we have held against others and walk in a state of forgiveness.

In this chapter, we will look at the last verse of the prayer. The first part of Matthew 6:13 reads, "And do not lead us into temptation, but deliver us from evil." The second part of this verse does not appear in the earliest Greek manuscripts: "For Thine is the kingdom, and the power, and the glory, forever. Amen" (Matthew 6:13). Whether it is in the original Greek manuscripts or not, it is still true and biblical (Luke 1:33; Romans 11:36; 1 Timothy 1:17; Jude 25; Revelation 5:13, 7:11-12, 11:15). We know that His is the Kingdom and the power and the glory, forever. However, for this study we want to focus on what Christ was saying when He taught His disciples to pray, "Do not lead us into temptation, but deliver us from evil."

The Greek word for "temptation" here is more specifically translated as "testing."[10] You could read Matthew 6:13 as, "Do not lead us into testing, but deliver us from evil." It is speaking about something that is difficult for our hearts to grasp concerning the spiritual reality between God and satan. We know that from the very beginning

---

Luke 1:33 "And He will reign over the house of Jacob forever; and His kingdom will have no end."

Romans 11:36 For from Him and through Him and to Him are all things. To Him be the glory forever. Amen.

1 Timothy 1:17 Now to the King eternal, immortal, invisible, the only God, be honor and glory forever and ever. Amen.

Jude 25 To the only God our Savior, through Jesus Christ our Lord, be glory, majesty, dominion and authority, before all time and now and forever. Amen.

Revelation 5:13 And every created thing which is in heaven and on the earth and under the earth and on the sea, and all things in them, I heard saying, "To Him who sits on the throne, and to the Lamb, be blessing and honor and glory and dominion forever and ever."

Revelation 7:11-12 And all the angels were standing around the throne and around the elders and the four living creatures; and they fell on their faces before the throne and worshiped God, [12] saying, "Amen, blessing and glory and wisdom and thanksgiving and honor and power and might, be to our God forever and ever. Amen."

Revelation 11:15 And the seventh angel sounded; and there arose loud voices in heaven, saying, "The kingdom of the world has become the kingdom of our Lord, and of His Christ; and He will reign forever and ever."

[10.] Ceslas Spicq and James D. Ernest, *Theological Lexicon of the New Testament* (Peabody, MA: Hendrickson Publishers, 1994), 80.

satan sinned against God and entered a fallen state; subsequently, Adam and Eve sinned (Isaiah 14:12-15; Genesis 2:16-17; 3:6-7, 13). What happened in the Garden of Eden may seem like a simple story, but the mysteries of what happened in the realm of spirit are very deep. What was put in motion at that time resulted in all of creation being subjected to futility (Genesis 3:16-19). As we discussed in an earlier chapter, Christ did not come and experience the cross solely for the removal and forgiveness of sin for man. He came to redeem all of mankind; because when man fell, all of creation was impacted (Romans 8:20-21). When we talk

---

Isaiah 14:12-15 "How you have fallen from heaven, O star of the morning, son of the dawn! You have been cut down to the earth, you who have weakened the nations! ¹³ But you said in your heart, 'I will ascend to heaven; I will raise my throne above the stars of God, and I will sit on the mount of assembly in the recesses of the north. ¹⁴ I will ascend above the heights of the clouds; I will make myself like the Most High.' ¹⁵ Nevertheless you will be thrust down to Sheol, to the recesses of the pit."

Genesis 2:16-17 And the LORD God commanded the man, saying, "From any tree of the garden you may eat freely; ¹⁷ but from the tree of the knowledge of good and evil you shall not eat, for in the day that you eat from it you shall surely die."

Genesis 3:6-7 When the woman saw that the tree was good for food, and that it was a delight to the eyes, and that the tree was desirable to make one wise, she took from its fruit and ate; and she gave also to her husband with her, and he ate. ⁷ Then the eyes of both of them were opened, and they knew that they were naked; and they sewed fig leaves together and made themselves loin coverings.

Genesis 3:13 Then the LORD God said to the woman, "What is this you have done?" And the woman said, "The serpent deceived me, and I ate."

Genesis 3:16-19 To the woman He said, "I will greatly multiply your pain in childbirth, in pain you shall bring forth children; yet your desire shall be for your husband, and he shall rule over you." ¹⁷ Then to Adam He said, "Because you have listened to the voice of your wife, and have eaten from the tree about which I commanded you, saying, 'You shall not eat from it'; cursed is the ground because of you; in toil you shall eat of it all the days of your life. ¹⁸ Both thorns and thistles it shall grow for you; and you shall eat the plants of the field; ¹⁹ by the sweat of your face you shall eat bread, till you return to the ground, because from it you were taken; for you are dust, and to dust you shall return."

Romans 8:20-21 For the creation was subjected to futility, not of its own will, but because of Him who subjected it, in hope ²¹ that the creation itself also will be set free from its slavery to corruption into the freedom of the glory of the children of God.

about our salvation and the crucifixion of Christ, we are dealing with tremendous mysteries in the realm of spirit, things that go beyond our ability to grasp. As we consider these mysteries, which we have only begun to approach in these chapters, we can sense with awe the wonder of our salvation, which is beyond our ability to comprehend.

During the Last Supper, the Lord prepared the disciples for His departure—His crucifixion. He said to Peter, "Simon, Simon, behold, Satan has demanded permission to sift you like wheat; but I have prayed for you, that your faith may not fail; and you, when once you have turned again, strengthen your brothers" (Luke 22:31-32). In the Greek text here, the expression "demand permission to sift you like wheat" is related to turning someone over from one person's hands to another's with the intent of torture and torment.[11] For Christ to say that satan had demanded permission meant that there existed a right on satan's part to have Peter turned over into his hands. It shakes our spirits to realize that satan had the kind of standing and access to God to demand that Peter be put in his hands[12] for the purpose of testing, which we could say was for the purpose of torment, because satan was determined to torment Peter. This is a difficult concept, and it is made even more difficult by the reality of Christ's response. In the Greek, the word "demand" means the granting of permission for what is being demanded.[13] Essentially, Christ was saying to Peter,

---

[11] Darrell L. Bock, *Luke: 9:51–24:53*, vol. 2, *Baker Exegetical Commentary on the New Testament* (Grand Rapids, MI: Baker Academic, 1996), 1742; Alfred Plummer, *A Critical and Exegetical Commentary on the Gospel According to S. Luke*, International Critical Commentary (London: T&T Clark International, 1896), 503.

[12] William Arndt, Frederick W. Danker, and Walter Bauer, *A Greek-English Lexicon of the New Testament and Other Early Christian Literature* (Chicago: University of Chicago Press, 2000), 344.

[13] Alfred Plummer, *A Critical and Exegetical Commentary on the Gospel According to S. Luke*, International Critical Commentary (London: T&T Clark International, 1896), 503.

"Satan has demanded, and it has been granted, that you be sifted, tested, and tormented." Our minds, immediately, are incapable of understanding why Christ could not refuse a request like that. We can only assume that if He could have, He would have.

What happened to Peter is similar to what happened to Job. Again, it is beyond our human ability to conceive that God the Father would allow satan the access to someone who was serving Him, in order to torture him and torment him, and to bring a test of his faith on that level. "Then Satan answered the LORD, 'Does Job fear God for nothing? Hast Thou not made a hedge about him and his house and all that he has, on every side? Thou hast blessed the work of his hands, and his possessions have increased in the land'" (Job 1:9-10). That is the way we think walking with God should be. We should be blessed. We should be protected by God. Everything should grow. All of the blessings should increase and things should get better and better and greater and greater. And in fact, that **is** the Kingdom; but there is something else that happens prior to the Kingdom. "'But put forth Thy hand now and touch all that he has; he will surely curse Thee to Thy face.' Then the LORD said to Satan, 'Behold, all that he has is in your power, only do not put forth your hand on him.' So Satan departed from the presence of the LORD" (Job 1:11-12). From that moment, satan went about destroying all that Job owned.

When Jesus told Peter of satan's request to test him, He added, "I've prayed that your faith not fail, and when you have turned, strengthen your brothers." All Christ could do was pray for Peter. Now, that might seem a little insipid if you are the one being tormented. Peter could have responded, "You must have more authority than that! Why are you allowing this in the first place?" It is hard to understand, but Christ was dealing with the things of the Kingdom. When we look at the experience that Peter went through, it was devastating. He was literally turned over to satan that he might have his way with Peter. We must recognize that Peter was getting ready to move as an apostle in the power of God, to move in miracles and the things of the Kingdom. When Jesus said to Peter, "After you have turned again, strengthen your brothers," the implication was that his brothers would also go through a similar experience. This also explains much of what we have lived under.

The same illustration is found in the story of Job. "And the LORD said to Satan, 'Have you considered My servant Job? For there is no one like him on the earth'" (Job 2:3). What God said about Job is what He is saying now about a people, the Body of Christ. What is happening to us is related to the fact that God is raising up a people, and there is no one like them in the earth (Joel 2:2). We live in a time when God is bringing forth the sons of the Kingdom, and we are a part of that. God said of Job, "For there is no one like him on the earth, a blameless and upright man fearing God and turning away from evil. And he still holds fast his integrity, although you incited Me against him, to ruin him without cause" (Job 2:3). God had allowed satan access to Job to test him. Do you feel like that is the story of your life? Do you feel like some force has been turned loose against you?

Search through the Body of Christ, and you will find that God is raising up a people. Yet their lives seem to be a disaster. Look at the ones who are chosen by God. Look at the ones who have some of the greatest words, promises, and prophecies over their lives, and it seems that their lives are the opposite of the promises. Yet God says about them what He said about Job: "I have no one like them, these sons of the Kingdom. There is no one like them on the earth. They are blameless. They are upright. They fear God and

---

Joel 2:2 A day of darkness and gloom, a day of clouds and thick darkness. As the dawn is spread over the mountains, so there is a great and mighty people; there has never been anything like it, nor will there be again after it to the years of many generations.

turn away from evil." No matter what they have gone through in the torment of satan against them, they hold fast the integrity of their faith. They believe God even though satan has been incited against their lives.

The sons of God that are coming forth worldwide are having similar experiences. In many churches there have been years of intercession and crying out to the Lord to release His appearing (2 Thessalonians 1:10). They are a people with a single focus: to see His presence and His Kingdom in the earth. No matter what the torment, no matter what has been turned loose against them, they live in the prayer, "Thy Kingdom come. Thy will be done, O Lord, in this earth—in my life." That cry has never ceased, and that is integrity. That is intensity. That is believing. Perhaps you have been through many devastating things and you believe that you are a failure. You are not. You are here on this earth holding fast with faith and integrity. Just as with Peter, satan has also demanded to sift you like wheat. He has demanded by some mystery we do not understand, an access to your life to torment you. What you need is nothing less than a miracle deliverance from the effects of satan's torture and torment.

These words "torture" and "torment" are not too strong to describe what many of you have suffered under satan's hand. "And Satan answered the LORD and said, 'Skin for skin! Yes, all that a man has he will give for his life. However, put forth Thy hand, now, and touch his bone and his flesh; he will curse Thee to Thy face'" (Job 2:4-5). This has been satan's claim against you. He says to God concerning you, "It is not enough that I destroy everything that they possess and everything that is around them. If You let me touch their flesh, then they will curse you." "So the LORD said to Satan, 'Behold, he is in your power, only spare his life'" (Job 2:6).

---

2 Thessalonians 1:10 When He comes to be glorified in His saints on that day, and to be marveled at among all who have believed—for our testimony to you was believed.

There are times when feelings will push us to say and condemn things that are not even rational. We will even condemn God, who is the answer for our distress.

Job's wife actually said, "Curse God and die!" (Job 2:9). Have there been times when you have felt like doing just that? "Lord, why aren't You protecting me? Where is the anointing to save me from these things?" The answer is to keep worshiping God. Every time that satan comes to kill us or touch us physically, instead of cursing God, we worship Him! We worship Him with a greater intensity and with a greater drive. Every time we do that we proclaim, "Satan, you are a liar! (John 8:44). We love God! If you kill us, we will love God. We will worship Him. We will not curse Him. We bless Him. He gave us life, and if you try to take it away, we will bless and worship Him." The greater the force from satan to touch us and destroy what we have and who we are—to make us sick, or touch our children, or even to kill us—we will worship God with more force! We will oppose satan in the force of our worship. If satan touches our flesh, we will not curse God; we will worship (Job 2:4). It will be in proclaiming that no matter what is happening, to God is the power, His is the glory, and His is the Kingdom.

God's people, His chosen ones who are the sons of God coming forth in His Kingdom, have experienced like Peter and Job the turning loose of satan against their lives. Throughout the earth today, when you look at the true ministries of God, you see satan

---

Job 2:9 Then his wife said to him, "Do you still hold fast your integrity? Curse God and die!"

John 8:44 "You are of your father the devil, and you want to do the desires of your father. He was a murderer from the beginning, and does not stand in the truth, because there is no truth in him. Whenever he speaks a lie, he speaks from his own nature; for he is a liar, and the father of lies."

standing at their right hand to accuse them (Zechariah 3:1). Where is the blessing that we need? Before the blessing there is an experience of testing; but after that, we cry out to the Lord, "Deliver us from evil! Deliver us from the evil one. Deliver us from this trial, from this torment that has been turned loose against our lives." At a point in time the trial is no longer necessary, and I believe that time is now. Now is the time for deliverance. I proclaim a release; I proclaim that the time of testing comes to an end for all the sons coming forth and for the entire Body of Christ, in the name of the Lord.

It may be hard for some people to understand this message, but for sons who have lived this reality, it is very easy to grasp the truth of this word. As we read in 2 Timothy 2:12 (KJV), if you suffer with Him, you will reign with Him. You are suffering with Him in the temptation, the trial, the testing of satan turned against your life. You are suffering with Christ.

Christ Himself was tempted in the wilderness, and satan was given access to touch Him.

> Again, the devil took Him to a very high mountain, and showed Him all the kingdoms of the world, and their glory; and he said to Him, "All these things I will give You, if You fall down and worship me." Then Jesus said to him, "Begone, Satan! For it is written, 'YOU SHALL WORSHIP THE LORD YOUR GOD, AND SERVE HIM ONLY.'" (Matthew 4:8-10)

There was a moment when Christ had the ability to say to satan, "Begone!" There was a moment when that temptation ended and

---

Zechariah 3:1 Then he showed me Joshua the high priest standing before the angel of the LORD, and Satan standing at his right hand to accuse him.

2 Timothy 2:12, KJV If we suffer, we shall also reign with him: if we deny him, he also will deny us.

the trial was over. Now is the time for us to say, "Begone" to satan. We have the ability to declare the end of the testing and the access of satan into our lives. That access must end, and the blessing must begin. We anticipate that what was taken away from us as a result of the experience of testing will be restored.

After his testing, Job was given a double portion of everything he had before (Job 42:10). It is the time for a restoration of everything that satan has desired to destroy. There is a very distinct experience in which Christ demands our return and we are turned back into His hands. Christ said to Peter, "I have prayed for you" (Luke 22:32), and He also ever lives to make intercession for us (Hebrews 7:25). Christ is praying us through our experience of testing, and there comes that moment when we have what is written in Colossians 1:13-14: "For He delivered us from the domain of darkness, and transferred us to the kingdom of His beloved Son, in whom we have redemption." There is a release in which we are transferred out of the trial, out of the testing, out of the possession of satan's hands to try us, and we are delivered into the Kingdom.

This concept of being delivered out of one place into another is very real. When Job was being tested, he was in another place. He had been possessed—not in the way we think of demon possession— but he had been locked up by satan into a certain place. That is why in spiritual warfare our weapons are mighty to the tearing down of fortresses (2 Corinthians 10:4). When you are tested, it is as if you are locked into a fortress—the dominion of satan; you cannot get out and nothing can get through to you. However,

---

Job 42:10   And the LORD restored the fortunes of Job when he prayed for his friends, and the LORD increased all that Job had twofold.

Hebrews 7:25   Hence, also, He is able to save forever those who draw near to God through Him, since He always lives to make intercession for them.

2 Corinthians 10:4   For the weapons of our warfare are not of the flesh, but divinely powerful for the destruction of fortresses.

our weapons are mighty to the tearing down of that stronghold, and God will transfer us out. He will translate us; He will deliver us from the dominion and the hands of satan's power, into His Kingdom, into another place where the access of satan does not exist. This is the day. This is the time. This is the hour for it to happen. We say, "Begone, satan! Begone, in the name of the Lord! We worship God and we serve Him only. Begone!" Then when we are turned back to the Lord—when we turn—we will strengthen our brethren (Luke 22:32). We will have the authority to deliver others from their testings. We will have the ability to get others out of the trials they are going through.

He is creating us to be a people of deliverance, but first we must be delivered (Joel 2:32). We know that all of creation is to be saved from futility, but the deliverance of creation will come through the glory and the release of the sons of God. Until we are delivered into this release, all creation remains in futility. In our worship, let us believe for a divine experience of ending futility. Whatever has happened to you, whatever has happened to your family, let there be restoration. Whether it has been physical, emotional, or spiritual; whether it has touched your possessions, your blessings, or the Word of God over your life; let there be restoration. The prophecy of Joel 2:25 is that God will restore that which has been stripped away. It is time to receive back that which has been devoured, including, and especially, our health. Let there be healings. Let there be deliverances from depression, from confusion, from mental problems, and from physical issues. Let there be deliverance from cancer, from every form of sickness,

---

Joel 2:32 "And it will come about that whoever calls on the name of the LORD will be delivered; for on Mount Zion and in Jerusalem there will be those who escape, as the LORD has said, even among the survivors whom the LORD calls."

Joel 2:25 "Then I will make up to you for the years that the swarming locust has eaten, the creeping locust, the stripping locust, and the gnawing locust, My great army which I sent among you."

and from everything that would touch us on a physical level. Lord, heal Your people! Deliver back to us our health! Restore unto us the joy of our salvation (Psalm 51:12). We really have not received back enough compared with what has been taken away. We are expecting more from the Lord. Demand the return of everything that has been stolen from you: all of your health, your wealth, and your children. Satan demanded to take Peter from Christ. It is time for us to demand release. We demand the return of God's blessing and God's prosperity to His people.

We are a people set to worship God. We have come out of our testings with a determination: we will worship our God and we will serve Him. Our cry has become, "Thy Kingdom come. Thy will be done, in earth as it is in heaven." Our heart to worship and our heart to serve is our deliverance. We should have a tremendous expectation that the Lord's presence can move through us, through our churches and our families in our worship. We should anticipate a great deal of deliverance, healings, and breakthroughs in worship. We do not need to wait for anything; we can appropriate His deliverance right now. Lord, be enthroned on the praises of Your people (Psalm 22:3). Let the spirit of Christ dwell in our places of worship, and as He does, let there be a touch from the Lord in each person's life. We worship the Lord for all that He will do in our midst. Our worship demands, "Deliver us from evil, in the name of the Lord!"

Psalm 51:12 Restore to me the joy of Thy salvation, and sustain me with a willing spirit.

Psalm 22:3 Yet Thou art holy, O Thou who art enthroned upon the praises of Israel.

16 | The End of Our Testing

In this chapter, we want to continue our study of Matthew 6:13, which is the last verse of the Lord's Prayer. It reads, "And do not lead us into temptation, but deliver us from evil." This idea of being delivered from evil is very important for us. As we learned in the previous chapter, "testing" is a better translation than "temptation" in this verse. We also learned that testing involves being held captive for the purpose of torment and torture. Thus we are able to pray to the Father, "Do not lead us into testing." At the same time, we know that God allows testing; but it is satan who brings torment into the testing. We have lived in testing, so there is an intense drive in our spirits to pray, "Deliver us from evil" (Matthew 6:13). Testing is not the same as spiritual warfare or satanic hindrance. Testing comes to a conclusion; it has a beginning and an end. We are already deep into testing, and for that reason we pray, "Lord, bring the end of the testing, and deliver us from evil."

The Scriptures contain many examples of people who were tested for a period of time, and then their testing came to an end. We read in Genesis 22:1-2 that God tested Abraham by telling him to sacrifice his son Isaac. Abraham, in his faithfulness, did not withhold Isaac from being sacrificed, and so his testing came to an end (Genesis 22:10-12). Job was severely tested, but at some point God delivered him from the testing and began to work with him. Job went through many tormenting tests, but those tests had a beginning and an end; the time came when the testing was finished. We read in Matthew 4 that Jesus was tested. Again, that testing had a beginning and then there was a point at which Jesus said, "Begone, Satan!" and the testing ended (Matthew 4:10-11). Peter also went through testing, and that testing had a beginning and an end (Luke 22:31-32). Deuteronomy 8:2 describes Israel's time in the wilderness as the time when God was testing them. That testing too had a beginning and an end.

Every time you read about a testing in the Scriptures, you also see that it ends with a blessing and with God ministering to those who

---

Genesis 22:1-2 Now it came about after these things, that God tested Abraham, and said to him, "Abraham!" And he said, "Here I am." ² And He said, "Take now your son, your only son, whom you love, Isaac, and go to the land of Moriah; and offer him there as a burnt offering on one of the mountains of which I will tell you."

Genesis 22:10-12 And Abraham stretched out his hand, and took the knife to slay his son. ¹¹ But the angel of the LORD called to him from heaven, and said, "Abraham, Abraham!" And he said, "Here I am." ¹² And he said, "Do not stretch out your hand against the lad, and do nothing to him; for now I know that you fear God, since you have not withheld your son, your only son, from Me."

Matthew 4:10-11 Then Jesus said to him, "Begone, Satan! For it is written, 'YOU SHALL WORSHIP THE LORD YOUR GOD, AND SERVE HIM ONLY.'" ¹¹ Then the devil left Him; and behold, angels came and began to minister to Him.

Luke 22:31-32 "Simon, Simon, behold, Satan has demanded permission to sift you like wheat; ³² but I have prayed for you, that your faith may not fail; and you, when once you have turned again, strengthen your brothers."

Deuteronomy 8:2 "And you shall remember all the way which the LORD your God has led you in the wilderness these forty years, that He might humble you, testing you, to know what was in your heart, whether you would keep His commandments or not."

were tested (1 Peter 5:10). At the end of Abraham's testing, the angel came to him (Genesis 22:15-18). At the end of Job's testing, his eyes were opened to see God and he received a double portion (Job 42:5-6, 10). At the end of Israel's testing in the wilderness, they received the blessing of Canaan land (Joshua 1:1-4). When Jesus was finished with His testing in the wilderness, the angels came and ministered to Him (Matthew 4:11). What about the end of Peter's testing? We know that his testing was ended by the Day of Pentecost, when he was filled with the Spirit, stood up with the eleven, and spoke a Word from God (Acts 2:14).

We have lived in testing, and so it is probably too late to ask, "Lead us not into testing"; but it is not too late to cry to the Lord, "Deliver

---

1 Peter 5:10 And after you have suffered for a little while, the God of all grace, who called you to His eternal glory in Christ, will Himself perfect, confirm, strengthen and establish you.

Genesis 22:15-18 Then the angel of the LORD called to Abraham a second time from heaven, ¹⁶ and said, "By Myself I have sworn, declares the LORD, because you have done this thing, and have not withheld your son, your only son, ¹⁷ indeed I will greatly bless you, and I will greatly multiply your seed as the stars of the heavens, and as the sand which is on the seashore; and your seed shall possess the gate of their enemies. ¹⁸ And in your seed all the nations of the earth shall be blessed, because you have obeyed My voice."

Job 42:5-6 "I have heard of Thee by the hearing of the ear; but now my eye sees Thee; ⁶ therefore I retract, and I repent in dust and ashes."

Job 42:10 And the LORD restored the fortunes of Job when he prayed for his friends, and the LORD increased all that Job had twofold.

Joshua 1:1-4 Now it came about after the death of Moses the servant of the LORD that the LORD spoke to Joshua the son of Nun, Moses' servant, saying, ² "Moses My servant is dead; now therefore arise, cross this Jordan, you and all this people, to the land which I am giving to them, to the sons of Israel. ³ Every place on which the sole of your foot treads, I have given it to you, just as I spoke to Moses. ⁴ From the wilderness and this Lebanon, even as far as the great river, the river Euphrates, all the land of the Hittites, and as far as the Great Sea toward the setting of the sun, will be your territory."

Acts 2:14 But Peter, taking his stand with the eleven, raised his voice and declared to them: "Men of Judea, and all you who live in Jerusalem, let this be known to you, and give heed to my words."

us from evil!" (Matthew 6:13). Testing is different than spiritual warfare. For instance, we see that satan still came against Peter in his ministry after he was tested. There are several examples in the Scriptures of people coming against Peter to destroy or hinder him; however, that was different than his testing (Acts 4:1-3, 18-21; 5:17-18; 12:3-4). Christ said to Peter that satan had demanded permission to sift him like wheat (Luke 22:31). As we studied in the previous chapter, the implication in the original Greek is that Peter was turned over to the hands of satan to be tortured and tormented. That is the way testing is. According to Mark 1:12-13, the Spirit drove Christ into the wilderness, where He was put into satan's hands for testing. Do you see the difference? Testing involves being captured or imprisoned for torment and torture. Spiritual warfare comes against a free son of God whom satan is trying to destroy or hinder, but the protection of God and the immunity

---

Acts 4:1-3 And as they were speaking to the people, the priests and the captain of the temple guard, and the Sadducees, came upon them, ² being greatly disturbed because they were teaching the people and proclaiming in Jesus the resurrection from the dead. ³ And they laid hands on them, and put them in jail until the next day, for it was already evening.

Acts 4:18-21 And when they had summoned them, they commanded them not to speak or teach at all in the name of Jesus. ¹⁹ But Peter and John answered and said to them, "Whether it is right in the sight of God to give heed to you rather than to God, you be the judge; ²⁰ for we cannot stop speaking what we have seen and heard." ²¹ And when they had threatened them further, they let them go (finding no basis on which they might punish them) on account of the people, because they were all glorifying God for what had happened.

Acts 5:17-18 But the high priest rose up, along with all his associates (that is the sect of the Sadducees), and they were filled with jealousy; ¹⁸ and they laid hands on the apostles, and put them in a public jail.

Acts 12:3-4 And when he saw that it pleased the Jews, he proceeded to arrest Peter also. Now it was during the days of Unleavened Bread. ⁴ And when he had seized him, he put him in prison, delivering him to four squads of soldiers to guard him, intending after the Passover to bring him out before the people.

Mark 1:12-13 And immediately the Spirit impelled Him to go out into the wilderness. ¹³ And He was in the wilderness forty days being tempted by Satan; and He was with the wild beasts, and the angels were ministering to Him.

of the Spirit are in place. This place of immunity is where we want to live.

Satan complained to God concerning Job: "Why wouldn't Job worship You? You have a hedge of protection all around him" (Job 1:9-10). In other words, satan was walled off from Job. What happened in the testing was that Job, just like Peter, was put outside of those walls and into satan's atmosphere. After their testing, both of these men were delivered from the hands of the wicked one, and their walls of immunity were restored. Satan was still there attempting to destroy or hinder them through spiritual warfare, but he was outside of God's walls of immunity. That is different than testing, which involves the concept of being captured and tortured in prison.

When someone is turned over to satan to be tested, it is tormenting and destructive (1 Peter 5:8-9). You get the sense of that in Job 2:3, where we find the Lord saying to satan regarding Job, "And he still holds fast his integrity, although you incited Me against him, to ruin him without cause." We understand this capability, in testing, for satan to ruin and destroy what God has given us, because that has been our experience. It is one thing for satan to remain outside of the walls, or hedges, that God builds, and attack us the way someone would attack a fort; that is spiritual warfare. It is completely different to be locked in a prison for satan to torture and torment us. The impact of the torment we have experienced is beyond our understanding, and it is **not** a result of spiritual warfare. It is the result of satan being released against us in a time

---

Job 1:9-10 Then Satan answered the LORD, "Does Job fear God for nothing? [10] Hast Thou not made a hedge about him and his house and all that he has, on every side? Thou hast blessed the work of his hands, and his possessions have increased in the land."

1 Peter 5:8-9 Be of sober spirit, be on the alert. Your adversary, the devil, prowls about like a roaring lion, seeking someone to devour. [9] But resist him, firm in your faith, knowing that the same experiences of suffering are being accomplished by your brethren who are in the world.

of testing, and it has been for our ruin and destruction.

It may seem repetitive to keep pointing out the difference between testing and spiritual warfare, but many have blended these two concepts together until they are the same experience in their minds. We have felt the full force of satan turned loose against us, and we have called that spiritual warfare. But it has not been spiritual warfare; it has been testing. And if we have been in testing, and thus in the hands of satan, then we have the prerogative to pray, "Deliver us from evil" (Matthew 6:13). Paul wrote that God has "delivered us from the domain of darkness, and transferred us to the kingdom of His beloved Son" (Colossians 1:13). That is the concept. When we understand the difference between testing and spiritual warfare, then we recognize that testing has a beginning and an end. Therefore, I believe it is time for us to pray, "Deliver us from evil. Translate us out of this prison into the Kingdom of Your beloved Son. Deliver us out of the evil one's control, and put us within the walls of immunity and protection of Your Kingdom." We know that satan will rage against the Kingdom of God, and that there will be spiritual warfare, but we want to be protected inside the walls of the fortress of God in that warfare.

This concept became real to me during a conversation I had with a pastor. I realized that his situation and problems in his walk with God were not spiritual warfare. As he was talking about how difficult it was for him to break through, I thought to myself, "I know this person. This man has hungered after the Lord. He has repented before God. He has sought the will of God for his life. He is determined to be a man of righteousness, and to be a shepherd to God's flock. Yet year after year, I have watched his incapacity to experience what he was seeking." And the Lord spoke to me, "This is the result of testing." And He reminded me of 1 Peter 4:12-13:

> Beloved, do not be surprised at the fiery ordeal among you, which comes upon you for your testing, as though

some strange thing were happening to you; but to the degree that you share the sufferings of Christ, keep on rejoicing; so that also at the revelation of His glory, you may rejoice with exultation.

Going back to Job 2:3, we read, "And the LORD said to Satan, 'Have you considered My servant Job? For there is no one like him on the earth, a blameless and upright man fearing God and turning away from evil.'" We know, from reading the story, that Job was not only perfect, but according to God he was blameless and upright. That was God's opinion of Job. I had that same experience while talking to this pastor. I thought, "This is an upright man. This is a righteous man. This is a man who has sought God." Even more than this one individual, the Spirit was speaking to me about many in the Body of Christ who are righteous and upright and are seeking the Lord. The Lord reminded me that this experience of testing is not something unique to our fellowship and our churches, but it is a common ordeal throughout the whole Body of Christ, where men and women are pressing in to walk blamelessly and in righteousness before the Lord.

God is bringing forth His sons in the earth and, just like Job, there are none like them. There is nothing like what God is doing in the Body of Christ to raise up sons. Someone could point to all of their problems and failures and say, "These are a destroyed people. Therefore, Christ must not be working in their lives, because if He was, their lives would not be ruined." When you are tested, you never look good. But let's get one thing straight, the ruin is satan's; the righteousness is ours. The judgment is satan's; the integrity is ours. The uprightness and the blamelessness are ours in Christ Jesus, and I know the same is true for all throughout the Body of Christ who have experienced testing. Together, we reject the ruin brought by satan, because we are blameless and upright, fearing God and turning away from evil.

Has any one of us ever done evil? Of course we have. We have all sinned and have fallen short of the glory of God (Romans 3:23). But what do we do when we sin? We turn away from evil and we reject it. We fear God and we turn our hearts to Him. We repent before Him and draw the blood of Christ to cover our sin. We pray, "God, save us from our sin because we fear You, we love You, and we trust in Your salvation."

God said of Job, "And he still holds fast his integrity" (Job 2:3). Many have held on to the Word of God by pure faith in the midst of testings, torments, and tortures.

We can read about Christ's temptation, but we cannot really grasp what that was like for Him. We cannot really understand Peter's torment. Imagine denying Christ at the very hour of the Lord's trial and crucifixion. What a torment he must have gone through! Yet at some point, God saw that he was an upright man and held fast his faith (1 Peter 1:6-7). Peter did not walk in condemnation. He walked in the grace of God as a man of God, as an apostle of God, and he performed the works of God. He came out of that time of testing freed from condemnation, not with emotional scars that continued to torture him for the rest of his life. I also loose you from the condemnation that tries to follow you and speak to you all day long. You must say as Christ did, "Begone, Satan!" (Matthew 4:10).

"There is therefore now no condemnation for those who are in Christ Jesus" (Romans 8:1). When Peter was free from his testing, he was free from the condemnation, because the condemnation was satan's lie. And I loose us from the condemnation of satan's

---

Romans 3:23 For all have sinned and fall short of the glory of God.

1 Peter 1:6-7 In this you greatly rejoice, even though now for a little while, if necessary, you have been distressed by various trials, [7] that the proof of your faith, being more precious than gold which is perishable, even though tested by fire, may be found to result in praise and glory and honor at the revelation of Jesus Christ.

lie. Everything that has been said to you, about you, and against you by satan, we bring into judgment, in the name of the Lord. We say, "Begone, satan! Begone from this family. Begone from the Body of Christ, in the name of the Lord." We are blameless. We are upright. We are fearing God. We are a people who turn away from evil. We are a people who hold fast to the Word of God (1 Corinthians 15:1-2). We are a people who walk in the integrity of Christ before God, despite the ruin that satan has brought. We understand that there is a difference between the testings we have experienced and spiritual warfare. We also understand that the testing has a beginning and an end. We pray, "Lord, if You have not finished testing us, then finish now!" Today, we declare the end of the testing, in the name of the Lord, and we cry out, "Deliver us from evil" (Matthew 6:13).

We read at the end of Abraham's test, "But the angel of the LORD called to him from heaven, and said, 'Abraham, Abraham!' And he said, 'Here I am.' And he said, 'Do not stretch out your hand against the lad, and do nothing to him; for now I know that you fear God, since you have not withheld your son, your only son, from Me'" (Genesis 22:11-12). We have not withheld anything from God. Therefore, at some point, He will say to us, "I know that you fear God and that you have not withheld anything from Me." God received Isaac from Abraham, and the testing ended. God also knows that you fear Him and that you will not withhold anything of your life from Him, so the testing must end. At the end of Abraham's testing, the angel came to minister to him. As the restoration of the Lord comes to us, the angels will begin to minister. Therefore we pray, "Lead us not into testing, but deliver us from evil."

---

1 Corinthians 15:1-2 Now I make known to you, brethren, the gospel which I preached to you, which also you received, in which also you stand, ² by which also you are saved, if you hold fast the word which I preached to you, unless you believed in vain.

Lord, send Your angels to minister refreshing to Your people. Bless us, Lord, so that our lives are able to fulfill Your Word, rather than be ruined. Allow Your power and Your promises to come forth from Your people. Let us finally be able to be for You, and for one another, what is in our hearts to be, and what Your Word says that we are. Let us live as Christ lived on this earth to do Your will, to speak Your Word, and to bring this age into Your Kingdom. We have lived under the absolute torment of not being able in our hearts to do Your will, but we establish this word as the reality for our lives today. Lord, bless us to do Your will. Fulfill Your promise in Jeremiah 31:33 that You will put Your Word in our hearts, and we will be able to live it, become it, and speak it. Amen.

Jeremiah 31:33   "But this is the covenant which I will make with the house of Israel after those days," declares the LORD, "I will put My law within them, and on their heart I will write it; and I will be their God, and they shall be My people."

17 | The Reason for Total Judgment

In this chapter, we continue our study of Matthew 6:13: "And do not lead us into temptation, but deliver us from evil." In the previous chapter, we related this verse to the scriptural examples of Job and Peter, who were both handed over to satan for testing. They were literally held captive and tormented by satan, just as many of us have also experienced. It is a mystery to us how satan is given such access to our lives, and it makes it more real to us why we need to pray, "Do not lead us into temptation [or testing], but deliver us from evil" (Matthew 6:13). The Lord knows that we must be delivered from the hand of evil, where we have been held captive. Living in a state of testing is not the fulfillment that God has for us. We have lived under the testing for many years, and through it all we have believed the prophecies that the Lord has spoken to us and have not let go of the Word. Today our declaration is that we are delivered from the testing into the fulfillment of that Word.

As long as we are in a time of testing, in which we are experiencing the reality of satan imprisoning us to try us and torment us, much of our energy and faith is expended in the process of just hanging on. It is true that during Job's testing, he never let go of his integrity;

that speaks of his ability spiritually to hang on to the Word and to hang on to faith (Job 2:3). However, that is different than moving in the effective outworking of ministry. Peter's time of testing was not a time when the Holy Spirit moved effectively through him; he was not yet moving in his destiny as an apostle. In the midst of his testing, he went back to Galilee, gathered the disciples, and they all went fishing (John 21:3). Now, there is nothing wrong with fishing, but it is not really the work of an apostle. Besides that, he did not catch any fish!

When we trust the Lord and believe who we are, believing the Word that is spoken, it is reckoned to us as righteousness (Romans 4:3). It is wonderful that we hang on to the Word during times of testing. Yet as good as that is, we are ready to do the Word, not just hang on to it. Look at the difference for Peter after the breakthrough came. As an apostle, he was delivering people, instead of fishing; he was speaking the Word; he was breaking down barriers and seeing thousands come to Christ (Acts 2:14, 41). Tremendous things happened through him after his testing was completed. He did miracles, signs, and wonders, and he stirred

---

Job 2:3 And the LORD said to Satan, "Have you considered My servant Job? For there is no one like him on the earth, a blameless and upright man fearing God and turning away from evil. And he still holds fast his integrity, although you incited Me against him, to ruin him without cause."

John 21:3 Simon Peter said to them, "I am going fishing." They said to him, "We will also come with you." They went out, and got into the boat; and that night they caught nothing.

Romans 4:3 For what does the Scripture say? "AND ABRAHAM BELIEVED GOD, AND IT WAS RECKONED TO HIM AS RIGHTEOUSNESS."

Acts 2:14 But Peter, taking his stand with the eleven, raised his voice and declared to them: "Men of Judea, and all you who live in Jerusalem, let this be known to you, and give heed to my words."

Acts 2:41 So then, those who had received his word were baptized; and there were added that day about three thousand souls.

up Jerusalem (Acts 5:12-15). He had visions and saw the Holy Spirit fall on the Gentiles (Acts 10:9-11; 44-45). That is better than fishing, and far more effective for the Kingdom of God.

It is a great blessing and credit to be reckoned as righteous because we believe, like Abraham believed (Romans 4:3, 23-24). Having faith and holding on to faith is a tremendous thing to do, and there is a blessing that comes back to us in that process. We rejoice when it is said of us, "They are a people of integrity. No matter what comes against them, they believe the Word." However, once we are released from our testing, it should then be said of us, "These who have turned the world upside down have come here also!" (Acts 17:6). There are two different realities. I thank God for the grace to be able to hang on through these years of testing, but that

---

Acts 5:12-15 And at the hands of the apostles many signs and wonders were taking place among the people; and they were all with one accord in Solomon's portico. [13] But none of the rest dared to associate with them; however, the people held them in high esteem. [14] And all the more believers in the Lord, multitudes of men and women, were constantly added to their number; [15] to such an extent that they even carried the sick out into the streets, and laid them on cots and pallets, so that when Peter came by, at least his shadow might fall on any one of them.

Acts 10:9-11 And on the next day, as they were on their way, and approaching the city, Peter went up on the housetop about the sixth hour to pray. [10] And he became hungry, and was desiring to eat; but while they were making preparations, he fell into a trance; [11] and he beheld the sky opened up, and a certain object like a great sheet coming down, lowered by four corners to the ground.

Acts 10:44-45 While Peter was still speaking these words, the Holy Spirit fell upon all those who were listening to the message. [45] And all the circumcised believers who had come with Peter were amazed, because the gift of the Holy Spirit had been poured out upon the Gentiles also.

Romans 4:23-24 Now not for his sake only was it written, that it was reckoned to him, [24] but for our sake also, to whom it will be reckoned, as those who believe in Him who raised Jesus our Lord from the dead.

Acts 17:6 And when they did not find them, they began dragging Jason and some brethren before the city authorities, shouting, "These men who have upset the world have come here also."

must come to an end and be replaced by the actual fulfillment of the Word of God through a people. There must be a complete release and deliverance from the testing of the enemy until we find the force and power and working of the Holy Spirit turned loose through us.

A passage of Scripture in Isaiah 49 describes the true nature of testing and how the deliverance comes.

> "Can the prey be taken from the mighty man, or the captives of a tyrant be rescued?" Surely, thus says the LORD, "Even the captives of the mighty man will be taken away, and the prey of the tyrant will be rescued; for I will contend with the one who contends with you, and I will save your sons. And I will feed your oppressors with their own flesh, and they will become drunk with their own blood as with sweet wine; and all flesh will know that I, the LORD, am your Savior, and your Redeemer, the Mighty One of Jacob." (Isaiah 49:24-26)

When Peter was tested, he was literally put into the hands of satan (Luke 22:31-32). He became a prey; he became "the captive of the mighty man." Once this happens to you, these verses in Isaiah 49 become your cry. You wonder, "Is there any way out of this? Is there any deliverance? Can I be released from the hand of the mighty man?" Peter must have felt that way. The only way we come back from being taken captive is that the Lord contends for us. Our deliverance literally requires that the Lord contends with our captor.

Luke 22:31-32 "Simon, Simon, behold, Satan has demanded permission to sift you like wheat; ³² but I have prayed for you, that your faith may not fail; and you, when once you have turned again, strengthen your brothers."

Isaiah 49 is a beautiful prophecy over Israel, and also over us, because we are grafted into Abraham through salvation in Christ (Romans 11:13-14, 17-18). The spiritual fulfillment of prophecy always follows the pattern of the natural that was manifested in the Old Testament Scriptures. When Judah was held captive in Babylon, they had a natural captor. When we are held captive in testing, our captor is spiritual. We are not talking about a struggle based on issues or arguments between people. We do not war against flesh and blood, but against principalities and powers (Ephesians 6:12). The weapons we use are spiritual, and they are mighty to the tearing down of strongholds (2 Corinthians 10:4). What we are talking about is bringing down the kingdom of satan into judgment, so that the Kingdom of God is free to reign on the earth. As we read in Isaiah 49, in order for Israel to be free, for God's people to be loosed, there had to be a corresponding response of the Lord contending against their oppressor. Judgment had to be turned loose. When we also come into this process of testing, of being held captive for the purpose of trial—as Abraham was, as Job was, and as Peter was—we understand that God is setting up the release of His judgments against our spiritual oppressor.

Romans 11:13-14 But I am speaking to you who are Gentiles. Inasmuch then as I am an apostle of Gentiles, I magnify my ministry, [14] if somehow I might move to jealousy my fellow countrymen and save some of them.

Romans 11:17-18 But if some of the branches were broken off, and you, being a wild olive, were grafted in among them and became partaker with them of the rich root of the olive tree, [18] do not be arrogant toward the branches; but if you are arrogant, remember that it is not you who supports the root, but the root supports you.

Ephesians 6:12 For our struggle is not against flesh and blood, but against the rulers, against the powers, against the world forces of this darkness, against the spiritual forces of wickedness in the heavenly places.

2 Corinthians 10:4 For the weapons of our warfare are not of the flesh, but divinely powerful for the destruction of fortresses.

Revelation 12:7-10 speaks of the war in heaven. That war happens for a reason—it is God who redeems His people who have been captured, and He brings judgment on their captor. The prophecies of the Hebrew Scriptures about the restoration of Israel and Jacob are always in the context of deliverance with judgment. This is because whenever you come under satan's dominion, he will never let you go. You must be delivered out of the dominion of darkness in order to be delivered into the Kingdom of the Son of His love (Colossians 1:13). Deliverance with judgment is required, because there is no way satan will ever let go of anything that is placed in his hands. Isaiah 14:17 describes this characteristic of satan: "Who made the world like a wilderness and overthrew its cities, who did not allow his prisoners to go home?" Satan does not allow his prisoners to go home. Anything that he has been given access to, in his mind, is his forever, and he will never let go of it. As far as satan was concerned, once Israel was in Babylon, he owned them forever. It is not his personality to let go of anything that he feels is under his dominion, and that is why there must be judgment.

Pharaoh is one of the greatest pictures of satan in the Old Testament. Pharaoh took Israel captive and he never planned to let them go. Therefore, the story of the Passover had to be the story of judgment. There was no other way. It began with a request. The Lord sent Moses with the Word of the Lord to Pharaoh and

---

Revelation 12:7-10 And there was war in heaven, Michael and his angels waging war with the dragon. And the dragon and his angels waged war, [8] and they were not strong enough, and there was no longer a place found for them in heaven. [9] And the great dragon was thrown down, the serpent of old who is called the devil and Satan, who deceives the whole world; he was thrown down to the earth, and his angels were thrown down with him. [10] And I heard a loud voice in heaven, saying, "Now the salvation, and the power, and the kingdom of our God and the authority of His Christ have come, for the accuser of our brethren has been thrown down, who accuses them before our God day and night."

Colossians 1:13 For He delivered us from the domain of darkness, and transferred us to the kingdom of His beloved Son.

requested, "Let My people go" (Exodus 7:16). The Lord said, "I am ready for My people to be free from Egypt. It is time for them to go." Pharaoh's response was, "No way!" (Exodus 7:22-23). In response to that, the Lord began a series of judgments, one judgment after another. Yet Pharaoh would never let them go. He was so set that he would even see his own kingdom destroyed before he would let the Israelites go. That is a picture of what is happening to us. Satan's kingdom in the heavens and on this earth will be destroyed by God in judgments because satan will never let mankind go. He will never let the sons of God go free, and so God will increase the judgments and the severity of those judgments, and they will happen progressively, one after another.

You are right in the middle of this story, because you are what God is asking for. In this generation, God is coming to the kingdom of satan, to satan himself, saying, "Let My people go. They may have been put in your hand, as was Peter, as was Job, in a time of testing. But now I am convinced of their faith." That is what God said about Abraham: "For now I know that you fear God, since you would have not withheld your son, your only son, from Me" (Genesis 22:12). God comes to us as well and says, "Now I know you fear Me, as I have seen your faithfulness over all these years." The only question is, will satan let us go? We know that it is not his personality to do so. This is seen in Exodus 14:1-4:

> Now the LORD spoke to Moses, saying, "Tell the sons of Israel to turn back and camp before Pi-hahiroth, between Migdol and the sea; you shall camp in front of

---

Exodus 7:16 "And you will say to him, 'The LORD, the God of the Hebrews, sent me to you, saying, "Let My people go, that they may serve Me in the wilderness. But behold, you have not listened until now." ' "

Exodus 7:22-23 But the magicians of Egypt did the same with their secret arts; and Pharaoh's heart was hardened, and he did not listen to them, as the LORD had said. 23 Then Pharaoh turned and went into his house with no concern even for this.

Baal-zephon, opposite it, by the sea. For Pharaoh will say of the sons of Israel, 'They are wandering aimlessly in the land; the wilderness has shut them in.' Thus I will harden Pharaoh's heart, and he will chase after them; and I will be honored through Pharaoh and all his army, and the Egyptians will know that I am the LORD." And they did so.

They were not in Egypt any longer. They were already free. They were delivered, and yet Pharaoh still pursued them, demanding, "I want them back!" (Exodus 14:5-8). Have you ever experienced a real deliverance, only to question, "Am I free? Did I really get delivered? It seems to me like it has gotten worse rather than better!" This is because satan's behavior is the same as Pharaoh's. Even when forced to let us go, he continues to pursue us. Therefore, we continue to believe; we continue to hold on; but we also cry out to the Lord, "Deliver us from evil! Bring judgment on our captor because he will never let us go. He will never release his hold, and it requires Your involvement." God said, "For I will contend with the one who contends with you, and I will save your sons. And I will feed your oppressors with their own flesh" (Isaiah 49:25-26). It is time, Lord. It is time that the satanic kingdom, that satan himself, our oppressor, is judged. We are saying, "Lord, all we can do is hang on; but You can contend with him who contends with us. You can rescue us from the tyrant. You can free us from the mighty man because he is not mightier than You. Lord, our hearts are crying unto You to free us from the oppressor and deliver us from

---

Exodus 14:5-8 When the king of Egypt was told that the people had fled, Pharaoh and his servants had a change of heart toward the people, and they said, "What is this we have done, that we have let Israel go from serving us?" 6 So he made his chariot ready and took his people with him; 7 and he took six hundred select chariots, and all the other chariots of Egypt with officers over all of them. 8 And the LORD hardened the heart of Pharaoh, king of Egypt, and he chased after the sons of Israel as the sons of Israel were going out boldly.

the hand of the tyrant by Your strength. It is not because of our strength. It is not because of our righteousness. It is not because we have hung on to Your Word in faith. It is for Your name's sake that You will contend with the oppressor who will never let us go. Lord, You will overpower him."

Jesus said,

> "But if I cast out demons by the finger of God, then the kingdom of God has come upon you. When a strong man, fully armed, guards his own homestead, his possessions are undisturbed; but when someone stronger than he attacks him and overpowers him, he takes away from him all his armor on which he had relied, and distributes his plunder." (Luke 11:20-22)

It seems impossible that anyone could overpower the strong man, but Christ did (Colossians 2:15). He has already won the victory (1 Corinthians 15:57). Now it is a matter of executing what is already the reality. We believe in the reality of deliverance, by the blood of Jesus Christ, from the testing and trials that satan puts upon us. It does not matter how strong the strong man is who binds us; there is one who is stronger than he. Therefore we pray, "Lord, attack our enemy and overpower him; take away his armor and disarm him. Strip away the armaments of satan, the armaments of principalities, the armaments of powers, and the armaments of the demons. Lord, disarm satan's kingdom and his entire army."

Christ taught us to pray, "Deliver us from evil" (Matthew 6:13). That is what we are asking. It seems like a simple thing to pray, but when you pray that prayer, you are initiating the war of the ages.

Colossians 2:15 When He had disarmed the rulers and authorities, He made a public display of them, having triumphed over them through Him.

1 Corinthians 15:57 But thanks be to God, who gives us the victory through our Lord Jesus Christ.

You are initiating God moving against the oppressor, because just like Pharaoh, satan will never let go. What the Passover tells us is that God and His Kingdom will win the struggle against the evil of satan and his nation. Satan's nation will be destroyed, along with its armaments and its armies, and it will never rise again. We are the ones whom God is asking satan to let go. We will not have a little deliverance; we will have a thorough and complete deliverance. As we read in 1 John 3:8, "The Son of God appeared for this purpose, that He might destroy the works of the devil." Satan himself will end up being destroyed in this process.

Have you ever asked, "Lord, how long will this go on?" That was the cry of those who had suffered because they held on to the testimony of Jesus: "How long, O Lord?" (Revelation 6:10). It seems to be taking a very long time. It is difficult to understand why it seems to take so long, but the reason is that it must be complete. When the Passover story was done, there was no Pharaoh, there was no army, there were no chariots, and there were no horses (Exodus 14:28). It was all gone. Our deliverance will be that thorough.

Although it may seem at times that we are wandering around in a wilderness and satan is pursuing us, we stand in faith. We are holding on to the Word of faith, and we ask the Lord to contend with our oppressor, the one who contends with us. We ask without doubting that the Lord is stronger. We say, "Overpower him, Lord! Take away his armor and take us as Your plunder. We are spoils

---

Revelation 6:10 And they cried out with a loud voice, saying, "How long, O Lord, holy and true, wilt Thou refrain from judging and avenging our blood on those who dwell on the earth?"

Exodus 14:28 And the waters returned and covered the chariots and the horsemen, even Pharaoh's entire army that had gone into the sea after them; not even one of them remained.

of war to You. You are our Father and we become Your sons. You have won us to Yourself. You are the strong man who is stronger than our captor. Move on our behalf, Lord. Move; deliver us from evil. It is the time."

18 | Don't Put the Lord, Your God, to the Test

In our study of the Lord's Prayer, we have devoted these last chapters to Matthew 6:13: "And do not lead us into temptation, but deliver us from evil." As we have said, the word "temptation" in this verse is better translated as "testing." We have lived in the testings of the Lord, and we have cried out in our hearts, "Lord, deliver us from evil." Yet we still have a lack of understanding of what the testings are all about. In this chapter, we want to solidify our understanding of what God is working in us through testing.

What is God doing by testing us? What is it that He is looking for? What is it that He is working in our hearts and spirits? When you are tested, it seems very confusing (1 Peter 4:12). The truth is that testing is very straightforward and simple to understand, if you view it from the perspective of what is happening in your heart where the Lord is concerned. God allows testings, which have a deep purpose in the perfection of our spirits and in the perfection

---

1 Peter 4:12 Beloved, do not be surprised at the fiery ordeal among you, which comes upon you for your testing, as though some strange thing were happening to you.

of our relationship with the Lord. Testing has a purpose; it has a reason. Testing has a beginning and an end, and God is looking for the fruit that the testing produces in us (Hebrews 12:10-11).

When you read the scriptural examples of people who were tested, you see that their testing always preceded the expression of God's ministry through them. Peter went through testing before moving in the apostolic ministry (Luke 22:31-32). Before Jesus began His ministry, He was baptized in water; the Holy Spirit rested upon Him and led Him into the wilderness to be tempted by the devil (Matthew 3:16—4:1). This word "tempted" is from the same Greek word as "temptation" in Matthew 6:13, which we understand means "testing."[14] Immediately following His testing, Jesus began moving in the three-and-a-half-year ministry as the Christ, the Anointed One. Even the Lord experienced testing before moving as the Anointed One in the earth. Testing has that same purpose for us in this day.

God is preparing a people for His use, to minister His Word, to minister His will, and to bring forth His Kingdom in the world. At a time when many people believe that they will be pulled out of this age in a "rapture," we believe that the Lord is preparing us to be His

---

Hebrews 12:10-11 For they disciplined us for a short time as seemed best to them, but He disciplines us for our good, that we may share His holiness. [11] All discipline for the moment seems not to be joyful, but sorrowful; yet to those who have been trained by it, afterwards it yields the peaceful fruit of righteousness.

Luke 22:31-32 "Simon, Simon, behold, Satan has demanded permission to sift you like wheat; [32] but I have prayed for you, that your faith may not fail; and you, when once you have turned again, strengthen your brothers."

Matthew 3:16—4:1 And after being baptized, Jesus went up immediately from the water; and behold, the heavens were opened, and he saw the Spirit of God descending as a dove, and coming upon Him, [17] and behold, a voice out of the heavens, saying, "This is My beloved Son, in whom I am well-pleased." [1] Then Jesus was led up by the Spirit into the wilderness to be tempted by the devil.

[14.] Ceslas Spicq and James D. Ernest, *Theological Lexicon of the New Testament* (Peabody, MA: Hendrickson Publishers, 1994), 80.

instruments in this age. Testing is a necessary part of becoming His instruments in the earth. Before this great anointing of the end time rests upon a body of people, they experience a testing. They experience a trial that is almost beyond imagination in what they suffer. It is the preparation for the anointing and for the ministry that will be released through God's people. From that standpoint we say, "Thank You, Lord, for putting us in this process."

An important point about testing is found in Deuteronomy:

> "And you shall remember all the way which the LORD your God has led you in the wilderness these forty years, that He might humble you, testing you, to know what was in your heart, whether you would keep His commandments or not." (Deuteronomy 8:2)

For the children of Israel, the wilderness was a testing. When you read about their wanderings, it can seem that God was just tormenting them. They went without water; they went without food; they were in the turmoil of the desert; but God was doing something in their hearts. God is also doing something in us. As much as these days of testing have not been a pleasant experience, we remember all of the way that the Lord has led us. We will look back on the days of testing and remember all that God has taken us through, because these testings will sustain us in the days of anointing. They will sustain us in the days of blessing so that we will not waver in our relationship to the Lord.

> "And He humbled you and let you be hungry, and fed you with manna which you did not know, nor did your fathers know, that He might make you understand that man does not live by bread alone, but man lives by everything that proceeds out of the mouth of the LORD." (Deuteronomy 8:3)

Not only did the children of Israel not know the manna, they also did not like it (Numbers 21:5). There are many times in the testing when you do not like what God is feeding you, either. But God was trying to teach them something. He was teaching them that life does not come from what man can produce or manufacture. Instead, life comes by every Word that the Lord speaks. We can talk about the Living Word, and we can talk about believing in the Word, but God wants us in the place where we truly live by the Word. He is making us aware that there is nothing we can do in ourselves, and there is nothing anyone else can do, because life and fulfillment come by every Word that the Lord speaks (John 15:5).

> "Your clothing did not wear out on you, nor did your foot swell these forty years. Thus you are to know in your heart that the LORD your God was disciplining you just as a man disciplines his son. Therefore, you shall keep the commandments of the LORD your God, to walk in His ways and to fear Him. For the LORD your God is bringing you into a good land, a land of brooks of water, of fountains and springs, flowing forth in valleys and hills; a land of wheat and barley, of vines and fig trees and pomegranates, a land of olive oil and honey; a land where you shall eat food without scarcity, in which you shall not lack anything; a land whose stones are iron, and out of whose hills you can dig copper. When you have eaten and are satisfied, you shall bless the LORD your God for the good land which He has given you." (Deuteronomy 8:4-10)

We need to lock this truth into our hearts: God is seeking to bless

---

Numbers 21:5 And the people spoke against God and Moses, "Why have you brought us up out of Egypt to die in the wilderness? For there is no food and no water, and we loathe this miserable food."

John 15:5 "I am the vine, you are the branches; he who abides in Me, and I in him, he bears much fruit; for apart from Me you can do nothing."

us. When you are in the wilderness you say, "All this testing is painful! This is horrible! I don't like it!" The wilderness is not a fun place. The point is that God is determined to bless you. He will bless you. He is bringing you to a good land, and He is bringing you into fulfillment. Highlight in your Bible verses 6 through 10 of Deuteronomy 8, because they describe what He is giving you. Then remember how He gives it to you: by the Word.

> "Beware lest you forget the LORD your God by not keeping His commandments and His ordinances and His statutes which I am commanding you today; lest, when you have eaten and are satisfied, and have built good houses and lived in them, and when your herds and your flocks multiply, and your silver and gold multiply, and all that you have multiplies, then your heart becomes proud, and you forget the LORD your God who brought you out from the land of Egypt, out of the house of slavery." (Deuteronomy 8:11-14)

He brings us out of the house of slavery. He sets us free. In the previous chapters, we talked about Peter's testing. Peter was turned over to the hands of satan; he was captured by him and enslaved. Our testing is like being enslaved. God will bring us out through judgment on our oppressor (Isaiah 49:24-26), but He wants us to learn something very important from our time of testing. He will

---

Isaiah 49:24-26 "Can the prey be taken from the mighty man, or the captives of a tyrant be rescued?" [25] Surely, thus says the LORD, "Even the captives of the mighty man will be taken away, and the prey of the tyrant will be rescued; for I will contend with the one who contends with you, and I will save your sons. [26] And I will feed your oppressors with their own flesh, and they will become drunk with their own blood as with sweet wine; and all flesh will know that I, the LORD, am your Savior, and your Redeemer, the Mighty One of Jacob."

deliver us from slavery (Hebrews 2:14-15), but first He works in our hearts a knowledge, an eternal memory, that none of this is from ourselves. He is the One who delivers us. He is the One who frees us. He is the One who blesses us. "Otherwise, you may say in your heart, 'My power and the strength of my hand made me this wealth.' But you shall remember the LORD your God, for it is He who is giving you power to make wealth, that He may confirm His covenant which He swore to your fathers, as it is this day" (Deuteronomy 8:17-18). God will confirm His covenant. Every Word that He has spoken to you He will confirm. He will fulfill every Word, and He will do it by Himself.

"Hear, O Israel!" The Hebrew word for "hear" is *Shema*,[15] which does not only mean "to hear," but "to obey."

> "Hear [and obey], O Israel! You are crossing over the Jordan today to go in to dispossess nations greater and mightier than you, great cities fortified to heaven, a people great and tall, the sons of the Anakim, whom you know and of whom you have heard it said, 'Who can stand before the sons of Anak?'" (Deuteronomy 9:1-2)

We have experienced spiritual warfare, but it is for a reason: we are going in to possess. We go in to possess nations in the heavenly places that are greater than us. We see the strong man who is protecting his house—like the sons of Anak, greater and mightier

---

Hebrews 2:14-15 Since then the children share in flesh and blood, He Himself likewise also partook of the same, that through death He might render powerless him who had the power of death, that is, the devil; [15] and might deliver those who through fear of death were subject to slavery all their lives.

[15.] James Swanson, *Dictionary of Biblical Languages with Semantic Domains: Hebrew (Old Testament)* (Oak Harbor: Logos Research Systems, Inc., 1997). *Shema* is not proper transliteration, however, it is the common usage today.

than us (Numbers 13:28, 31). Nevertheless, He said, "You will dispossess them."

> "Know therefore today that it is the LORD your God who is crossing over before you as a consuming fire. He will destroy them and He will subdue them before you, so that you may drive them out and destroy them quickly, just as the LORD has spoken to you. Do not say in your heart when the LORD your God has driven them out before you, 'Because of my righteousness the LORD has brought me in to possess this land,' but it is because of the wickedness of these nations that the LORD is dispossessing them before you." (Deuteronomy 9:3-4)

When we bring down the principalities and powers over the nations, it will not be because of our righteousness. It is only because of their wickedness that the Lord will use us as His instruments. He has emptied us to use us as instruments to speak His Word. We do not live by bread alone—it is not by what we do. It is only by His Word, His force, His power and His righteousness that He brings an end to the wickedness.

> "Know, then, it is not because of your righteousness that the LORD your God is giving you this good land to possess, for you are a stubborn people. Remember, do not forget how you provoked the LORD your God to wrath in the wilderness; from the day that you left the land of Egypt until you arrived at this place, you have been rebellious against the LORD." (Deuteronomy 9:6-7)

Numbers 13:28 "Nevertheless, the people who live in the land are strong, and the cities are fortified and very large; and moreover, we saw the descendants of Anak there."

Numbers 13:31 But the men who had gone up with him said, "We are not able to go up against the people, for they are too strong for us."

These passages that we read in Deuteronomy chapters 8 and 9 describe how Moses exhorted the children of Israel before they crossed the Jordan. They were getting ready to cross over and move as conquerors, to possess the land and to receive the blessing and fulfillment of what God had spoken. Similarly, when Jesus began His ministry, He went to the Jordan. After He was baptized and the Spirit descended upon Him, the Spirit drove, or impelled, Him into the wilderness (Mark 1:9-12). There God took Christ through exactly the same pattern of testing that He took Israel through in the wilderness, because He was working the same thing in Jesus as He was working in Israel. Remember that the testing precedes the anointing.

> And Jesus, full of the Holy Spirit, returned from the Jordan and was led about by the Spirit in the wilderness for forty days, being tempted by the devil. And He ate nothing during those days; and when they had ended, He became hungry. And the devil said to Him, "If You are the Son of God, tell this stone to become bread." And Jesus answered him, "It is written, 'MAN SHALL NOT LIVE ON BREAD ALONE.'" (Luke 4:1-4)

Satan said, "Make bread. Provide for yourself." And Jesus answered, "Man cannot provide for himself. He lives by the Word of God." It has to be God's Word fulfilled by God.

> And he led Him up and showed Him all the kingdoms of the world in a moment of time. And the devil said to Him, "I will give You all this domain and its glory; for it has been handed over to me, and I give it to whomever

---

Mark 1:9-12 And it came about in those days that Jesus came from Nazareth in Galilee, and was baptized by John in the Jordan. [10] And immediately coming up out of the water, He saw the heavens opening, and the Spirit like a dove descending upon Him; [11] and a voice came out of the heavens: "Thou art My beloved Son, in Thee I am well-pleased." [12] And immediately the Spirit impelled Him to go out into the wilderness.

I wish. Therefore if You worship before me, it shall all be Yours." And Jesus answered and said to him, "It is written, 'You shall worship the Lord your God and serve Him only.'" (Luke 4:5-8)

Satan tested Christ with the exact dominion that God had promised Him. The Father already was going to give all of creation into the hands of Christ. Satan came and said, "Let me give it to you. Do it another way. Don't get the promise by worshiping God, by giving Him the credit." Do you remember those verses in Deuteronomy that describe all the blessings and everything God wants to give you? Satan is always trying to give you what God has already promised that He will give you. One of the biggest challenges you grapple with is how to think about what God has already promised you. The blessings that God has promised you can become such an issue in your own heart that you start to think, "The Lord promised me blessings. He promised me a blessing on my children and a blessing on my finances"; and you can become tempted to grasp for those things, but in a way that is not believing that God will do what He said. In contrast, worship says, "Lord, You are everything. You are the only thing. You are all there is, and for me in my life there is nothing else other than that which comes from You."

When you are tested, you are being tested to see how you will receive the promises of God. Will you try to get them another way? Will you credit yourself, or credit the world, or credit some other means of appropriating the blessings of God? Jesus said, "There is no other way." As we read in Deuteronomy, the Lord said to the children of Israel, "Once you have all of these blessings, will you say, 'My hand did it'? Will you say, 'Someone else gave this to me'? Or will you bless the Lord your God and worship Him only?" When you experience the fulfillment of His Word, will you give yourself in service back to Him, and worship Him because you understand that all you have only comes from Him

(John 3:27)? Your fulfillment involves nothing from you. There can be no pride of the flesh. That is why He said, "I humbled you" (Deuteronomy 8:3). Why does He humble us? Humiliation is not very fun, but He humbles us so that in our hearts we can distinguish between what He has given us and what we have done for ourselves. Through all eternity we will worship God. Through all eternity we will serve God, because everything that we have is from Him. This is what Christ had in His spirit.

> And he led Him to Jerusalem and had Him stand on the pinnacle of the temple, and said to Him, "If You are the Son of God, throw Yourself down from here; for it is written, 'HE WILL GIVE HIS ANGELS CHARGE CONCERNING YOU TO GUARD YOU,' and, 'ON their HANDS THEY WILL BEAR YOU UP, LEST YOU STRIKE YOUR FOOT AGAINST A STONE.'" And Jesus answered and said to him, "It is said, 'YOU SHALL NOT PUT THE LORD YOUR GOD TO THE TEST.'" (Luke 4:9-12)

You have to remember who is testing whom. God is testing you. Sometimes it becomes easy to try to test God with His own Word. Satan quoted Scriptures that were prophecies written of Christ: "I will give the angels charge, lest You strike Your foot against a stone" (Psalm 91:11-12). Then he said to Jesus, "Okay, make this happen. Test the Lord. Make God come through with His Word." We cannot turn any of our prayer or prophecy or crying out to God into a test of Him and His Word. We cannot be testing Him. We must be the ones who receive testing from Him. We must be living in a faith that says, "You spoke these things, and You will

---

John 3:27 John answered and said, "A man can receive nothing, unless it has been given him from heaven."

Psalm 91:11-12 For He will give His angels charge concerning you, to guard you in all your ways. [12] They will bear you up in their hands, lest you strike your foot against a stone.

manifest them to me. You will bless me. I do not live by bread alone. I live by Your Word—Your Word fulfilled by Your hand." It is God who will give us the land. It is God who will bring the end of the testing. He will bring the fulfillment of the Word, of the prophecies, and of all that He has spoken to us.

Position yourself in humility before the Lord. Check your spirit and make sure that you are not falling into the error of testing the Lord. The Lord was angry with the children of Israel because they tested Him in the wilderness. We must make sure we are free from this in our own hearts and spirits. Psalm 95, written years after the events of the wilderness, warned a new generation against testing God (Psalm 95:7-11). The Book of Hebrews contains the same warning (Hebrews 3:7-11). These Words apply to us today. Do not be like those who failed to enter the promised rest because they tested God (Hebrews 4:1-3).

Psalm 95:7-11 For He is our God, and we are the people of His pasture, and the sheep of His hand. Today, if you would hear His voice, ⁸ do not harden your hearts, as at Meribah, as in the day of Massah in the wilderness; ⁹ "When your fathers tested Me, they tried Me, though they had seen My work. ¹⁰ For forty years I loathed that generation, and said they are a people who err in their heart, and they do not know My ways. ¹¹ Therefore I swore in My anger, truly they shall not enter into My rest."

Hebrews 3:7-11 Therefore, just as the Holy Spirit says, "TODAY IF YOU HEAR HIS VOICE, ⁸ DO NOT HARDEN YOUR HEARTS AS WHEN THEY PROVOKED ME, AS IN THE DAY OF TRIAL IN THE WILDERNESS, ⁹ WHERE YOUR FATHERS TRIED ME BY TESTING ME, AND SAW MY WORKS FOR FORTY YEARS. ¹⁰ THEREFORE I WAS ANGRY WITH THIS GENERATION, AND SAID, 'THEY ALWAYS GO ASTRAY IN THEIR HEART; AND THEY DID NOT KNOW MY WAYS'; ¹¹ AS I SWORE IN MY WRATH, 'THEY SHALL NOT ENTER MY REST.' "

Hebrews 4:1-3 Therefore, let us fear lest, while a promise remains of entering His rest, any one of you should seem to have come short of it. ² For indeed we have had good news preached to us, just as they also; but the word they heard did not profit them, because it was not united by faith in those who heard. ³ For we who have believed enter that rest, just as He has said, "AS I SWORE IN MY WRATH, THEY SHALL NOT ENTER MY REST," although His works were finished from the foundation of the world.

Numbers chapter 14 tells us about God's response to being tested on His Word. Moses said to the Lord,

> "But now, I pray, let the power of the Lord be great, just as Thou hast declared, 'The Lord is slow to anger and abundant in lovingkindness, forgiving iniquity and transgression; but He will by no means clear the guilty, visiting the iniquity of the fathers on the children to the third and the fourth generations.' Pardon, I pray, the iniquity of this people according to the greatness of Thy lovingkindness, just as Thou also hast forgiven this people, from Egypt even until now." So the Lord said, "I have pardoned them according to your word; but indeed, as I live, all the earth will be filled with the glory of the Lord. Surely all the men who have seen My glory and My signs, which I performed in Egypt and in the wilderness, yet have put Me to the test these ten times and have not listened to My voice, shall by no means see the land which I swore to their fathers, nor shall any of those who spurned Me see it." (Numbers 14:17-23)

Ten times Israel tested God. They saw His glory, and they saw His signs. They saw His miracles in Egypt and in the wilderness. Yet they continued to test Him. They said, "Are You taking us out of Egypt just to kill us in the wilderness?" (Exodus 17:3). They murmured and complained about what they did not have and what the Lord had not provided. This unbelief, which required the Lord to provide a sign or to provide a promise, was their downfall. It was their destruction. Our hearts need to be freed from this unbelief that tests the Lord. There is a way in which, in our unbelief about His Word, we come back to Him and say, "Why haven't You

---

Exodus 17:3 But the people thirsted there for water; and they grumbled against Moses and said, "Why, now, have you brought us up from Egypt, to kill us and our children and our livestock with thirst?"

done this thing? Why did You bring me to this place? Why are You leading me through this testing?" He is leading you through the testing because He is going to bless you. He is testing you; you are not testing Him. He is testing your spirit to see how you will walk before Him. He must bring us to the place where we are vessels who understand and know how to stand before Him and how to appropriate from Him all that He has spoken.

Our intercession cannot be about testing God. We do not bring the Word back to Him and say, "You spoke this. Now where is it? Why isn't it manifested for me yet?" We must be vessels to speak His Word like watchmen on the wall, prophesying by faith day by day what He has said and what He has promised, knowing in our hearts that He will bring to pass that which He has spoken (Isaiah 62:6-7). Do you see the difference? His Word is faithful, and it will always manifest what He has spoken. It will always bring into being what He has determined (Isaiah 55:10-11). We do not have to try to manipulate Him through our own will. We have to understand that, in this testing, He is creating our hearts before Him. If there are delays, then we must face those with faith and say, "I cannot produce this. Man does not live by bread alone, but by every Word and every promise that He has spoken. Lord, 'give us this day our daily bread' (Matthew 6:11). Give us today, by Your hand, today's fulfillment by Your Word. You bring the blessings. You bring the promises. You bring the fulfillments. And where it seems that it is taking too long, we realize that You are humbling our hearts."

Isaiah 62:6-7 On your walls, O Jerusalem, I have appointed watchmen; all day and all night they will never keep silent. You who remind the LORD, take no rest for yourselves; [7] and give Him no rest until He establishes and makes Jerusalem a praise in the earth.

Isaiah 55:10-11 "For as the rain and the snow come down from heaven, and do not return there without watering the earth, and making it bear and sprout, and furnishing seed to the sower and bread to the eater; [11] so shall My word be which goes forth from My mouth; it shall not return to Me empty, without accomplishing what I desire, and without succeeding in the matter for which I sent it."

There are ministries in the Church who try to manipulate God into moving in signs and wonders. That is not what we are to do as we cry for an outpouring of His Spirit. We are not looking for some way to manipulate the moving of God. Our cry is a cry of faith and a cry of worship that knows He will give us what He has spoken. When we find ourselves in a wilderness, and there is no water and we are thirsty, what do we do? Do we say, "I need You to move now! You said You were going to do this, so You had better do it. You are either doing it, or You are lying to me." No, we say, "We have a promise of water. We have a promise that You will sustain us. Give us this day our daily bread. We believe You. We trust You. We worship You. We serve You. We do not manipulate You, and we do not test You."

It is easy to focus on the many promises and many Words that we do not yet see fulfilled, but the Lord told the children of Israel to focus on what He had already done for them. He said to them, "I have revealed My presence to you. You who are complaining and testing Me have seen Me, and you have seen My works in Egypt and in the wilderness. I provided for you the cloud by day and the pillar of fire by night" (Exodus 13:21). They witnessed all the things that He provided, and yet, at the same time, they were saying, "Yes, but You made this promise, and I want to manipulate You into moving right now. I have to have it right now!" God is looking for a different heart than that.

Jesus was tested on the same issues that Israel was tested on in the wilderness. He was tested until He said, "I do not live by bread alone, but I live by every Word from God." In fact, Christ was the

---

Exodus 13:21 And the LORD was going before them in a pillar of cloud by day to lead them on the way, and in a pillar of fire by night to give them light, that they might travel by day and by night.

Word of God (John 1:1, 14). That is how thoroughly it was worked in His Spirit. We should look for the same thing to happen in us. It is not that we speak the Word; it is that we become the Word. He is testing us so that we become the Word of God because it has become everything to us. Jesus knew what God was going to give Him, and He refused the fulfillment of those promises except by the hand of God. He said, "I receive it from You, Lord, and then My response is to worship You forever because it came from You. All that I have comes only from You—not from Me, not from the hand of satan, not from the world, and not by any other provision." Jesus rejected the promise except by the hand of God, and that same faith has to be in us. We reject the blessings and the promises except by His hand. Everything happens by a Word from God: life, health, provision, food, fulfillment, and the land of promise. It is all by a Word from God. It is not that we get a Word and then set about to fulfill it ourselves. No, we believe Him and we believe His Word. We become the atmosphere of drawing Him in His fulfillment.

In our prayer, in our worship, and in our relationship with the Lord, we need to understand the difference between taking from God and receiving from Him. When you take it, then you can give yourself credit for appropriating. Do you see the difference? The expression of the nature of satan is that he takes what God is going to give before God gives it. Therefore he is the usurper. He is a false authority because he took it. We are to receive from God. Ask, and you will receive (Matthew 7:7-8). You do not take from His hand

---

John 1:1 In the beginning was the Word, and the Word was with God, and the Word was God.

John 1:14 And the Word became flesh, and dwelt among us, and we beheld His glory, glory as of the only begotten from the Father, full of grace and truth.

Matthew 7:7-8 "Ask, and it shall be given to you; seek, and you shall find; knock, and it shall be opened to you. [8] For everyone who asks receives, and he who seeks finds, and to him who knocks it shall be opened."

what He will give you. Allow God to be the giver and the provider. We cannot grab the fulfillment from Him; that is satan's nature. He is a false authority in the sense that he took the authority without God giving it to him. Our prayers and prophecies cannot be based on a perverted concept of appropriating from God. We know that He has these things for us, but we absolutely must receive everything by His hand, by His choosing, and by His giving. Until that happens, we must know that He has provided it and He will give it to us.

We must know that the promises are ours but refuse to usurp them. We must not attempt to rob God of the glory and honor and worship that belongs to Him alone as the provider of all things for us. As soon as we reach out our hand and take His provision in a wrong way, then we have robbed God of glory. We have robbed Him of honor. We must be as Christ was in the days of His flesh.

> Have this attitude in yourselves which was also in Christ Jesus, who, although He existed in the form of God, did not regard equality with God a thing to be grasped, but emptied Himself, taking the form of a bond-servant, and being made in the likeness of men. And being found in appearance as a man, He humbled Himself by becoming obedient to the point of death, even death on a cross. (Philippians 2:5-8)

As thirsty as you get, do not grab from Him the glass of water. That was one of the testings. He was going to provide, by a miracle, water from the rock that followed them through the wilderness (1 Corinthians 10:4); but they were thirsty, and instead of asking the Lord and letting Him provide it, they had to grab it. "Give us this water!" That is the example of what not to do. Do not test the

---

1 Corinthians 10:4 And all drank the same spiritual drink, for they were drinking from a spiritual rock which followed them; and the rock was Christ.

Lord, but ask Him to provide by His Word every miracle, every blessing, and every promise that He has for you.

No matter how hard it becomes, we refuse to test God. He can test us, but we cannot test Him. We have phenomenal Words of promise and blessing, and we need only to believe the Word that He has spoken. We repent of any way that we have used His Word to test Him. Instead, we say, "Lord, by Your Word which You have sworn, by Your name, by Your grace and love, fulfill Your promises and bring Your blessings. We believe Your Word. We believe in Your promises. We believe in the goodness of the Lord in the land of the living—but it must come by Your hand." We reject and refuse any arrogant attitude that would test God over His Word. We ask the Lord to root it out of our hearts in every area where it exists in us. Our focus is upon Him and His Word, and we simply believe that today is the day of His fulfillment. Today, what He has spoken manifests for His people. Our worship of Him is a focus that cuts through all confusion, all battle, and every distraction that would take our minds, our hearts, our souls, and our spirits off of the fact that it is God who will bring about the fulfillment of every good Word that He has spoken. We draw that fulfillment from His presence, because we believe in Him.

Lord, You are the answer, and You are the source for all of our release and blessing. We will not test You, Lord. By Your grace, put a new heart in Your people so that we may walk in Your ways and know You (Jeremiah 31:33-34).

Jeremiah 31:33-34 "But this is the covenant which I will make with the house of Israel after those days," declares the LORD, "I will put My law within them, and on their heart I will write it; and I will be their God, and they shall be My people. 34 And they shall not teach again, each man his neighbor and each man his brother, saying, 'Know the LORD,' for they shall all know Me, from the least of them to the greatest of them," declares the LORD, "for I will forgive their iniquity, and their sin I will remember no more."

19 | The Kingdom of God Dawns Through His Sons

When one of the disciples asked Jesus, "Lord, teach us to pray" (Luke 11:1), His response was to teach them what we know as the Lord's Prayer. What Jesus taught His disciples at that time has been preserved and handed down to us in the Bible, and it has become very familiar to us. However, because the words of this prayer are so familiar, it is easy for us to recite them by rote and skim over the depth of meaning contained in those words. In this book, we have endeavored to break through the dullness that comes with familiarity, and to reach in for an impartation of what the Holy Spirit is revealing in Christ's teaching about prayer. The Lord commanded us to pray, "Thy kingdom come. Thy will be done, on earth as it is in heaven" (Matthew 6:10). Those words have to be more than something we recite. We want the Lord to impart to our spirits a cry for the Kingdom of God to be on this earth. The drive to stand in the Father's presence and become those who

---

Luke 11:1 And it came about that while He was praying in a certain place, after He had finished, one of His disciples said to Him, "Lord, teach us to pray just as John also taught his disciples."

release His Kingdom on earth is central to the Lord's Prayer, but that thought is not on the minds of most Christians when they recite it. We can pray the words, "Thy Kingdom come; Thy will be done on earth," and yet be completely disconnected from what that really means.

As a prelude to Christ's ministry, John the Baptist came and preached, "Repent, for the kingdom of heaven is at hand" (Matthew 3:1-2). Then, from the time that John was arrested, Jesus began preaching the same message of the Kingdom (Matthew 4:12-13, 17). Jesus picked up the mantle, in a sense, and the Kingdom of God became a focal point of His ministry. Knowing its importance to Christ, why do we, as Christians, distance ourselves from the idea of the Kingdom of God? We have a tremendous awareness of what God is doing in our hearts and lives through the cross of Jesus Christ, and through the work of salvation in us. Yet we have disconnected the concept of salvation from what Christ taught about the Kingdom of God. Clearly, Christ is our salvation. He is the sacrifice for our sin, and yet He came preaching the Kingdom of God. He understood the connection between the two. We cannot separate the Kingdom of God from salvation, because the two are very much one. Think of the Kingdom of God as the final outworking of salvation. If you take salvation to its final conclusion, the outcome is the Kingdom of God.

Matthew 3:1-2   Now in those days John the Baptist came, preaching in the wilderness of Judea, saying, [2] "Repent, for the kingdom of heaven is at hand."

Matthew 4:12-13   Now when He heard that John had been taken into custody, He withdrew into Galilee; [13] and leaving Nazareth, He came and settled in Capernaum, which is by the sea, in the region of Zebulun and Naphtali.

Matthew 4:17   From that time Jesus began to preach and say, "Repent, for the kingdom of heaven is at hand."

When we think of our salvation, we do not see it as a progressively growing reality. We tend to look back on a time and a place, at the moment when we were saved. It is absolutely true that when we repent of our sins and ask Jesus Christ to come into our hearts, He enters our hearts and lives in us. From that moment we know that we are saved, but it does not stop there. The Scriptures describe salvation in terms of growing. We come into Christ as babes, and then we grow up to be mature sons. Ephesians 4:13-15 makes this abundantly clear:

> Until we all attain to the unity of the faith, and of the knowledge of the Son of God, to a mature man, to the measure of the stature which belongs to the fulness of Christ. As a result, we are no longer to be children, tossed here and there by waves, and carried about by every wind of doctrine, by the trickery of men, by craftiness in deceitful scheming; but speaking the truth in love, we are to grow up in all aspects into Him, who is the head, even Christ.

We are born into Christ, but then we must progress; we must grow; we must mature. Everything about our salvation must increase, because the truth is, it will increase throughout eternity. The process of salvation is not a one-time event. There is an approach to salvation in which you tell someone, "You are a sinner, and you need to be saved." Then you get that person to accept Christ, and you walk away saying, "That's done. That person's soul is now saved!" But that picture really does not describe salvation. Salvation is maturing. Salvation is something that is growing and progressing; it is ongoing in the heart of the believer. In this chapter, we will look at some Scriptures that show this biblical principle of salvation, and we will see how salvation and the Kingdom of God are truly one.

The Book of 2 Peter describes how a believer grows in Christ. In the first chapter, Peter writes about his experience with James and John on the Mount of Transfiguration. There they beheld the glorification of Jesus Christ, and saw Moses and Elijah as they appeared alongside Him (Matthew 17:1-3). Peter explains, "For we did not follow cleverly devised tales when we made known to you the power and coming of our Lord Jesus Christ, but we were eyewitnesses of His majesty" (2 Peter 1:16). There was a maturity in those apostles that did not exist in the rest of the believers.

> And we ourselves heard this utterance made from heaven when we were with Him on the holy mountain. And so we have the prophetic word made more sure, to which you do well to pay attention as to a lamp shining in a dark place, until the day dawns and the morning star arises in your hearts. (2 Peter 1:18-19)

This is a great picture that Peter is giving of salvation. According to Peter, the salvation process is like the dawning of the day. To understand how salvation works, simply get up while it is still dark and wait for the dawn. It is beautiful to watch. At some point you can see a little bit of sunlight on the tops of the mountains. Then the light moves down and gradually the dark valleys begin to brighten up. The light increases and spreads out until the sunlight bathes everything you can see. Eventually, everything is consumed by sunlight. The salvation process is the same. It is like a new day dawning in your life, and the day does not begin in full sunlight; it begins in darkness and then progressively becomes light. It is true that salvation happens at a certain moment, but at that moment there is still a lot of darkness.

Matthew 17:1-3   And six days later Jesus took with Him Peter and James and John his brother, and brought them up to a high mountain by themselves. ² And He was transfigured before them; and His face shone like the sun, and His garments became as white as light. ³ And behold, Moses and Elijah appeared to them, talking with Him.

When you first receive Christ, you are only at the beginning of the process. There are still many things in your life that God needs to work out before you experience the full light of day. That is why Peter wrote, "You need to listen to me, because there is something that I have. I have more of the light and more of the dawn rising in me than you do, so listen to what I am telling you until the same experience happens in you." He did not mean by this that he had an exclusive ministry and no one else could be like him. He was simply saying, "Give it some time. Submit to what I am teaching you, because that same experience will happen in you and you also will be bathed in light. You will be filled with the same new day, the same morning star that I have experienced."

Paul's writings contain this idea as well. "For I am confident of this very thing, that He who began a good work in you will perfect it until the day of Christ Jesus" (Philippians 1:6). Again you can see the progression. What happened at the moment you were saved was the beginning of something, and what God started in you, He is determined to perfect. He is going to finish the work (1 Thessalonians 5:23-24). This is what we experience as we come more and more into a relationship with the Father. In Philippians 2:13, we read another great example of this: "For it is God who is at work in you" (Philippians 2:13). You see, it is the Father who is at work in you. It is easy to focus on Christ and say, "I received Christ, so I have salvation." Yes, but Christ opened the door for you to be reconciled to the Father (Romans 5:10; 2 Corinthians 5:18). Jesus told His disciples, "My Father and I will

---

1 Thessalonians 5:23-24 Now may the God of peace Himself sanctify you entirely; and may your spirit and soul and body be preserved complete, without blame at the coming of our Lord Jesus Christ. ²⁴ Faithful is He who calls you, and He also will bring it to pass.

Romans 5:10 For if while we were enemies, we were reconciled to God through the death of His Son, much more, having been reconciled, we shall be saved by His life.

2 Corinthians 5:18 Now all these things are from God, who reconciled us to Himself through Christ, and gave us the ministry of reconciliation.

take up Our abode in you" (John 14:23). He was saying, "Open your heart and receive Me. If you open your heart and let Me in, you will be restored to the Father; then something will progress in your life unto a completed salvation." When the Father comes in, you realize, "My salvation is not something that happened one time and now the experience is over"; you recognize that the Father, when He is in your life, is working. He is working in you "both to will and to work for His good pleasure" (Philippians 2:13).

God is working in us to progressively bring us into the perfected experience that started with the simplicity and wonder of our salvation. From that very first moment, God is looking for His work to progress in us. God is doing something in us and through us that will affect the entire world, and at some point, there will be a completely new day that is fully dawned. This new day is what the Bible refers to as the Kingdom of God. This is why Jesus came preaching the Kingdom of God. He did not just say, "Be saved!" When Jesus came as the salvation of the world, He taught about the Kingdom of God, because He was seeing more than just the beginning of things. We need to connect in a greater way with how salvation works through us to become the Kingdom of God. Romans the 8th chapter brings out this principle:

> For you have not received a spirit of slavery leading to fear again, but you have received a spirit of adoption as sons by which we cry out, "Abba! Father!" The Spirit Himself bears witness with our spirit that we are children of God, and if children, heirs also, heirs of God and fellow heirs with Christ, if indeed we suffer with Him in order that we may also be glorified with Him. For I consider that the sufferings of this present time are not worthy to be compared with the glory that is to be revealed to

---

John 14:23 Jesus answered and said to him, "If anyone loves Me, he will keep My word; and My Father will love him, and We will come to him, and make Our abode with him."

us. (Romans 8:15-18)

We cannot worry about the sufferings, because they are what is maturing us. "For the anxious longing of the creation waits eagerly for the revealing of the sons of God" (Romans 8:19). Here again is the idea of progressing. The process is to grow from being children into being mature sons, and the sons of God are what creation is waiting for. This is an important point. Creation is not crying out for our salvation; it is crying out for the sons of God to come forth. It is crying out for those who have matured from birth into something that is fully grown. Creation is literally crying out for what Jesus spoke; it is crying out for the Kingdom of God.

"For the anxious longing of the creation waits eagerly for the revealing of the sons of God" (Romans 8:19). Why does creation care about the sons of God? "For the creation was subjected to futility, not of its own will, but because of Him who subjected it [speaking of the Father], in hope that the creation itself also will be set free from its slavery to corruption into the freedom of the glory of the children of God" (Romans 8:20-21). Salvation manifests in us and grows in us. We grow from being children to being matured sons. This is what Christ did, but something else happens along the way. As we mature, all of creation is being set free from its futility. Creation also receives salvation. It does not receive it on its own, however; it receives salvation through what the children of God are doing in their daily lives, in the progression and the working of God to mature them. Why is God so focused on maturing us? Why does He care about us growing and maturing and becoming sons? The reason is because without us becoming mature sons, all of creation is stuck in futility.

The Greek word translated as "creation" in Romans 8:21 is *ktisis*,[16] and

---

[16.] Timothy Friberg, Barbara Friberg, and Neva F. Miller, *Analytical Lexicon of the Greek New Testament*, Baker's Greek New Testament Library (Grand Rapids, MI: Baker Books, 2000), 239.

the depth of its meaning is significant. This word conveys a different idea than our concept of creation as being the entire universe.

The Greek word for the "universe" is *kosmos*.[17] This word can mean the universe, the physical earth, or it can mean people or humanity. Because *kosmos* encompasses everything that surrounds us in the physical universe, why is it not the word used for creation in Romans 8? The Greek word *ktisis* means creation, and the creation includes more than the physical created things around us.

In God's creation, there is more than just the *kosmos*, which is everything we can relate to around us as pertaining to us and our world. Man, the earth, even the universe, are all physical things. The universe is a very big concept; it is all of that which encompasses us physically, but it is still that which we are seeing with our eyes and measuring. The salvation that God is working through you is bigger than that. It goes back to the first chapter of Genesis, and it deals with everything that was created by God from the moment of creation. In fact, the meaning of *ktisis* includes the act of creation itself, the very moment when God created all things. Everything created by God is included in that which is saved through the manifestation of the sons of God. That is the *ktisis*; it is all created things, the things in the heavens—the unseen realm including principalities and powers (Ephesians 3:10; 6:12)—as well as the things in the physical realm, the earth. This is what Jesus meant by the Kingdom of God. He was talking about all of creation. He was talking about all things that God has ever created. There is nothing that God ever created that does not come within the city limits of

---

Ephesians 3:10 In order that the manifold wisdom of God might now be made known through the church to the rulers and the authorities in the heavenly places.

Ephesians 6:12 For our struggle is not against flesh and blood, but against the rulers, against the powers, against the world forces of this darkness, against the spiritual forces of wickedness in the heavenly places.

the Kingdom of God.

When Jesus came to save mankind, by the definition of the word, you could say that He came to save the *kosmos*. In fact, according to the Scriptures, He came specifically to the Jewish people. When He spoke to the Canaanite woman, He said, "I have come to those that are of the house of Israel. I cannot give this bread to dogs" (Matthew 15:24-26). How then is salvation applied to the *ktisis*, to all of creation? As salvation is worked through us, then all of creation participates in that salvation experience. Romans 8:19 does not say that creation is waiting for Jesus to manifest in the earth as the Son of God; it does not say that all creation was longing for Christ to go to the cross and die for our sins. It says that all creation is waiting for the manifestation of the sons of God—because as we come into the glory and the release that God has for us, and as we progress in our salvation experience, the world progressively is being set free from its futility. That is why you become the focus of the Father. That is why God is at work in you to will and to do of His good pleasure. Do you know what His good pleasure is? It is the Kingdom of God. It is all things being set free from futility. It is the total release of all creation. Can you see then why God cares about maturing us? Can you see why He is working with us and in us and through us? As He is working in you, you must realize also that things are happening outside of you. You have to see the connection. Your experience of a breakthrough, or a maturing, or a release in your spirit is also a release to God's creation. When Jesus came, He had this as His drive, and this same drive is being worked in us.

---

17. James Strong, *Enhanced Strong's Lexicon* (Bellingham, WA: Logos Bible Software, 2001).

Matthew 15:24-26 But He answered and said, "I was sent only to the lost sheep of the house of Israel." 25 But she came and began to bow down before Him, saying, "Lord, help me!" 26 And He answered and said, "It is not good to take the children's bread and throw it to the dogs."

This maturity that God is working in us is far more than simply praying, "O God, help me; I sinned again. Please get me out of my sin. I repent. I want to mature." We can pray that way from too small of a vision, missing the very point of why God would even bother to work in us. After all, we have salvation. We have been included in eternal life. Why don't we just relax? Why should we worry about the Kingdom of God? We have everything that we need—we have all that the Father provided through Jesus Christ in our lives. Why would we be pressing in to something more? We are pressing in because the Lord is working in our spirits a deep burden for the Kingdom of God, even as Christ had.

Christ went to the cross knowing what He was doing. He knew why He was suffering. He understood the plan of God. He realized that it would not be fun for Him. It would involve tremendous suffering and pain, but He did not do it for Himself. The sons of God coming forth cannot do it for themselves either. What we are going through, and what God is working in our spirits, bringing the progression of His Kingdom, is not for us on a personal level. Paul wrote, "For I consider that the sufferings of this present time are not worthy to be compared with the glory that is to be revealed to us" (Romans 8:18). That is the way it was for Jesus. What He suffered could not be compared to what God had planned in saving mankind through that suffering. We may want to make our suffering be about ourselves, but it is not. We do not grow and mature because we think it would be really cool to be sons of God. The maturing process includes suffering. If we suffer with Him, we will be glorified with Him (Romans 8:17).

It is not necessarily fun to have God work in you to will and do of His good pleasure. When He works things out in your life, it is often embarrassing. It is painful. You suffer. You have to give up of yourself and give up your will and desires. Why do that? Is it just to have something better for yourself? No, God wants you to have a revelation of His Kingdom. The Lord is looking for us to experience our maturing with a vision of the Kingdom of God. He wants us to recognize the Kingdom of God in what is happening to us. He wants us to understand that what is happening through us by becoming sons of God is releasing all of creation. It is releasing **all** creation. That is far beyond the *kosmos*, far beyond anything we can even understand. Everything that God created is being released from futility. God put that futility on all creation because of man's fall, and He will release all creation because of man's breaking through to become the sons of God. The sons of God were with the Father before the fall ever happened (Job 38:4-7), and it was at that moment when He commissioned man to be over the earth. That is why, today, God is using the base things of this world—and out of everything He created there is nothing more base than mankind (1 Corinthians 1:28). Yet, through us, He will release all of creation from futility. This is what is happening in our spirits. This is where God is taking us. We have to live our lives now on a natural level with this as our focus because creation will not be free until God completes the maturing process in us.

Mankind, as we are now, will never bring about the Kingdom of God. Without question, there are many problems in the world that need to be fixed. However, whenever man tries to solve one problem, he cannot seem to do it without creating more problems. What we understand as believers is that man will never fix the problems in the culture or laws of any country. Man will always mess it up somehow. Why? Because of what is in man. If we could find the perfect system of government, the problem with it would

---

Job 38:4-7 "Where were you when I laid the foundation of the earth? Tell Me, if you have understanding, ⁵ who set its measurements, since you know? Or who stretched the line on it? ⁶ On what were its bases sunk? Or who laid its cornerstone, ⁷ when the morning stars sang together, and all the sons of God shouted for joy?"

1 Corinthians 1:28 And the base things of the world and the despised, God has chosen, the things that are not, that He might nullify the things that are.

be that humans would be administrating it. Someone without morals and without righteousness would be able to get in and steal from it or pervert it. Man keeps passing more and more laws trying to take the Adamic nature out of what they are trying to fix, but constantly passing laws will not fix the fact that man in his fallen state will never bring about the Kingdom of God.

It is easy to get caught up in social issues and social causes through organizations or politics, but do not mistake that for the Kingdom of God. Somewhere along the line, in whatever program man comes up with to try to emulate the Kingdom of God, his flesh nature will ultimately make it not work, or even destroy it, because someone will come along and abuse the system. We have to differentiate between the Kingdom of God and doing good works, or just being good Christians. The Kingdom of God comes as God is working in us to perfect that which He started with our salvation, and it is out of that perfection process that things change in the world. Jesus was hung on a cross. That does not seem like an action that would impact the entire planet; yet it did. Why? Because Christ allowed the Father to perfect and mature Him, as Hebrews 5:9 states: "And having been made perfect, He became to all those who obey Him the source of eternal salvation." Because Christ allowed the Father to perfect Him and He hung on the cross in obedience, salvation was triggered by His actions.

We must commit our lives to this prayer: "Thy Kingdom come. Thy will be done, on earth as it is in heaven" (Matthew 6:10). The Kingdom of God is something beyond humanity, because the nature of man, as it is, will never produce the Kingdom of God. The Kingdom of God will only happen when God is on the inside of mankind changing man. Mankind will never vote the Kingdom of God into office. They did not vote Jesus into office, did they? They did not vote for Him to be a ruler in the Temple. They did not vote for Him to be a ruler of any kind. They did not do anything except hang Him on a cross, because that is man's thinking. We need our thinking to be transformed (Romans 12:2). We need to start relating to salvation as part of the Kingdom of God, and living it out in our daily lives. We need to be preaching the Kingdom of God through our lives. The world around us needs the Kingdom of God very badly, and we should be burdened to see it come forth. At the same time, we should understand how it comes; otherwise, we will get caught up in a lot of ideas and humanistic endeavors that will never come to pass. The greatest force for change in the world is that God is working in the Body of Christ to mature a people through the process of their salvation. There is only one way to change the world, and that is to set creation free from its slavery to corruption into the freedom of the glory of the children of God. I must change; you must change; and every moment that God is working in your life is changing creation. We should understand that, and dedicate our lives to be a people burdened for the Kingdom of God to manifest in the earth!

Romans 12:2 And do not be conformed to this world, but be transformed by the renewing of your mind, that you may prove what the will of God is, that which is good and acceptable and perfect.

NOTES

NOTES

NOTES

NOTES

NOTES

ABOUT THE AUTHOR

Gary Hargrave has a passion for leading people into spiritual maturity. Gary effectively ministers the life-changing truth of God's Word through Bible teaching and prophetic revelation that emphasizes the Lordship of Christ.

Gary embraces the teachings and insights of the Hebrew Scriptures as the essential foundation of God's Kingdom and the roots of Christian faith.

By cultivating spiritual maturity in Christians, Gary is deeply committed to teaching and inspiring unity in the body of Christ and between Christians and the Jewish people.

Throughout decades of ministry, Gary has worked closely with leaders in the Jewish, Catholic and Protestant communities to build relationships based on commonality and understanding. He frequently leads study tours to Israel and the lands of the Bible.

Gary is the host of a weekly podcast entitled Growing In God, and is the founder of Shiloh University, an accredited online Bible college and seminary.

Gary and his family reside in Hawaii.